Praise for *Well-Being*

Bravo to authors Hargreaves and Shirley f̶ well-being and happiness! In a style that is accessible and free of jargon, this book teaches us that children cannot learn when they are lonely, alienated, or unhappy. Drawing on research and plain common sense from before and during the COVID-19 pandemic, this book reminds us what really matters in education. The thoughtful lessons apply not only to schools but also to community centers, sports clubs, and anywhere else that young people congregate.

—**Dr. Ruth K. Westheimer,** author, media personality, therapist, and adjunct professor, Columbia University

Well-Being in Schools is an inspiring and *revolutionary* book. It's about far more than the title suggests. Readers of this fine work will come to view the public school as a metaphor for all of society. Applied to schools and beyond, the three powerful forces it identifies—including a call to renew our relationship with nature—can reshape the lives of children and adults right now, while offering us hope for a newer world.

—**Richard Louv**, author of *Last Child in the Woods: Saving Our Children from Nature-Deficit Disorder* and *Our Wild Calling*

Andy Hargreaves and Dennis Shirley's *Well-Being in Schools* is a brilliant journey through the global and local landscapes, fields, and foibles of well-being theory and practice in education. In a highly readable way, the authors take us through every different permutation of thinking about young people's well-being, examine its limitations, and offer new insights about ways to prioritize well-being in policy and practice. I thoroughly recommend this book to all those who are interested in placing well-being in schools much higher up the policy agenda.

—**David H. Edwards,** PhD, General Secretary, Education International

This timely and highly accessible book is extremely important in these volatile times. Focusing on three core forces—*social prosperity*, *ethical technology use*, and *restorative nature*—Hargreaves and Shirley make it clear that schools can no longer rely only on content delivery with occasional forays into social and emotional learning if we want to prepare students for the increasingly tumultuous world in which they live.

—**Jean Clinton**, clinical professor, Department of Psychiatry and Behavioural Neuroscience, McMaster University, Canada, and **Michael Fullan**, professor emeritus and former dean, OISE/University of Toronto

Well-Being in Schools provides a comprehensive road map for teachers and leaders alike to firstly understand and secondly create the conditions for student well-being and achievement. Rich and vivid examples of emergent and promising practice from school systems around the world drive home the reciprocal relationship between well-being and student success. This is a must read for school and system leaders.

—**Kevin Godden,** EdD, superintendent

How can our schools enable young people not just to achieve academically but also to "live long and prosper?" And what can we learn from education systems that do both of these things well? Andy and Dennis outline how the pandemic is showing us what really matters in education and is sharpening our thinking about what needs to change. This timely and wide-ranging book pulls no punches. Full of international analysis and insights, it inspires us to believe not only that it is imperative for our young people that we build back better but also that it might just be possible to do so. I loved it.

—**Steve Munby,** visiting professor, University College London and former CEO, National College for School Leadership, England

Student well-being has become the key element of successful education systems. This important book shows how learning to be well is not just about your well-being or mine, it is a social condition that includes all of us. There is no better time than now to dive deeper in the meaning of student well-being. I recommend this book to teachers, school leaders, and policymakers as a guide how to build a better and healthier world through education.

—**Pasi Sahlberg,** author of *Finnish Lessons 3.0: What Can the World Learn from Educational Change in Finland?*

Andy Hargreaves and Dennis Shirley capture the art and science of student well-being as the fundamental building block to our present and future. They weave theory, practice, and policy together to give us practical and relevant next steps to our work in *Well-Being in Schools*. Student well-being is a timeless focus for all of us and essential to our post-pandemic recovery.

—**Joshua J. Garcia,** EdD, superintendent

Well-Being in Schools

ASCD MEMBER BOOK

Many ASCD members received this book as a
member benefit upon its initial release.

Learn more at: **www.ascd.org/memberbooks**

Andy Hargreaves
Dennis Shirley

Well-Being in Schools

Three Forces That Will Uplift Your Students in a Volatile World

ascd

Alexandria, Virginia USA

1703 N. Beauregard St. • Alexandria, VA 22311-1714 USA
Phone: 800-933-2723 or 703-578-9600 • Fax: 703-575-5400
Website: www.ascd.org • Email: member@ascd.org
Author guidelines: www.ascd.org/write

Ranjit Sidhu, *CEO & Executive Director;* Penny Reinart, *Chief Impact Officer;* Genny Ostertag, *Managing Director, Book Acquisitions & Editing;* Susan Hills, *Senior Acquisitions Editor;* Julie Houtz, *Director Book Editing;* Liz Wegner, *Editor;* Thomas Lytle, *Creative Director;* Donald Ely, *Art Director;* Georgia Park, *Senior Graphic Designer;* Cynthia Stock, *Typesetter;* Kelly Marshall, *Production Manager;* Shajuan Martin, *E-Publishing Specialist*

All web links in this book are correct as of the publication date below but may have become inactive or otherwise modified since that time. If you notice a deactivated or changed link, please email books@ascd.org with the words "Link Update" in the subject line. In your message, please specify the web link, the book title, and the page number on which the link appears.

PAPERBACK ISBN: 978-1-4166-3072-2   ASCD product #122025
PDF E-BOOK ISBN: 978-1-4166-3073-9; see Books in Print for other formats.
Quantity discounts are available: email programteam@ascd.org or call 800-933-2723, ext. 5773, or 703-575-5773. For desk copies, go to www.ascd.org/deskcopy.

ASCD Member Book No. FY22-3 (Dec. 2021 P). ASCD Member Books mail to Premium (P), Select (S), and Institutional Plus (I+) members on this schedule: Jan, PSI+; Feb, P; Apr, PSI+; May, P; Jul, PSI+; Aug, P; Sep, PSI+; Nov, PSI+; Dec, P. For current details on membership, see www.ascd.org/membership.

Library of Congress Cataloging-in-Publication Data

Names: Hargreaves, Andy, author. | Shirley, Dennis, 1955- author.
Title: Well-being in schools : three forces that will uplift your students in a volatile world / Andy Hargreaves and Dennis Shirley.
Description: Alexandria, VA : ASCD, 2022. | Includes bibliographical references and index.
Identifiers: LCCN 2021037691 (print) | LCCN 2021037692 (ebook) | ISBN 9781416630722 (paperback) | ISBN 9781416630739 (pdf)
Subjects: LCSH: School psychology. | School children--Psychology. | Affective education. | Well-being. | School environment.
Classification: LCC LB1027.55 .H369 2022 (print) | LCC LB1027.55 (ebook) | DDC 370.15--dc23
LC record available at https://lccn.loc.gov/2021037691
LC ebook record available at https://lccn.loc.gov/2021037692

31 30 29 28 27 26 25 24 23 22   1 2 3 4 5 6 7 8 9 10 11 12

For all the teachers, administrators, and other educators who did everything in their power to keep 1.6 billion of the world's children engaged with their learning, despite being cut off from school for weeks and even months on end during the coronavirus pandemic

"Education is the point at which we decide whether we love the world enough to assume responsibility for it and by the same token save it from that ruin which, except for renewal, except for the coming of the new and young, would be inevitable."

—Hannah Arendt

Well-Being in Schools

Preface:
Live Long and Prosper

If you had a choice to be healthy or successful, which would you choose? Of course, most of us wouldn't want to choose at all. Who wouldn't prefer to be healthy *and* successful? But what if you were really forced to pick one over the other?

Well, if you look at most educational policies since the 1990s, you might imagine that success is what really matters and sometimes practically *all* that matters. Test scores, examination results, and international comparisons of educational performance have all exalted literacy, mathematics, and science scores as the be-all and end-all of education. There have been some attempts to update these metrics with 21st century skills or global competencies, but even these have been primarily driven by economic and modern workforce needs.

The focus on achievement, success, and high performance in education and the economy has been like a never-ending story about what's most important in education and in life. Health and well-being have seemed like an afterthought—a luxury that our scarce attention and resources can't always afford.

The early years of the 2020s changed all that. They will be etched indelibly in our memories for the rest of our lives. These were the years the COVID-19 pandemic took millions of lives, disrupted economies, robbed young people of more than a year of regular learning, and plunged families and communities into depression, anxiety, poverty, and isolation.

COVID-19 turned our assumptions about what matters in schools and society upside down. The fantasy that learning could be accessed on devices anytime, anywhere, and that the walls of schools in the 21st century should come down, was confounded by having to face the simple fact that children need to be looked after for numerous reasons, including so that their parents can go to work. The poverty that the pandemic exposed and exacerbated made many children vulnerable to sleeplessness, stress, violence, and abuse. One poll conducted in the United Kingdom, for example, reported a rise in issues related to mental health and well-being for at least one in three of the 4,000 children and young people who responded.[1]

Not everyone suffered from being at home. Peace and contentment came to children who were no longer targets of teasing and bullying. Those who found it hard to sit still and concentrate for hours on end in a regular classroom environment could now fidget and wander around at will. Nobody missed the dreary rituals of test preparation. Although many students closing in on the end of high school worried about how they would be graded and how this would affect their futures, there were no reports that they hankered after high-stress examinations.

Well-being was no longer at the back of the school bus. It was in the driver's seat. How could teachers get food to children in poverty when meals at school were no longer available? What could schools do to keep an eye on the most vulnerable children and their families, who might be struggling, squabbling, or getting caught up in intensifying custody battles, for example? More and more school and system leaders began to realize that when children and families were figuring out how to learn on devices (or in other ways) at home, it was time to put aside worksheets and to give up worrying about kids falling behind in their measured achievement. It was better instead to ensure that children were at least learning something, that they were enjoying what they were doing, and that they were productively occupied, whether by chatting with their parents, participating in family activities, or just playing together.

It took all of this to get policymakers and the public to pull up short and appreciate what famed psychologist Abraham Maslow had pointed out in 1943—that before people could engage with the possibilities for personal growth and "self-actualization," as he called it, they needed to be safe and physically well.[2] As our own parents often reminded us, health is everything.

In truth, in the five years or so before the pandemic, most educational systems had already started to pay a lot more attention to their students' well-being. A look at Google's N-Gram viewer makes it clear that although the term *well-being* has a 70-year history, its frequency of use shot up after 2010 (see Figure P.1).

The growing attraction of well-being and wellness is evident in everyday life. We see it in the opening of spas and wellness centers on high streets and in shopping malls; in smartwatches that count our calories and our steps; in apps that display our sleep patterns and heart rate; in obsessions with diet and nutrition; in celebrity websites that provide wellness advice and market well-being products;[3] and in the boom in self-help books on subjects such as how to master emotions, change tiny habits, and even how to breathe![4]

In a different way, the rising prominence and provenance of well-being have also been apparent in schools. In research we present in this book, educators reported that children were starting school less prepared to learn compared to earlier generations.

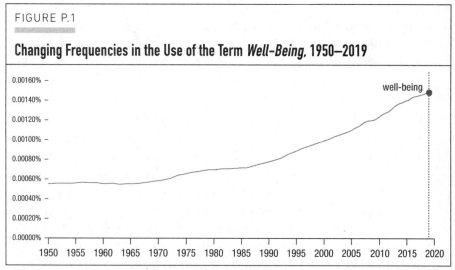

FIGURE P.1

Changing Frequencies in the Use of the Term *Well-Being,* 1950–2019

Source: From Google Books, NGram Viewer for "well-being." https://books.google.com/ngrams/graph?content=well-being&year_start=1950&year_end=2019&corpus=26&smoothing=3

Children found it hard to listen, line up, and take turns when they had to. Biting, kicking, and other antisocial behaviors appeared to be increasing. Many young learners seemed to be exhibiting early signs of restlessness, inability to concentrate, and overall attention deficits. Levels of anxiety and depression were rising in all age groups, from small children to young adults.

Teachers sensed the origins of these changes. More children were living on the edge of poverty or in families where the necessity to work two or three jobs in the modern economy meant that children were left on their own a lot more. Kids were more connected to technology, but not always in a good way. Video games and social media were consuming many children's lives with excessive hours of screen time. Overworked and overscheduled parents had little or no time to organize or oversee alternatives. Some parents occupied their children with digital devices rather than converse with them. A surge in refugees from countries at war or in conflict also brought growing numbers of children with little or no experience of schooling into the classrooms of receiving countries. Teachers had to learn how to cope with the emotional and behavioral manifestations of students who were traumatized as a result of violence, bereavement, homelessness, fear, and chaos they had experienced in their former countries.

Children were suffering, and their teachers were struggling. Schools, policy systems, and foundations started to respond, leading to an explosion of initiatives, programs, and publications in social and emotional learning (SEL). Teachers' professional vocabulary expanded to include terms such as *growth mindset, emotional regulation,* and *mindfulness.* Educational policies started to assign high priority to well-being. Political leaders and their economic advisers began to insist that society had more important goals than economic growth. Quality of life—and the policies that supported it—should be the chief priorities, they said. This view was what the original *Star Trek*'s Mr. Spock meant when he urged people to "live long and prosper"—not to get rich, but to flourish as human beings.[5]

After 40 years of chasing bigger numbers in everything from economic productivity to student test scores, we are now witnessing the emergence of a new way of thinking about what is most important in our lives. This is a kind of *Prosperity Doctrine*—a belief in the value of thriving in all aspects of life, not just economic ones. Prosperity in this sense is about the development of the whole child rather than just the parts of the child that can remember bits of knowledge, pass tests, and eventually get jobs. Prosperity is about having a sense of purpose and meaning in life, about feeling fulfilled and being a positive force for good in the lives of others too.

The Case for Well-Being

Given these developments, this book about well-being is fortuitously timely, because we didn't set out to write about well-being—or even to research the subject. Instead, in the early stages of a project with 10 of the 72 school districts in Ontario, Canada, the provincial government released a report that identified four policy pillars as its priorities.[6] One of these was improving students' well-being. As part of our collaborative relationship, the districts then asked us to examine their efforts to promote student well-being in response to the new policy direction.[7]

This book draws on what we discovered to set out arguments, evidence, examples, and implications concerning how we can and should address issues of children's well-being in schools. Our intention is not to add to the many how-to books on well-being with specific ideas and strategies about what teachers can do in their classrooms right now. Rather, we want to provide a deeper yet accessible understanding of the subject of well-being and SEL, and the main ideas behind them. To do this, we draw not only on our own evidence but also on research and writing on well-being across a number of disciplines.

Using this interdisciplinary approach, our book sets out to stimulate new thinking and to challenge existing ideas about well-being and SEL. It presents inspiring examples of well-being initiatives in action. It examines the relationship between well-being and student success. It defines bold new directions for well-being. Our book also raises critical questions about the well-being agenda—not to undermine it, but to put it on a firmer footing. Throughout our book, we show that well-being and SEL are not just psychological matters but also relate to how our institutions and societies enhance or impede everyone's well-being.

The book is organized in eight chapters. The opening chapter explores and explains what most people mean when they talk about well-being. It connects psychological interpretations of well-being to understanding the role that it plays in the world. The chapter closes by describing three programs and policies that address these micro and macro aspects of well-being together. These show the relationships between interpersonal processes, such as bullying and empathy inside schools, and big-picture issues in society, such as conflict, genocide, and peace.

Chapter 2 introduces six of the most widely used and psychologically based theories of well-being and SEL that have influenced the work of teachers worldwide in their attempts to address young people's development.

Chapter 3 then asks readers to inspect some of their most fundamental beliefs about the value of well-being and to examine what may be wrong with the concept. The more we are attached to something in education—a curriculum, a program, or a strategy—the more we should examine it for any flaws. As in romantic or business partnerships, when we embrace something or someone, we should do so in full knowledge of the drawbacks and limitations. In our quest to improve well-being, we must not shrink from acknowledging some of the more difficult issues that the well-being agenda has raised. This effort can actually temper commitment with realism and help avoid disappointment later on.

Chapter 4 examines what it is that has led to the eruption of interest in well-being in education during the second decade of the 21st century. The need for educators to pay more attention to well-being, we argue, has resulted from the combined pressure of two great movements in education and society—a chaotic and uncertain one emerging from the imminent future, and a controlling and restricting one of testing and standardization derived from an outworn past. Together, these pressing movements are thrusting well-being issues up in front of us, where they can't be missed. The COVID-19 pandemic, we note, has added to these pressures and uncertainties. It has ensured that well-being will remain at the top of our educational priorities for years to come.

Chapters 5, 6, and 7 paint a big-picture perspective of well-being and SEL in society. They describe three powerful forces that are changing well-being policy and practice: The first is a quest for personal and social prosperity, the second is a drive toward more ethical uses of digital learning technologies, and the third is a call to renew our relationship with nature. Chapter 5 describes the goal of *prosperity for all,* which abandons economic obsessions with growth and austerity and educational preoccupations with achievement targets in favor of creating a better quality of life for everyone. Chapter 6 takes an approach to *ethical technology use* that sets aside overly exuberant commitments to hybrid and blended forms of digital technology in order to make way for digital learning strategies that have a uniquely valuable impact and that take full account of all associated dangers and risks. Chapter 7 then argues for the power of *restorative nature.* It proposes increasing the amount of time devoted to learning outdoors to reconnect people with Indigenous heritages, strengthen young people's physical and mental health, and establish early relationships with nature that build a foundation for environmental sustainability.

In Chapter 8, using evidence from the 10 school districts we studied in Ontario, we examine the relationship between students' well-being and their academic success. This is a topic where strong opinions abound. Is well-being essential as a basis for academic success? Or is it peripheral to—or even a distraction from—the serious study of academics? And what about the reverse relationship? Does well-being result from success, or can too much stress about being academically successful actually undermine students' well-being? This chapter invites readers to examine their own assumptions about well-being and achievement, and to rethink how to create the most productive relationship between these things.

The Epilogue considers the future of well-being in the work of teaching and the world beyond it. How can we get better at helping our students and societies get better? What do we now know that can help us improve everyone's quality of life? How can we attend to our own well-being so that we will be fully equipped to help all our young people be healthy, prosperous, and successful? How can all of us see and strengthen the connection between well-being in ourselves, our schools, and the world? After the greatest pandemic in a century, how can we build everyone back to be better-educated people who know *how to live together?*

Our Evidence and Research

Our ideas and the evidence in this book draw on a range of sources. These include existing research literature on well-being in schools and society; and our research, advisory, and evaluative work with policy reforms in Canadian provinces and US states, as well as in other countries. The prime source, though, is a four-year study of educational change in Ontario, Canada, in relation to a 2014 government policy titled *Achieving Excellence.*[8]

With a population closing in on 15 million, Ontario is the most populous of Canada's 10 provinces. It has nearly 5,000 schools.[9] The province's public schools have been the envy of the world. Apart from Ireland and the city-state of Singapore, Canada is the highest performer among all English- and French-speaking nations, and Ontario is one of the top four performing provinces in that country.[10] Especially considering Ontario's high levels of immigration, the province's performance remains exceptional.[11] Test results on OECD's Program for International Student Assessment (PISA) show Ontario consistently ranking in the top dozen school systems. On the 2018 PISA results, Ontario tied for 5th in the world in reading, marginally behind Alberta, among other Canadian provinces.[12] International visitors have flocked to see a diverse public system that serves almost 94 percent of the province's students and that enjoys strong public confidence in its schools and teachers.[13]

Between 2002 and 2013, Ontario's drive to raise achievement and narrow achievement gaps concentrated on students' performance in literacy and mathematics, especially in the elementary grades.[14] In 2013, although Ontario's government continued to be led by the Liberal Party, a new premier—Kathleen Wynne, the former education minister—assumed office. Wynne's education policy, *Achieving Excellence,* took the province in new directions.[15]

Achieving Excellence set out four priorities. One was to maintain public confidence in a system that had raised student performance on test results by 17 percentage points over the previous decade. Second, although excellence was still a clear priority, other academic areas, such as the arts and STEM (science, technology, engineering, and mathematics), were now added to literacy and mathematics as priorities. Equity was a third priority, but it was no longer interpreted just as narrowing achievement gaps; it now encompassed inclusion of diverse and vulnerable groups and their identities, such as Indigenous, refugee, and LGBTQ students, so they could see themselves, their communities, and their needs reflected in the life and learning of their schools. The fourth pillar of Ontario education reform was that "Ontario is committed to the success and *well-being* of every student and child" (emphasis added).[16]

Before the release of the policy report, we were approached by a consortium of 10 of Ontario's 72 school districts. The Council of Ontario Directors of Education (CODE) created the consortium. We were asked to collaborate with the consortium in documenting projects that they also wished to share with one another to advance their learning through regular meetings that we facilitated. After the release of *Achieving Excellence,* most of these projects focused on aspects of students' well-being.

Our research team used semi-structured interviews to elicit information about the improvement initiatives in the 10 school districts and to gauge how they were learning from one another in the consortium. We visited each district over one or two days in the spring of 2016. Teams of two or three were mixed and rotated to enhance cross-validation of interpretation. We conducted in-depth interviews and focus group discussions with more than 220 teachers, principals, central office staff, affiliated school-based personnel, project leaders, and civil servants from the Ministry of Education. We visited classrooms to observe, firsthand, how projects were being implemented and with what consequences. We also gathered documents such as district-level and ministerial reports to supplement our research findings. More details of our methodology are described in our technical research report.[17]

Building Everyone Back Better

Even before US President Joe Biden was elected in 2020, he pledged that his administration would "build back better" after a raging pandemic that claimed more than half a million US lives and led to unemployment and poverty levels that were unprecedented in modern times.[18] The phrase *getting better,* of course, has a double meaning. It refers to recovery of health after being sick and to improving over time. *Building back better* has to mean more than mere recovery, important as that is. All was far from well beforehand. Building back better, in the United States and everywhere else, must therefore also see a determination to improve people's health and well-being compared to how it was *before* the pandemic.

The global pandemic didn't just make people sick. It exposed how sick so many aspects of modern society were already. Think of the underresourced, for-profit care homes, or nursing homes, as they are variously called, that placed seniors in thinly disguised waiting rooms for their final journey to the funeral home. Consider the care staff in these homes, living a gig-economy existence that require them to move from home to home, picking up and carrying infection with them, as they try to hold down multiple jobs to make ends meet. What about the migrant farm laborers, huddled together in little more than shacks, with no rights or protections, earning pitifully low wages, just so the rest of us could get our fresh fruits and vegetables? What about all the essential workers on zero-hours contracts, who, we have learned, are often living in a world with no security, just one paycheck away from destitution?

The world has reached a parlous state when starving children tear open deliveries from the local food bank because school closures mean that their schools can no longer feed them. At the same time, it is outrageous to hear that some children have actually been relieved to be learning at home because they no longer have to endure taunts and bullying at school. It is shocking to discover that schools and school districts in the United States and the UK were threatened with fines or withdrawal of funding if they didn't open up their schools again—even when infection rates that governments were failing to control remained perilously high.[19]

Let's hope that after the pandemic the predictions of epidemiologist Nicholas Christakis, in *Apollo's Arrow*—that we will relive the Roaring 20s that followed the 1918 pandemic—will turn out to be wrong.[20] Let's extend the inspiring spirit of community that arose at times during the pandemic to offer one another help and solidarity. Let's not forget that one of our prime directives in schools is to help young people feel safe, cared for, fulfilled, and thriving, so that they prosper within the school and beyond it. Let's bring the public good, in equitable schools for all, back to the fore. Let's not go back to the worst of what we had before, but instead *build back better* for all young people's well-being for the future. As a start, in this book, we now turn to what the best of well-being can look like and to how we can set about developing it.

1

What Is Well-Being?
Why Does It Matter?

Before 2020, if you'd asked people what first came to mind if you mentioned "the Who," they likely would have thought of the aging British rock band of that name. But another WHO—the World Health Organization—became a household name when it responded to the COVID-19 pandemic. Created by the United Nations in 1947 as an organization responsible for global health issues, the WHO's constitution defined health as "a state of complete physical, mental and social *well-being* and not merely the absence of disease or infirmity" (emphasis added).[21] The WHO established new professions such as psychiatric social work and school counseling. Following World War II, it brought well-being onto the world stage alongside economic performance, peace, and global security.

Well-being is important in all areas of life, but especially in young people's development. We know that young people feel well when they enjoy their learning, look forward to coming to school, and feel valued by their families and friends. We all want them to experience joy, to thrive physically and emotionally, and to have a voice in their learning and their future.

It's not always immediately obvious when young people feel well, though. This is why well-being can be hard to measure sometimes. Well-being can be effervescent and expressive, but not all of us wear our heart on our sleeve. Well-being can just as easily be calm, reflective, and understated. Well-being might be manifested in a bursting sense of pride that accompanies an athletic accomplishment or a successful dramatic performance. But it can also be expressed in the quiet contentment found in reading an engrossing book or just playing quietly with a friend.

We're most likely to grasp the value of well-being when it's not there, when we witness all the signs of being ill instead. We notice when children are hungry or haven't slept. We are alert to young people being isolated, left out, or bullied. We have become increasingly vigilant about vulnerable children who are at risk of neglect or abuse at home. We provide specific help for young people with diagnosed conditions such as autism spectrum disorder, ADHD, anxiety, or fetal alcohol spectrum disorder. More and more schools and school systems have developed policies and strategies to deal with racism, homophobia, and other prejudices. And one of the basic competencies of teaching is to be able to be empathetic toward and supportive of children who have more transient experiences of ill-being such as losing a family member, experiencing the death of a pet, worrying about a parental breakup, or falling out with a best friend.

Well-being, happiness, and fulfillment are not just the icing on the cake of learning and achievement. As we will see in Chapter 8, they are essential to meeting academic goals. It's hard to be successful when you're tired, worried, hungry, fearful, or depressed. Conversely, breakthroughs in accomplishment and mastery can lead to surges in self-confidence and satisfaction.

In addition to their contribution to learning, well-being and fulfillment also have immense value in their own right. Mental health data collected during the COVID-19 pandemic revealed that the group whose well-being often suffered the most was teenagers.[22] At a time in their lives when an important part of growing up is about being with friends and developing a sense of identity and hope for the future, teenagers were cut off from their peers in the neighborhood and from their teachers, mentors, and friends at school. For all the talk about online learning being able to be organized anywhere, anytime after the pandemic, the undeniable truth is that if physical schools are taken away, children and teenagers may become disconnected from many of the people who are important to them and their development. Well-being is an essential part of education and an invaluable part of growing up. We ignore it at our peril.

Learning to Be

Officially, and obviously, the prime purpose of education is not well-being, but learning. Understanding an intriguing idea, learning something new, developing a difficult skill, mastering a challenging concept—this seems to be the essence of education. It's what attracts many teachers into the profession—to switch on light bulbs for children, enable them to grasp or do something they thought was beyond them, help them progress, or introduce them to interests that can turn into lifelong passions.

But schools are not only about academic learning. They promote young people's emotional and moral development too. If we act as if learning and achievement are the only things that matter, we fall into the trap of what Dutch professor Gert Biesta calls learnification.[23]

Learnification means that anything and everything has to be justified in terms of its impact on learning. Want to secure more time for music in your school? Then point to the evidence that music raises mathematics achievement. Interested in developing meditation and biofeedback among your children? Then demonstrate that the resulting calmness will improve performance on test-taking days. And if you are extending the school day, don't emphasize the value of being with peers, practicing leadership, or developing new interests. Just set out the evidence that extended learning time can increase measured achievement.

Alongside learning as we usually understand it, though, schools are also about how children develop. They are about how students experience and express awe, wonder, excitement, compassion, empathy, moral outrage at injustice, courage, playfulness, commitment, self-respect, self-confidence, and many other emotional and moral qualities in their education. Young people need to experience these things not just because of who they will become *in the future* but also because of who they are *now*.

In 1996, the United Nations established an education commission led by a former president of the European Commission, Jacques Delors. Its report was titled *Learning: The Treasure Within*.[24] It built on a preceding UN report, issued 25 years earlier, called *Learning to Be.*[25] The Delors report made a powerful case for humanistic educational goals and purposes that, it claimed, had been overlooked and left behind.

The commission was concerned about growing unemployment, rising rates of exclusion, increasing inequality, and widespread damage to the natural environment. "All-out economic growth," it argued, "can no longer be viewed as the ideal way of reconciling material progress with equity, respect for the human condition and respect for the natural assets that we have a duty to hand on in good condition to future generations."[26] With these concerns uppermost, the Delors report began:

> Education has a fundamental role to play in personal and social development. The Commission does not see education as a miracle cure or a magic formula opening the door to a world in which all ideals will be attained, but as one of the principal means available to foster a deeper and more harmonious form of human development and thereby to reduce poverty, exclusion, ignorance, oppression and war.[27]

The commission's report rested on four pillars of learning.[28] *Learning to know* involved engaging in a broad education and developing subject-specific knowledge. *Learning to do* was about acquiring skills and competencies, including modern skills such as teamwork that we now understand as representing global competencies. These two kinds of learning are what schools and universities have emphasized the most and can be easily examined and tested. However, Delors's team stressed, the other two pillars— *learning to be* and *learning to live together*—are at least as important in a rapidly changing and increasingly imperiled world. Yet they receive far less attention in formal educational systems.

Learning to be is about unearthing the buried treasure of people's hidden talents. These include "memory, reasoning power, imagination, physical ability, aesthetic sense, the aptitude to communicate with others."[29] *Learning to be* requires the development of essential "self-knowledge" among group leaders.[30]

At a time when the collapse of the Berlin Wall had not put an end to national and international conflicts, the most important yet most neglected of all the four pillars, Delors argued, was *learning to live together,* to secure "mutual understanding, peaceful interchange and, indeed, harmony."[31] Learning to live together amounted to developing "an understanding of others and their history, traditions and spiritual values and, on this basis, creating a new spirit which would induce people to implement common projects or to manage the inevitable conflicts in an intelligent and peaceful way."[32]

On January 6, 2021, an insurrectionist mob stormed the US Capitol, tearing up the already fraying fabric of the nation's historic democracy. After the initial shock, who asked how Americans had failed to educate their citizens to *learn to live together?* Who regretted the decades-long atrophy of social studies and civics at the expense of more and more testing? Did technology executives in a digital industry dominated by white men accept responsibility for the profit-driven algorithms that divided people, reinforced their preferences and prejudices to communicate only with others like them, and spread sedition and hate?

Can Americans, and others of us in similarly compromised democracies, ask how we have failed to learn to live together? How can we put things right in our schools, technology and media companies, politics, and society? How can these divisions be healed with courage, empathy, truth, knowledge, critical thinking, and common cause? These things should be as much a part of the well-being agenda as mindfulness, self-regulation, positive mindsets, and resilience.

Learning to Be Well

The Delors report taught us that well-being is about more than feeling healthy, happy, mindful, or resilient. Nor is well-being only about feeling safe and protected from harm. It is not a purely psychological matter. Well-being is also a social condition that involves inclusion, belonging, peacefulness, and human rights. Strong well-being programs and policies see and secure the connections between the psychological states of children and the eventual state of the world. Well-being is a social as well as a psychological phenomenon. It's hard to be well if you live in a sick society.

Let's look at three examples of programs and policies that address both the social and psychological aspects of well-being and their interconnections. They are a high school history program that draws connections between bullying in schools and genocide; an elementary education initiative that develops empathy among young people as a basis for peace in society; and a systemwide policy on child well-being that is a central pillar for also developing excellence, inclusion, and equity.

Facing History and Ourselves

If the broader argument about well-being and society feels like something that belongs only in a world history course or in a peace education curriculum, it is important to acknowledge that the capacity for global conflict begins in our families and communities. At times, it has also been exacerbated in the classrooms and hallways of our schools. This is the essential insight of a curriculum initiative developed in Brookline, Massachusetts, that is now recognized and used all over the world. Its name is Facing History and Ourselves (FHAO).[33]

In 1974, Margot Stern Strom and William Parsons, two secondary school social studies teachers in Brookline, found themselves dissatisfied with how their students were learning about the Holocaust. Try as they might, they felt that their students approached the horrors of genocide almost as if it were any other school subject that needed to be mastered for the college admissions grind. Strom and Parsons acquired a grant to develop a program that would "link a particular history to universal questions, those timely yet timeless questions that resonate with every generation."[34]

Strom became the founder and executive director of FHAO. She later wrote that she wanted "students to confront not only their own potential for passivity and complicity, but also their courage and resilience. And we must teach them to value their rights as citizens and take responsibility for their actions."[35]

In April 1978, NBC television released a miniseries, *Holocaust,* that was viewed by more than 120 million people, many of them secondary school students.[36] Strom and her colleagues wanted to respond to the newfound interest in the Nazis' genocide of

European Jews by helping students to develop their moral reasoning and applying it to how they interacted with others. They developed new lesson plans, swapped them, observed each other's classrooms, and provided each other with critical feedback.

By 1994, FHAO had developed a curriculum and resource book called *Facing History and Ourselves: Holocaust and Human Behavior.*[37] FHAO didn't want students to learn about the Holocaust as just another historical incident. The teachers also wanted students to ask themselves what kinds of people they were, who they wanted to become, and how they would act when confronted with injustices.

A central theme in FHAO is that students have to examine how they themselves treat outsiders in their classrooms and schools. Do they welcome or shun them? Are they passive when they see unpopular students being bullied? Students learn about stage-theory approaches to genocide that begin with what can appear to be relatively minor acts of labeling and ranking others but can escalate into wholesale persecution—and ultimately genocide. In the process, students learn to identify with those who are persecuted, whether in Nazi Germany or in their own schools and communities.

FHAO rapidly gained traction in schools. Curriculum materials expanded to include the Armenian genocide, the US civil rights movement, and topics related to democracy and human rights. What are the results? Teaching about the Holocaust has statistically significant impacts on students' moral reasoning, their abilities to empathize with others, and overall school climate.[38] Even teachers' self-efficacy is enhanced after teaching the FHAO curriculum.[39]

FHAO demonstrates that teaching is about more than getting students to feel good about themselves. It takes students seriously as moral beings and empowers them to look critically at their own lives. It also teaches students that their own well-being is linked with that of others. It urges them to speak up and speak out against injustice, whether in the form of outright bullying or more casual incidents of meanness. It helps young people learn how to be and how to live together.

By 2020, FHAO had become a global network with more than 100,000 teachers in 134 countries.[40] It developed webinars, podcasts, and protocols to help teachers to discuss controversial issues with their students. Most recently, FHAO created content on the spread of the coronavirus and its disproportionate impact on people of color and the poor.[41]

FHAO exemplifies two important points about well-being. It demonstrates that intellectually demanding learning and student well-being can and should go together. It also shows that well-being is a social responsibility as well as an individual lifestyle or a positive health choice.

Roots of Empathy

In 1996, social entrepreneur Mary Gordon established a program called Roots of Empathy for elementary school students in Ontario.[42] The program is designed to increase empathy, caring, and other prosocial behaviors and to reduce aggression, cruelty, meanness, and bullying. Roots of Empathy is now used in countries around the world. In addition to Canada, these include Costa Rica, Germany, Ireland, the Netherlands, New Zealand, Norway, South Korea, Switzerland, the United Kingdom, and the United States.[43] For several years running, it has been recognized as one of the 100 leading educational innovations in the world.[44]

Like most outstanding innovations, Roots of Empathy has a simple but compelling design. Parents of infants between 2 and 4 months old visit a classroom regularly for an entire school year and bring their baby with them. A trained instructor coaches the class to observe the infant and name the baby's feelings.[45] This interaction helps children understand their own feelings and the feelings of others around them too. Who could not be charmed, intrigued, and disarmed by a curious, cute, and defenseless infant? Using the knowledge and insight gained through observing and interacting with a tiny human, children learn to master and moderate as well as understand their own and one another's feelings.

Research in several countries, including rigorous blind-control studies, shows that the Roots of Empathy program significantly increases rates of empathy, sharing, helping, and including, and decreases levels of bullying and other kinds of aggression.[46] Mary Gordon believes that her program doesn't just create a safer and more nurturing school environment for all students. In a world that "is becoming increasingly less democratic and more violent," where children see how "we are failing to understand and support one another," Roots of Empathy's open-ended methods enable children to see the world through the eyes of others, beginning with the baby's.[47]

Kids who have picked on other kids and teased them—or worse—for being too fat, too skinny, too smart, too dumb, having an unusual accent, or wetting the bed, learn through their interactions with and around a baby the importance of inclusion and belonging. They come to understand that "making someone feel like they don't belong is a really cruel thing to do."[48] In the end, like FHAO, but operating with a very different age group and methodology, Roots of Empathy aspires to connect improved classroom well-being to the creation of a more inclusive and empathetic society. As Scottish philosopher and economist Adam Smith once recognized, sympathy is the emotional foundation of democracy.[49]

Ontario Education Policy, 2014–18

The concerns about young people's well-being have led to well-being policies and strategies becoming part of system policy frameworks in a number of places. Ontario—the source of much of our evidence—is one of them. Although Canada is a global leader in educational achievement and equity, its record on student well-being is less impressive. For example, in 2020, UNICEF placed Canada 30th out of 38 better-off nations on a table measuring the well-being of 15-year-olds across three indicators of mental well-being, physical health, and skills.[50] On OECD indicators of life satisfaction, Canada's students are "not significantly different from the OECD average."[51] As in a number of countries in East Asia, Canada's record on student achievement is not matched by its performance in student well-being.

By 2014, the Ontario government and many of its educators were realizing that all was not well with the well-being of their students. For a dozen years, Ontario had, with considerable success, focused on increasing achievement and narrowing achievement gaps in literacy and numeracy. Ontario was and is the highest achieving of Canada's 10 provinces in most areas of education. But by 2013 or so, the decade-long upward curve of improvement was starting to flatten.[52] There were growing concerns that there was more to students' learning and development than literacy and mathematics and high school graduation rates alone. Something had been missing in Ontario's push to improve its achievement record. A big part of that missing piece was young people's well-being.

Field workers in the Ministry of Children and Youth Services were encountering increasing evidence that young people in Ontario were struggling. In response, they developed a "youth engagement process" that entailed "extensive youth dialogue" in "face-to-face" and "interactive workshops" throughout the province, along with an online survey.[53] A Youth Development Committee of 25 young Ontarians was created from a pool of more than 400 applicants to inform the ministry's findings. The resulting report, *Stepping Stones: A Resource on Youth Development,* from the Ministry of Children and Youth Services, was published in 2012.[54] It had a large impact on the province's policies on youth well-being.

From February 2013, after Kathleen Wynne became the premier of Ontario, she and her government made well-being one of Ontario's four educational policy pillars. The ministry's *Achieving Excellence* policy communicated that "students cannot achieve academically if they feel unsafe at school or are bullied online. They cannot be expected to reach their full potential if they have mental health issues and if we do not provide them with the support they need."[55]

Why did one in eight students in Ontario have serious thoughts about suicide? More than one in five students reported being cyberbullied. One in eight worried about being threatened or harmed at school.[56] These percentages were even greater for vulnerable populations such as LGBTQ students and students from Indigenous communities (known in Canada as *FNMI*—First Nations, Métis, and Inuit).[57] These unsettling statistics helped to explain "why the well-being of children and students needs to move to the center of the education system's priorities."[58]

As a result, the ministry encouraged teachers and school administrators to "increase interest among children and youth in being physically active, and to increase their motivation to live healthy, active lives." *Achieving Excellence* called on a broad range of partners to "build safe and accepting schools" and to help students develop as full human beings and contributors to society.[59]

Well-being in Ontario was now regarded as a foundation for educational achievement and equity. Equity was no longer equated just with narrowing achievement gaps in tested literacy and mathematics. Equity involved inclusion of all young people and their identities as well. If students could not see their cultures and identities in the life and curriculum of the school, the reasoning went, they would find it hard to achieve there. Feeling safe and being included, valued, and respected were inalienable parts of the province's bold new agenda of educational improvement.

In 2016, the Ontario Ministry of Education adapted a graphic of student well-being from the 2012 *Stepping Stones* report. The image was based on consultation with children and youth and also developed through discussions with Indigenous elders, to ensure that their culture was visibly represented in the final product (Figure 1.1).

The ministry explained its graphic by observing that "'Self/Spirit' is situated at the center of the four interconnected domains"

FIGURE 1.1

Well–Being Graphic

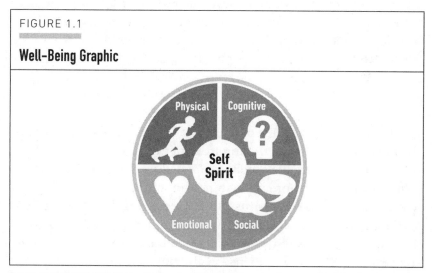

Source: From *Ontario's Well-Being Strategy for Education Discussion Document* (p. 3), by Ontario Ministry of Education, 2016, Queen's Printer for Ontario. Copyright 2016 by Ontario Ministry of Education, Ontario, Canada. Reprinted with permission.

represented by the cognitive, emotional, social, and physical quadrants.[60] It noted that "concepts of self and spirit have different meanings for different people," indicating that in some communities, "cultural heritage, language and community are central to identity."[61] For instance, the ministry noted, "According to Indigenous ways of knowing, well-being is based on the balance of the mental, physical, spiritual, and emotional aspects of the individual, seen not as separate domains but as elements combined and centered within Spirituality and connected by community."[62] The spiritual core of well-being was relevant not just for Indigenous communities but for members of other faiths, and even those of no religious faith, who pursue spiritual development through a reverence for humanity or nature, for example.[63]

This multifaceted and multicultural understanding of well-being is missing from the universal and seemingly culture-free definitions expressed in international rankings and indicators of well-being, happiness, and quality of life. Ontario's ideas about well-being have been rooted in the nature of and vision for the province as a distinctive culture and society. Without this explicit grounding, other schools and school systems may fall into the trap of promoting some norms of well-being that are actually Western and individualistic, for example, compared to other alternatives. We will take up this issue in more detail in Chapter 3.

Conclusion

Well-being is a big deal. Even before the COVID-19 pandemic, it was already moving closer to the forefront of policy priorities in education. Then the pandemic cruelly reminded us that health and well-being must come before everything—in society as well as in our schools. But it is not just viruses that threaten our well-being. War, conflict, environmental devastation, intolerance, prejudice, and division also harm our well-being. So do loneliness, isolation, and living in a virtual world at the expense of the physical world.

Learning to be and *learning to live together* are not just abstract ideals. They are achievable in real programs and policies that help us connect our own health to the health of the world. Yet opportunities to be healthy and to be well are not distributed evenly. Well-being does not mean the same thing for everyone, in every culture. It may be "loud and proud" in Texas, "as bold as brass" in Northern England, or much more humble and self-effacing in East Asian cultures with Confucian heritages and Buddhist associations. There is a lot to learn about what well-being is, what it looks like, how we can recognize it when we see it, and how it is affected by inequality and diversity. These are some of the big questions we raise in this book.

Let's turn first to how mainstream psychological thinking has been approaching well-being. What advice do some of the most popular and well-regarded theories of well-being have to offer? How can they help us? At the same time, what are they missing? We'll come to grips with these issues in the next chapter by outlining and exploring six of the most widely used theories of well-being.

2

Theories of Well-Being:
Evidence and Influence

Practically all teachers want their students to feel happy, experience joy, and achieve a sense of fulfillment. Although we went to school in a time when more than a few teachers were unfair, mean, bullying, and indifferent to our happiness and well-being, most of us would be hard-pressed to find teachers these days who come to school wanting their students to be miserable failures.

For a long time, one of the most widely cited pieces of evidence on what makes an effective school has been the establishment of a safe and orderly environment for learning.[64] But this factor is now just the minimum requirement for children's well-being.

Schools today have an obligation to go far beyond Abraham Maslow's basic levels of safety if they are going to help their students know how to be and how to live together. Attaining well-being involves much more than reaching those minimal thresholds. So what *is* well-being?

Portraying Well-Being

The US Centers for Disease Control and Prevention (CDC) concluded a literature review of health and well-being by noting that there is "general agreement" that "well-being includes the presence of positive emotions and moods (e.g., contentment, happiness) and

14

the absence of negative emotions (e.g., depression, anxiety), satisfaction with life, fulfillment and positive functioning."[65]

In this respect, well-being is an optimal condition that we all should aspire to, both for ourselves and for others. This is why ASCD's Whole Child Network stresses the importance for everyone of "learning to live for universal well-being" as a positive condition of thriving rather than only an absence of individual pain.[66]

Well-being has come into prominence in education following its inclusion in indicators from the OECD, UNESCO, and elsewhere that rank countries in relation to well-being and happiness. Well-being initiatives are now proliferating around the world through a range of programs and practices. In our investigation into how Ontario's well-being strategy was being interpreted by teachers and leaders in 10 school districts, we came across an array of activities that were meant to improve students' well-being. They included the items in Figure 2.1.

Many of these initiatives were introduced by individual teachers and schools in particular grades or subjects. Inevitably they were uneven in their spread and implementation. In an attempt to offset this problem, systems across the world, from individual schools to entire nations, have produced comprehensive frameworks that try to capture and represent all conceivable approaches to improving student well-being. These frameworks and the graphics that accompany them enable teachers and leaders to see where and how well-being can and should receive attention in all areas of their work, in relation to all aspects of well-being. They are useful for monitoring existing practice and developing new interventions.

The framework depicted in Figure 2.2 was developed by one of the school districts in our study. It shows the many ways in which well-being can be addressed. Valuable though they are, however, such frameworks are also like overly detailed maps that can be overwhelming as a basis for plotting the way forward. They can cause educators to overplan, on the one hand, or to feel they are always falling short somewhere, on the other. Alongside frameworks like these, therefore, something else is needed: clear theories

FIGURE 2.1

Well-Being Activities in 10 Ontario School Districts

Focus	Activity
Design	Calming spaces for kindergarten children
Curriculum	Emotional self-regulation
	Social justice projects on refugees or homelessness
Mindfulness	Breathing, meditation, and yoga
Monitoring	Phone apps for students to draw teachers' and counselors' attention to peers experiencing health issues
Student Voice	Mental health committees comprising students with mental health issues of their own
	Student-designed posters on mental health solutions
	Gay-straight alliances to support LGBTQ students
Poverty Alleviation	Breakfast, laundry, and clothing support for children in poverty through support worker positions and charitable funding drives
Identity	Acknowledging and celebrating identities of vulnerable groups such as the French-speaking linguistic minority, refugees, students with special needs, Indigenous communities, and LGBTQ students

that underpin people's understandings of well-being and how it can be improved through particular interventions and courses of action.

Kurt Lewin, who is often credited with establishing the entire discipline of social psychology, once wrote that "there is nothing as practical as a good theory."[67] Theories are statements about how things are interrelated, about where there are patterns of cause and effect. Theories enable us to understand why things are the way they are, and either directly or indirectly, they suggest how those things might be changed. We all have working theories about why people behave the way they do. Sometimes, through disciplines such as action research (which Lewin also invented) or collaborative inquiry, teachers and other people formalize those theories, test them, and refine them through evidence and experience.

FIGURE 2.2

The "Continuum of Care" in an Ontario School District

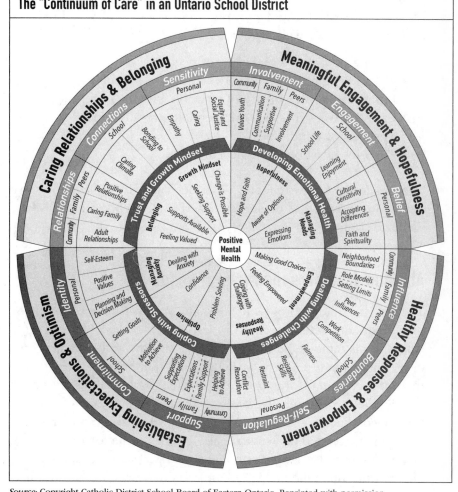

Source: Copyright Catholic District School Board of Eastern Ontario. Reprinted with permission.

People working in scientific disciplines develop formal theories—through experiments, surveys, observations, and other methods—that become established in their fields of operation and that influence practitioners who work in those fields. Researchers in social psychology have had a strong influence on the field and practice of well-being. The findings of some of the most prominent social psychologists have led to a booming industry of self-help books, TED Talks, professional development workshops, and apps to promote their ideas.

Six of the most popular and impactful bodies of social psychological research on well-being are

- Abraham Maslow's hierarchy of needs,
- Martin Seligman's framework of positive psychology,
- Daniel Goleman's theory of emotional intelligence,
- Carol Dweck's research on fixed and growth mindsets,
- Theories of mindfulness, and
- Theories of whole child development.

The remainder of this chapter describes each theoretical approach and shows how it has been manifested in the schools and districts we have studied.

Abraham Maslow's Hierarchy of Needs

The US psychology professor Abraham Maslow set out one of the most frequently referenced and widely used theories of human motivation in his famous *hierarchy of needs*. Maslow argued that people everywhere want to satisfy basic human requirements. These needs, he proposed, can be arranged in a hierarchy of human development (see Figure 2.3). Originally, Maslow contended that each of five distinct needs had to be satisfied before the next in the hierarchy, so that they proceeded in a sequential order from one to another.[68] The general view today is that although one need may be dominant at any point in time, the needs can and do often overlap. For instance, not everyone always puts safety first, or even second, as Maslow claimed. Believers in a cause will go on hunger strike or be willing to die for their country. People will throw themselves in front of their partners or their children during a mass shooting. Some people will risk absolutely everything, in fact, to sacrifice themselves for causes they believe in or people they love. Writers and other artists will go night after night without sleep in order to bring a creative project to fruition. Part of what made COVID-19 so challenging was that so

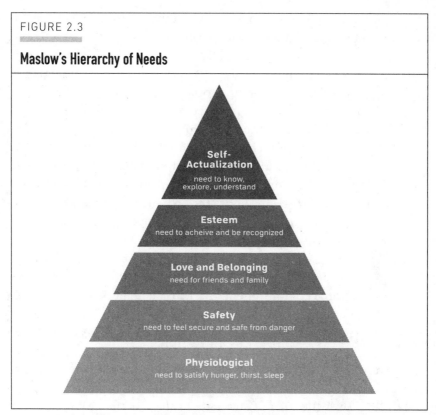

FIGURE 2.3

Maslow's Hierarchy of Needs

Self-Actualization
need to know, explore, understand

Esteem
need to acheive and be recognized

Love and Belonging
need for friends and family

Safety
need to feel secure and safe from danger

Physiological
need to satisfy hunger, thirst, sleep

Source: From *The Learning Compact Renewed: Whole Child for the Whole World* (p. 15), 2018, ASCD.

many needs had to be addressed at once, which made it difficult for educators to know where to set their priorities.

According to Maslow, the different stages in his hierarchy of needs are as follows:

1. *Physiological,* in terms of the basic survival needs for food, shelter, clean air and water, clothing, and sleep. When the COVID-19 pandemic happened, everyone was reminded that even before learning and achievement, the physical and mental health of young people is paramount.
2. *Safety,* with regard to protection from violence, abuse, and disease. All children want to go to a school in a safe environment that is free from bullying and mindful of child protection.

3. *Love and belonging,* in terms of needs for attachment to social groups and communities as protections against loneliness, anxiety, and depression. Belonging is a big part of what it means to experience well-being, whereas lack of belonging is a prime reason for young people's experiences of ill-being.

4. *Esteem,* as experienced in acceptance, recognition, and being valued by others in the community. Being esteemed is a fundamental issue of inclusion in schools. These days, we would also say that there are risks not just of insufficient self-esteem as a result of being excluded or ignored, but also of inflated levels of self-esteem at others' expense. Esteem should be based on real effort and accomplishment rather than mere presence and participation.

5. *Self-actualization,* in terms of the realization of personal potential, fulfillment, and a sense of worth through deliberate quests for accomplishment as a learner, an athlete, a gardener, or a parent, for example. For Maslow, the ultimate form of self-actualization was a quasi-religious "peak experience."[69]

Toward the end of his life, Maslow added a sixth level, "self-transcendence," to his hierarchy of needs. He expressed "deep uneasiness" over the idea of self-actualization as the culmination of human development and wrote that there was something in "the higher stages of human nature" that impelled people to reach "*beyond* health."[70] The pursuit of "ultimate verities" such as "truth, goodness, beauty"[71] seemed to have a magnetic force all their own for which people were prepared to sacrifice even their health and their happiness. People "who are struggling and reaching upward really have a better prognosis than the ones who rest perfectly content at the self-actualization level," he observed.[72] Maslow's existential and even spiritual insights about this sixth level have, however, received little follow-up or recognition.

The resonance and utility of Maslow's hierarchy of needs for teachers and educational leaders, especially in terms of the primacy of the first two or three levels in relation to vulnerable students, were clearly apparent in our 10 districts. For example, an assistant principal of a school where 85 percent of students self-identified as

Indigenous and that was "the hub for 23 First Nation tribes" stated, "We have a lot of kids that are high-anxiety, with a lot of developmental trauma. A lot of kids are in [foster] care." A principal in the same district explained, "We look at our role as addressing the whole student. Sometimes we clothe them, feed and shower them, and love them, really. It takes a lot of work and a lot of empathy and understanding."

One of the teachers in this district asked, "You really start off the day, you are looking at Maslow's hierarchy of needs. How did they sleep? Are they hungry? Are they feeling OK? Are they happy? You are starting bare bones and you work your way up until [they] are ready to learn." When students at this school joined a cookout for teachers after school hours, one of them asked her teacher, "Do you mind if I get a plate for my mom? She's really hungry and she's too embarrassed to ask."

The principal in this school attributed the vulnerability of her students to parents who are "unemployed, uneducated, living in extreme poverty." "We have one of the highest suicide-rate areas in all of Canada," one service provider in this district noted. People are pushed to the brink as a result of "a lot of despair, hopelessness, depression." Many students had witnessed suicide in their families or seen family members self-harming. Some students had attempted suicide themselves.

Attending to Maslow's hierarchy of needs is essential for all students who struggle. It matters not only in Indigenous communities like the one we just described but also among various other communities. In our own research, these included refugees who manifested the effects of post-traumatic stress in hitting and biting behaviors, poor white working-class students in communities where factories had closed down and employment prospects had disappeared, LGBTQ students who were subject to bullying, and Old Order Mennonite communities whose children left school early to marry or work on the farms (which led principals to put their priority on building relationships with families by walking home with them and carrying their shopping purchases, or by using their produce for school meals). Outside our own research samples, we could also add African American, African Canadian, and, in the UK, BAME (Black,

Asian, and Minority Ethnic) students and their historic subjection to racism and oppression, which frequently leads to underachievement. The same could be said for many high-achieving, first-generation immigrant students from East Asia who nonetheless experience emotional tension in managing the peer cultures of Western high schools and traditional expectations from their parents.

Putting Maslow's hierarchy before achievement goals is essential in the middle of a crisis, especially for the most vulnerable students. Maslow usually tends to be invoked when the more basic needs of food, safety, and belonging are prioritized. It's really important to not stop there, though. Students bring assets and potential as well as deficits. All students, and especially those who are struggling due to reasons beyond their control, have the right to aspire to self-actualization and self-transcendence. Indeed, in Indigenous cultures, self-transcendence is often not the last level that has to be attended to but comes close to being the first. Perhaps spiritual hunger for something better, higher, and more worthy of all of us is one of the greatest hungers of all.

Cindy Blackstock, Canadian First Nations activist and professor of social work at McGill University in Montreal, points out that Maslow developed his final stage of spiritual transcendence after staying with the Blackfoot Indians in Canada. Here, she notes, Maslow learned about and was inspired by the importance of spirituality in Indigenous ways of knowing and being. However, Blackstock continues, Maslow failed to "fully situate the individual within the context of community" and to see human needs in relational, cultural, contextual, and intergenerational terms, rather than purely individual ones of self-actualization and self-transcendence.[73] This critique of Maslow underlines how well-being is a social and cultural phenomenon, not merely an individual and psychological one.

Martin Seligman's PERMA Framework

Martin Seligman is the Zellerbach Family Professor of Psychology at the University of Pennsylvania's Department of Psychology. Like Maslow, he is a former president of the American Psychological

Association. Along with his doctoral dissertation chair, Steven Maier, he is famous for his early research into *learned helplessness,* which explains why people are often passive in the face of factors that seem beyond their control.[74] But it is his landmark studies on what he called *positive psychology,* and his advocacy for well-being interventions, for which he will likely be most remembered.

Some years ago, Seligman and his colleagues were concerned that the field of psychology had become preoccupied with people's mental and emotional dysfunctions and was neglecting joy and other positive emotions.[75] Seligman wasn't the first to have this opinion. Maslow had already argued that the two major schools of psychological thought—psychoanalysis and behaviorism—conceived of human beings as being riddled with pathologies.[76]

Seligman has taken Maslow's forays into well-being and turned them into an impressive program of theory and research. Seligman concentrated on mental and emotional states that were positive in nature when things were going well. He boldly stated that "the time has come to resurrect character" as a key psychological construct and to understand that humans have much more "decision latitude" when it comes to shaping their lives than they ordinarily believe.[77]

With concepts such as *learned optimism* and Carol Dweck's *growth mindset,* this approach has emphasized how to develop positive states of mind and real-world approaches to problem solving that can be adopted at scale to build better schools and societies. Seligman and his colleagues developed a battery of interventions to infuse "positive education" into schools by asking students to identify their "signature strengths" and to write journal entries on "what went well" during their school day.[78]

Business CEOs, self-help specialists, transnational organizations such as the OECD, and even government leaders such as former UK Prime Minister David Cameron have seen in Seligman's work a practical basis for providing psychological supports and interventions to significantly improve people's overall quality of life.[79]

Seligman's ideas are expressed in a mnemonic of five principles known as PERMA (see Figure 2.4). The state of well-being embodied in these elements of PERMA is found in

- *Positive emotions,* such as joy or happiness;
- *Engagement,* which reaches what Mihaly Csikszentmihalyi describes as being in a state of *flow,* when we are so absorbed by an activity that we lose track of everything else going on around us;[80]
- *Relationships* of human connection and intimacy;
- *Meaning,* purpose, and a sense of fulfillment in being part of something greater than ourselves; and
- *Accomplishment* of goals and purposes that lead to pride and satisfaction.

Together, Seligman claims, these elements create a sense of human flourishing that amounts to more than evanescent happiness or superficial fun.[81] They are also more positive and active than simply avoiding ill-being and harm by establishing senses of safety or preventing bullying.

With research findings demonstrating the impact of PERMA interventions in countries as disparate as Bhutan, Mexico, and Peru, the framework's influence as a way to understand and develop

---

FIGURE 2.4

Seligman's PERMA Framework

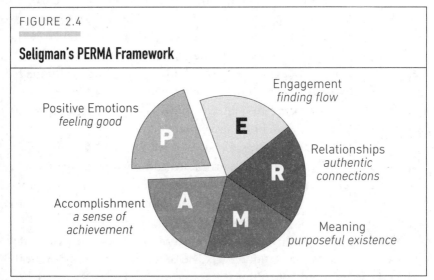

Source: Adapted from "Positive Psychology Theory in a Nutshell," by Catarina Lino. https://positive psychology.com/positive-psychology-theory/. PERMA® is a registered trademark of Martin E. P. Seligman.

well-being has become considerable.[82] The PERMA framework is, in this respect, describing not just a state of mind but a way of life that is purposeful, meaningful, ethical, and relational. It validates the importance of human worth and the creation of a better life in which human beings are able to thrive and flourish.

None of our 10 Ontario districts made explicit use of Seligman's PERMA framework, but a lot of their practices were consistent with it. For example, one of the largest districts in the province had shifted from a language of "marker students," who were failing to achieve measured proficiency for one reason or another, to "students of wonder," whom educators felt were wonderful as human beings but nonetheless they struggled with aspects of their learning. Educators in multidisciplinary teams identified students of wonder whom they wanted to help to flourish more, gathered and analyzed samples of their work, and developed interventions to respond to their needs.

What was the impact of these teams? Educators in one school wrote:

> In the beginning, our student of wonder showed no confidence, limited communication skills, and played alone. We chose to give her more opportunities to communicate, such as small oral language groups and dramatic play opportunities. The impact of this was that she became more confident when she became more responsible for her learning and belonging. Her confidence has led to her playing with other students, participating in class, and communicating in different ways. Our next steps are to continue to run small oral language groups with various students, and to encourage her to take on a main role in the dramatic play center to increase her vocabulary.

All the principles of PERMA were evident here. The student experienced *positive emotions* as she grew in confidence. She became more *engaged* with her learning as her opportunities to communicate were expanded. This engagement helped her to build *relationships* with other students. She also came to appreciate how *meaningful* it was to become "more responsible for her learning and belonging." By taking on the "main role in the dramatic play center," she would increase her growing sense of *accomplishment* in being a valued member of her class.

In relation to older students, the district with the Continuum of Care model shown in Figure 2.2 created student well-being surveys that it used to design suggested "action plans" that were published in a reader-friendly flip book. Some of the proposed activities were to

- "Encourage students to write three positive things that happened that day."
- Ask students "to engage in positive self-talk and limit themselves participating in negative self-talk."
- "Model and teach optimistic and positive attitudes, language, and actions."

Educators were especially concerned about students who were bullying one another on digital devices, so the district trained teachers "to develop a **P**ositive, strength-based attitude." Students were to be brought into a "culture of **E**ngagement" in which they would "feel optimistic, positive, confident, and capable." Principals would "go around to all the classrooms" at "the beginning of the year" to promote an antibullying app the district had developed. They encouraged students to use it to build healthy **R**elationships with one another. Teachers adapted assignments to give them real **M**eaning for students by focusing on something the "struggling student is passionate about, further emphasizing strength." They helped students to gain a sense of **A**ccomplishment, so that they associated school with "feelings of success."

Theories of Social and Emotional Learning (SEL) and Regulation

In the United States, well-being in education is typically described as "social and emotional learning," or SEL. SEL is best known through the work of the Collaborative for Academic, Social, and Emotional Learning (CASEL).[83] CASEL was cofounded by US academic, *New York Times* journalist, and bestselling author Daniel Goleman. Goleman is famous for his theory of *emotional intelligence* in individuals, relationships, organizations, and education. Without question, his

1995 blockbuster book, *Emotional Intelligence,* and its sequels, *Working with Emotional Intelligence* and *Primal Leadership,* have changed how people think about the role that emotions play in our learning, our well-being, and our lives.[84] Goleman's groundbreaking idea has affected thousands of schools around the world.

Emotional intelligence, Goleman argues, is different from the kind of intelligence we think can be easily measured by multiple-choice IQ tests. Emotional intelligence, he says, is a trainable competence. It comprises people's capacity to recognize and label human emotions, including their own, and then to manage and control their own and others' emotions, such as anger or anxiety, in order to improve relationships and effectiveness. Emotional intelligence, Goleman claims, adds value to cognitive intelligence, improving people's ability to learn, reason, judge, and perform effectively.

Goleman identified five different domains of emotional intelligence:

1. *Self-awareness:* people's ability to recognize and understand their moods, emotions, and drives, as well as their effect on others.
2. *Self-regulation:* the ability to control or redirect disruptive impulses and moods, and to think before acting.
3. *Motivation:* a passion to work or learn for reasons that go beyond money or status and to pursue goals with energy and persistence.
4. *Empathy:* the ability to understand the emotional makeup of other people in all their diversity, and the skill to manage conflicts and differences accordingly.
5. *Social skill:* proficiency in executing the previous four domains and putting them into action.

CASEL has evolved the original areas identified by Goleman into five core competencies:[85]

1. Self-awareness
2. Self-management
3. Social awareness
4. Relationship skills
5. Responsible decision-making

According to the CASEL website, these five core competencies make up the essence of social and emotional learning (see Figure 2.5). This learning is defined as "the process through which all young people and adults acquire and apply the knowledge, skills, and attitudes to develop healthy identities, manage emotions and achieve personal and collective goals, feel and show empathy for others, establish and maintain supportive relationships, and make responsible and caring decisions."[86] Research on the impact of SEL programs points to positive effects on student achievement and engagement, mental health, and the kind of work ethic that leads to greater success in gaining meaningful employment and to living healthier lives after school is over.[87]

Through the work of CASEL and other organizations, SEL initiatives have spread widely throughout North America. By 2013, all US states had identified preschool competencies for SEL. A growing number of states had also developed age-appropriate competencies for K–12 education.[88] Countless professional development courses have been taken by teachers eager to promote SEL.

FIGURE 2.5

The CASEL Framework

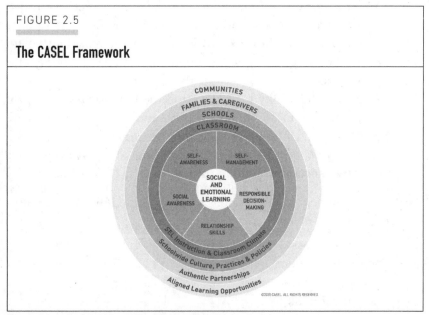

Source: Copyright © 2020 by CASEL. All rights reserved.

The spirit and substance of many of these initiatives were pop-
ularized in the 2015 Disney animated children's movie *Inside Out.*[89]
Informed by the advice of University of California, Berkeley, psychologist Dacher Keltner, author of *Born to Be Good: The Science of
a Meaningful Life,* the movie revolves around an 11-year-old child
and the inner turmoil and ultimate resolution she experiences when
she takes flight from a family crisis and finds her emotions battling
for supremacy with each other in the control room of her brain.[90]
Five of the six basic emotions that Charles Darwin claimed were
culturally universal—joy, sadness, anger, fear, and disgust (Darwin
also included surprise)—take on individual personalities in the
movie.[91] These characters also encounter different zones during
their journey together that are colored according to their emotional
nature, such as red for anger and blue for sadness.

This "Wizard of Oz" of the emotions has provided children, families, and schools with clear reference points. Children as young as
5 can now label and then discuss their own and others' emotions as
a basis for emotional self-regulation. In Ontario we came across at
least nine different programs addressing well-being through emotional regulation. Several made explicit reference to and based curriculum content and lesson plans on the association of emotions
with colors. Teachers referenced these repeatedly throughout the
school day with their students.

One of the most widely used programs in Ontario is called
Zones of Regulation. This provides students with "a framework to
foster self-regulation and emotional control."[92] The zones were created when researchers found that students were being punished for
misbehavior largely because teachers had not understood the pre-
cipitating events. Sometimes these events could be something as
easy to alter as lowering the level of external stimulation for students with autism spectrum disorder. One district described this as
an "early emotional literacy project teaching kids to identify their
emotions and getting more vocabulary than *happy, mad, sad.*"

In this program, students are taught to identify their emotions
with reference to four categories or colors:

1. The *Red Zone* describes extremely heightened states of alertness and intense emotions. A person in this zone may be

elated or experiencing anger, rage, explosive behavior, devastation, or terror. Students in this zone do not find it possible to advance their academic learning.

2. The *Yellow Zone* also describes a heightened state of alertness and elevated emotions, but people in this zone have some control over their actions. A person in this zone may be experiencing stress, frustration, anxiety, excitement, silliness, "the wiggles," or nervousness.

3. The *Green Zone* describes a calm state of alertness. A person here may be happy, focused, content, or ready to learn. This is the zone that teachers aim for, where optimal learning occurs.

4. The *Blue Zone* describes low states of alertness, such as feeling sad, tired, sick, or bored. Students in this zone need teachers to rouse them to life with exciting curricula that can take their minds off their troubles and reengage them by expanding their imaginations.

Teachers and administrators have been enthusiastic about Zones of Regulation. One elementary teacher's students had a little strip on their desks with the four colors that they could use to check in with their teacher. She explained:

> I will just say to everyone, "What zone are you in?" If they're not in the green zone, which is ready to learn, ready to go, we've got to figure out what we can do. I do have a couple of kids that would say, "I'm in the yellow. Can we have a body break?" That goes to one of the strategies to get you out of the yellow and into the green, just to move, to exercise.

A teacher in a different district explained how Zones of Regulation was "teaching little children at the age of 3 'Are you in the red zone? If you're in the red zone, this is what you can do.'" She continued, "Teachers are actually loving it as well. It's something across the district." Another teacher described how "we're also working on labeling feelings, because if they don't know what it is that they're feeling, they don't know how they can help themselves." Here, the teacher believes, better emotional intelligence improves students' self-determination by giving them ways to describe what they are feeling throughout the school day.

The four zones provide an easy way to discuss emotional topics that come up as a matter of course in the early childhood classroom. "I think giving everybody a consistent language is helping, because working with students, they're able to identify the zones a lot easier than they're able to identify what emotion it is," one teacher said. The program also give teachers a framework to think about the children's emotional well-being, how that affects learning, and how they might change their own teaching accordingly. One teacher said:

> Right after Christmas, I'd done a lesson and I just felt it didn't go well, and after I came back I realized the reason was because most of the kids were in the yellow zone. When I went back the next day and said, "Who can tell me what we did yesterday?" none of them could remember. I think when I'm teaching, I'm more aware of what's going on with the students, and if I'm seeing that the students are not in the green zone, maybe the whole class needs a body break.

According to one principal, educators were "seeing some gains" because of this approach. Suspension numbers had dropped since implementing the Zones of Regulation. "Kids are able to take responsibility for behavior a little more easily than they used to," the principal said. "They're able to articulate what went wrong."

We will see other ways of approaching emotional self-regulation later on in this book. The point to stress now is that it has become a central component of the SEL programs that are spreading rapidly in schools today. This expansion, in turn, springs from the success of Goleman's idea that emotional intelligence is real and measurable. The premise is not only that emotional intelligence can be taught and learned in deliberate ways, but also that schools have a social responsibility to develop it in their students.

Carol Dweck's Mindsets

Carol Dweck is the Lewis and Virginia Eaton Professor of Psychology at Stanford University. Her book *Mindset: The New Psychology of Success* has earned her top rankings on TED Talks and a Distinguished Scientific Contribution Award from the American Psychological Association.[93] Dweck is also the inaugural winner of the

$4 million Yidan Prize for "significant contribution to the science of education."[94]

Like Maslow's hierarchy of needs and Seligman's positive psychology, Dweck's research has worked its way into the heart of the education profession. These days, people in various fields, from politics to sports, effortlessly use the language of "growth mindsets" and "fixed mindsets." At a surface level, these categories resonate with everyday distinctions we all make between can-do people and people who seem unable or unwilling to change or improve. Of course, there is more to these two mindsets than meets the eye.

For Dweck, a generative "growth mindset" is predicated "on the belief that your basic qualities are things you can cultivate through your efforts."[95] People with growth mindsets love challenges. When they fail at tasks, they view their difficulties as opportunities for growth. "The passion for stretching yourself and sticking to it, even (or especially) when it's not going well, is the hallmark of the growth mindset," Dweck writes.[96]

Those with "fixed mindsets," on the other hand, think of intelligence as a static attribute. This assumption is devastating for students who struggle in school, because once they've fallen into a pattern of receiving low marks, they become preoccupied with "distracting thoughts" and "secret worries" about whether they are smart or not.[97] Even students who score well in school are unhappy if they have fixed mindsets. When their schools tell them they are smart, they love the approval, of course. But when they are confronted with evidence that they still have a lot to learn, they suffer because they've been socialized to believe that "imperfections are shameful."[98] As the lyrics of Céline Dion's hit song *Imperfections* express it, students like this feel they have got their "own set of scars to hide."[99]

The conundrum of the mindset research is that more praise doesn't get people out of fixed mindsets or out of the failure or worry that accompanies them. Indeed, Dweck warns against "the danger of praise and positive labels." "Telling children they're smart, in the end, made them feel dumber and act dumber, but claim that they were smarter," her research has shown.[100]

What does all this mean? Choosing between positive or negative evaluations isn't the issue. What matters is whether students think of themselves as people who can get smarter through perseverance and curiosity or whether they think that their intelligence is fixed and not much can be done about it. Dweck asks, *What could put an end to the fixed mindset?* To improve schooling, she says, we need to start by acknowledging "how changing people's beliefs—even the simplest beliefs—can have profound effects" on students' learning.[101]

The power of growth mindsets is exemplified in the work of legendary African American teacher Marva Collins, who welcomed inner-city students into her Chicago classroom and got them reading at such high levels and with such palpable joy that she became a national celebrity. Dweck quotes Collins as saying, "I have always been fascinated with learning, with the *process* of discovering something new." When a reporter asked a boy in Collins's class what made her teaching special, he answered, "We do hard things here. They fill your brain."[102]

So who is responsible for kids having fixed mindsets? Dweck never comes straight out and blames teachers. Still, for Dweck, the role of the teacher is absolutely key. If a student says, "I can't do this," teachers should amend their statement to be "I can't do this *yet.*" If students don't like algebra or say "I hate math," teachers should encourage them to consider the alternative "I'm learning by getting better at working hard on difficult challenges" or should coach them to change their beliefs by affirming that "you can always substantially change how intelligent you are."[103]

Researchers have tried to replicate Dweck's studies but have been unable to get the same decisive results.[104] As we shall see in Chapter 3, the argument that teachers can transform student achievement by altering their own and their students' beliefs about learning is open to exaggeration and misuse, as is also the case with positive psychology as a whole.

Although beliefs and mindsets play a role in learning and achievement, social structures of poverty and insufficient support for public services and safety nets cannot be ignored. Indeed, downplaying the social and political factors that create barriers for students' proclivities to want to grow in confidence and skill can tempt some administrators into using growth mindsets to gaslight their teachers into believing that they alone are responsible for failures of students in poverty. In 2015, Dweck acknowledged that this kind of misinterpretation is "what keeps me up at night."[105]

Almost half the projects in our 10 districts put a priority on developing growth mindsets among students and their teachers. "A lot of the dialogue now is about the growth mindset and how important that is," one teacher said. A growth mindset was linked to improving mathematics achievement, students' self-regulation, and resiliency. One special education consultant spoke about "building in mindset activities in every single coaching session" with teachers. Teachers accordingly said that they were learning how to shift their feedback to students so that they would be more able to appreciate "how mistakes are learning opportunities."

Another teacher took the idea of mindsets further, to include engagement with parents. She showed her students videos about growth mindsets to encourage them to not give up on tough problems so quickly. "The kids are going home and there's some YouTube videos [on the topic] that they're actually playing for the parents at home," one said. By promoting the belief that everyone can achieve, educators treated well-being and academic success as the results of hard-won effort.

However, despite these positive initiatives, it is also important to heed Dweck's warning that many educators "claim to have a growth mindset" simply because it "had become the right thing to have, the right way to think," even though they "continued to react to their children's mistakes as if they are problematic or harmful."[106] The point of growth mindsets is to change actual practice and not just people's professed beliefs.

Mindfulness

In 2018, an extraordinary phenomenon occurred in bestselling nonfiction. The top books were not business guides, biographies of celebrities, or even self-help texts. They were coloring books—for adults. With calming titles such as *Moments of Mindfulness: Anti-Stress Coloring and Activities for Busy People,* these runaway bestsellers tapped into a readership that was overwhelmed with work, digital demands, and consumerism.[107] They were aimed at people who just wanted to sit quietly, color, be left alone, and be in the present moment. As an antidote to our crazy-busy world, the masses had discovered and embraced mindfulness.

A glance at Google's N-gram viewer shows that the word *mindfulness* first emerged around the 1950s and '60s, started to get broader adoption in the 1990s, and then really took off in the early 2000s.[108] Why? Mainly, there seems to have been a convergence of two developments: the acceptance of mindfulness in popular culture and the emergence of new findings in neuroscience.

On the one hand, ever since the Beatles brought meditation into the mainstream in the 1960s, through being tutored by the Maharishi Mahesh Yogi, exploring alternate states of mind captured the attention of popular culture. In *Be Here Now,* former Harvard psychology professor Richard Alpert (later known as Ram Dass, which means "servant of God[109]") described how he and his colleague Timothy Leary (famous for urging 30,000 hippies at a "Human Be-In" in San Francisco's Golden Gate Park in 1967 to "turn on, tune in, drop out") had shared LSD with their students at Harvard University.[110] This was before Alpert dedicated himself to meditation. Even though Alpert emphatically rejected the use of hallucinogens after his commitment to meditation, the association of meditation with drugs meant that it was sometimes regarded as an escapist indulgence. This old stereotype of meditation and mindfulness persists to this day among some parents and members of the public who want schools to abandon well-being and get back to basics.

A second approach to meditation took a more minimalist and ascetic path. It is personified in the teachings of Vietnamese Zen master Thich Nhat Hanh. The nonagenarian Thich Nhat Hanh has been an antiwar activist, was nominated by Martin Luther King Jr. for a Nobel Peace Prize, and espouses a form of "engaged Buddhism" in pursuit of inner peace that puts social ethics at the forefront.[111]

Thich Nhat Hanh's followers are invited to focus in minute detail on following their in-breaths and out-breaths. "The mind is like a monkey swinging from branch to branch through a forest," Thich Nhat Hanh says, yet it can be brought to peace through disciplined practice.[112] With the help of extended retreats and through guided meditation tapes, millions have sought a greater sense of equilibrium by dedicating themselves to daily meditation. Thich Nhat Hanh's mindful meditation is not just meant to benefit the individual. It is also supposed to ensure that, through open-minded "nonattachment from views," practitioners "will respect the right of others to be different and to choose what to believe and how to decide."[113] Mindful meditation, then, is a way to fuse inner peace of the self with outer peace in the world.

At the time of Abraham Maslow's death in 1970, research into what he described as "the farther reaches of human nature" was in its infancy.[114] Since then, however, neuroscientists have conducted thousands of experiments on people's ability to influence and control their ways of thinking and feeling. For example, Dennis's former neighbor, Professor Jon Kabat-Zinn, has conducted research at the University of Massachusetts Memorial Medical Center in Worcester on what he calls "mindfulness-based stress reduction" (MBSR).[115] By teaching a simplified form of meditation in an eight-week program, Kabat-Zinn and his colleagues showed that when patients increased their capacity to manage their own stress and anxiety, they benefited not just in terms of positive psychological developments but greater physical health as well. In one study, for example, meditating patients with psoriasis healed at four times the rate of a nonmeditating control group.[116]

By 2005, more than 16,000 people—including Dennis—had been served by Kabat-Zinn's clinics and at his retreats. A free MBSR clinic was established in inner-city Worcester, and more than 100 scientific papers were published on this secularized version of mindfulness. Simultaneously, other neuroscientists began using CT scans, MRIs, and PET scans to ascertain exactly what was happening in the brains of experienced meditators. Studies by Richard Davidson and Antoine Lutz at the University of Wisconsin found that meditation not only stimulated the growth of new neurons in distinct local areas of the brain but also improved how neural pathways were strengthened across them, thereby helping people to respond to adversity more quickly and adaptively.[117]

Concurrent with the emergence of this research, educators and the general public also developed an interest in mindfulness.

Dennis was among them. In 2005, with a teacher leader, Elizabeth MacDonald, he established a seminar for a group of Boston Public School teachers. One result was their book on *The Mindful Teacher.*[118] Other writers have followed with titles including *Mindful Learning, Mindfulness for Teachers,* and *The Way of Mindful Education.*[119] A booming industry of websites, social media apps, and nonprofit organizations concerned with mindfulness also sprouted up before and during the COVID-19 pandemic. Just one of them, www.mindfulschools.org, "has trained over 50,000 educators, parents, and mental health professionals from across the globe, reaching an estimated 3 million children worldwide."[120]

What does the research say about the impact of mindfulness interventions in schools? One randomized control study of a "mindfulness-based kindness curriculum" in a sample of 68 preschool children found that "the intervention group showed greater improvements in social competence and earned higher report card grades in domains of learning, health, and social-emotional development, whereas the control group exhibited more selfish behavior over time."[121] Another randomized control study, this time of elementary school students, found that "children in the Mindful Awareness Practices group who were less well-regulated showed greater improvement in executive function compared with controls."[122] At the secondary level, a randomized control study of 198 students of low socioeconomic backgrounds compared ones who were taught mindfulness meditation with a control group. "Results revealed a significant increase in working memory capacity for participants in the meditation group." The research team concluded "that certain mindfulness practices may be uniquely associated with aspects of cognitive functioning and physical health."[123]

In some places, mindfulness initiatives are expanding system-wide. For example, 370 schools in England have begun teaching mindfulness meditation to generate "new, robust evidence about what works best for their students' mental health and well-being," according to a government website.[124]

Back in our Ontario schools, we observed many ways in which teachers were exploring mindfulness with their students. "There's breathing, body scanning, and learning techniques, and recognizing arousal," one teacher said. In her school, teachers taught

> the students about full body listening with your mind. What did that look like? What did that sound like? Your ears, your eyes, just your whole body. We have many new teachers who are very interested. They introduced it in their classroom with some high-needs kids. It's very interesting to see the kids that are "up here" one minute, and put that mindfulness practice into place, and they can come right back down. We can get back into teaching then.

Schools across the districts were also experimenting with "calming spaces," where students could retreat for a little restorative time before returning to a class. Educators had begun teaching students the basics of meditation so they could learn to settle their bodies and quiet down their minds to prepare for learning. Some teachers introduced simple yoga exercises so that students had the benefits of increased blood flow to enhance optimal levels of cognition.

Mindfulness interventions were especially popular in early childhood classrooms. Some teachers invited students to try out simple activities such as following their breath when they were stressed or anxious. Others used imaginative play to demonstrate different ways students could manage conflict. Mindfulness wasn't a stand-alone experience but was linked with learning. As Figure 2.6 indicates, one kindergarten classroom's calming area not only encouraged children to "take 10 deep breaths" but also to "read a book" or to "draw and write" if they were "tird," "angre," or "hppr" (tired, angry, or hyper).

Mindfulness practices do not solve large-scale problems by themselves. But they do promote and support children's social competencies and academic learning. Moreover, Dennis's work on mindful teaching in Boston enabled teachers to open up, support each other, and be highly critical about controversial issues such as neighborhood violence and top-down administrative control that were affecting their students' and their own well-being.[125] Social approaches to well-being needn't compete with psychological ones but can complement them in powerful ways. The thoughtful use of mindfulness is just one example of how this kind of synergy can happen.

FIGURE 2.6

Calming Area in a Kindergarten Classroom

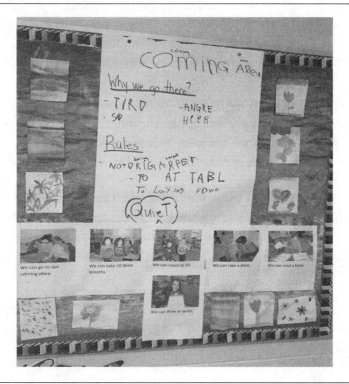

Source: Courtesy of Dennis Shirley.

The Whole Child

In recent years, as the influence of top-down accountability and standardized testing has started to be challenged, a broad educational philosophy and diffuse set of practices have begun to emerge as an alternative. Labeled *whole child education* or *whole child learning,* this approach draws on a number of historical and theoretical traditions.

The world's Indigenous cultures, for example, have approached education holistically for eons by integrating spiritual, physical, mental, and social dimensions of growth.[126] The rise of modern educational systems has often sidelined or suppressed these eternal considerations, though—especially in eras driven by standardization, competition, and testing. From time to time, however, humanistic interpretations of the purpose of education recapture, redefine, and reassert the more ancient understandings of human development. One such movement occurred more than a century ago among a rising generation of educators worldwide, as demonstrated by these examples:

- At the University of Chicago, John Dewey's Laboratory School gave children opportunities to explore the arts, cook, knit, and dance, within a philosophy that regarded practical tasks and intellectual work not as "dualisms" but as things that enriched one another.[127]
- In 1901, Bengali poet Rabindranath Tagore, who went on to win the 1913 Nobel Prize in Literature, founded an experimental ashram to counteract the influence of colonialist models of education that had excluded spiritual development from other dimensions of learning.[128]
- In Rome in 1907, Maria Montessori launched *Casa dei Bambini,* or "Children's Homes," with ergonomic furniture and tasks adjusted for active young minds that were keen to explore their natural environment.[129] Montessori's legacy remains in her eponymously named schools that address the whole of young children's development all over the world.
- In England in 1892, a women's teacher-training college known as Froebel College (now the University of Roehampton) was established to promote the ideas and practices of the German educational theorist Friedrich Wilhelm August Froebel. Froebel was a lover of nature, had previously invented the concept of *kindergarten,* and had established play and activity centers to advance the idea that education should be based on children's unique needs and capabilities.[130]

These innovations were promoted and disseminated through the New Education Fellowship (NEF), an independent professional association started in 1921 in England that continues to this day under the name of the World Education Fellowship.[131] The NEF published the *New Era* journal and held conferences for educators from all over the world.[132] These reformers wanted to learn from others so they could bring their practices back to schools in their own countries.

In general, the Great Depression, World War II, and the ensuing decades were not kind to these sorts of whole child initiatives, however. In the first years after the devastation of the war, most of the involved countries experienced various degrees of austerity and emphasized a return to normalcy. In the 1950s McCarthy era in the United States, for example, experimentation in schools fell out of favor. Attempts at innovation in mathematics and science followed the Soviet Union's launch of the Sputnik satellite in 1957, but implementation efforts largely failed.[133] In the 1960s and 1970s, there were some bottom-up initiatives in the United States—a university-based laboratory school here or an alternative "school-within-a-school" somewhere else—but these efforts were scattered, and even in these cases, the innovative promise was often accompanied by poor implementation in practice.[134]

Circumstances in the UK were better disposed to philosophies consistent with whole child approaches. From the late 1950s through the 1970s, educators from all over the world, including the United States, flocked to see what was happening in English primary schools. Andy's best teacher in primary school, Mary Hindle—who inspired him to become an educator himself—recalled how in Andy's class in 1961 and others like it, "The children studied the local nature of pond life and such," where "each group . . . planned the work under a leader." The children also worked on four class newspapers every week, each with its own editor. They were "completely free to develop as the group wanted," she wrote decades later. "They were fascinating to read with drawings and letters to the editor—and me sometimes."[135] Andy even wrote the travel section for one of the papers! A government inspector's report on Andy's school, at the time, referred to its "stimulating atmosphere." The written work was linked closely with "the children's environment and interests." "A successful beginning has been made with expressive movement to music," the inspectors added.[136]

Nationally, a 1967 British parliamentary commission's report titled *Children and Their Primary Schools,* known as the *Plowden*

Report, brought together disparate experiences such as these across many UK schools and school districts into a philosophical whole. The report memorably referred to how the curriculum in the best primary schools "lays special stress on individual discovery, on first-hand experience and on opportunities for creative work."[137] Presaging future policymakers' exhortations for schools to develop global competencies and prepare children for jobs that didn't exist yet, the report's authors cautioned that "the best preparation for being a happy and useful man or woman is to live fully as a child."[138]

From the 1970s onward, in the UK and elsewhere, a world oil crisis, global recession, and growing unemployment moved the UK government to emphasize education for work, in basic skills, monitored by top-down accountability. But whole child education never disappeared in England. It just went underground.

In the early 1980s, Andy's young children attended a village primary school in Oxfordshire. With a reputation stretching back decades, the school hosted many international visitors who came to see outstanding learning in visual arts, expressive and imaginative writing, and small-group work. Andy's 6-year-old son, for example, worked in a group of four children who would pull the school's sole computer on its trolley from the other end of the building to compose stories collaboratively. Their teacher printed out their drafts, then provided feedback led by questions such as "How long ago?" or "What did they look like?" The children developed further drafts through conversation and joint writing, until the final versions were complete. Under the leadership of an iconoclastic chief education officer, Sir Tim Brighouse, these practices were common throughout the county.[139]

Now, whole child education is reemerging on a more systemwide basis in the form of schools within a Whole Education (WE) network. The network was started in 2010 by English educators "who are united in their belief that all children and young people deserve a fully rounded education."[140] The network engages professionals who seek to be "values-led," not data-driven, by experienced colleagues who "don't tell you what to do or do it for you."[141] Reciprocal school visits by teams of fellow teachers and leaders from schools in other parts of England provide a foundation for mutual learning and staff development. The network provides "inspiration and challenge to help you discover what works best in your context."[142]

The Whole Education network more than proved its worth during the COVID-19 pandemic. At Braunstone Frith Primary School in the city of Leicester, head teacher Amelia Smith and her colleagues wanted to let the children know that "we still love and care for them." Believing that it was "important for staff to continue working" during this critical time, teachers visited families at their homes (while wearing masks and preserving physical distancing) to make sure that everyone was OK.[143] They provided families with food packs the staff had assembled for them. When home conditions were too difficult for children and their caretakers to manage, teachers brought these vulnerable children to school.

Braunstone Frith teachers adapted quickly to online learning. They informed parents about effective ways to tutor their children at home. They taught parents to use success criteria so they would know when children had completed assignments accurately. They sometimes lent their own digital devices they used at school to children who didn't have the necessary equipment at home. When the home lacked adequate Wi-Fi, teachers either brought children to school or adapted assignments for use in printed learning packs that they dropped off at children's homes.

Before and during the pandemic, the Whole Education approach in England has improved learning and well-being by going beyond the limitations of a narrow academic curriculum. It offers a coherent strategy and philosophy that draws on its network to support, encourage, and protect it within a wider context that is driven by market competition, top-down accountability, and examination results.

Across the Atlantic, especially because of the onset of accountability-driven policies such as No Child Left Behind and Race to the Top, approaches consistent with whole child philosophies have been scattered and sporadic.[144] For that reason, in 2007, ASCD launched a Whole Child Initiative to "change the conversation about education from a focus on narrowly defined academic achievement to one that promotes the long-term development and success of all children."[145] It asserted a humanistic philosophy of learning and development that is about the importance of the whole child *now* and not just those parts of the child that might be economically useful in the future or that would comply with accountability demands in the present.

ASCD generated a Whole Child newsletter, organized a Whole Child podcast, and published a Whole Child blog. It hosted five Whole Child symposia, one in partnership with our colleagues and us at Boston College in 2017. Five Whole Child tenets (see Figure 2.7), based upon Maslow's hierarchy of needs, have underpinned ASCD's framework:[146]

1. "Each child enters school healthy" and is taught how to develop "a healthy lifestyle."
2. "Each child learns in an environment that is physically and emotionally safe."
3. All students are "actively engaged in learning and connected to the school and broader community."
4. Every student "is supported by qualified, caring adults" with proper professional qualifications.
5. "Each student is challenged academically" and is poised for "success in college or further study and for employment" as well as for "participation in a global environment" after completing high school.

FIGURE 2.7

ASCD's 5 Whole Child Tenets

In the first decade of the Whole Child Initiative, ASCD forged 75 partnerships with states, districts, and nonprofit organizations to undertake systemic changes "toward a more well-rounded approach to education."[147] It advocated for a wholesale transformation of federal policies that eventually helped to secure the passage of the Every Student Succeeds Act and its partial pullback from standardized testing in 2015.[148] It has also extended its work with international organizations to focus on "the whole child for the whole world," linking children's development to the betterment of the world in which they and we live.[149]

How has the Whole Child Initiative played out in practical terms in its partnership schools? One example is Hamilton Elementary School in Port Angeles, Washington, where principal Gary Pringle and his staff wanted to create an environment "where high performance, kindness, self-responsibility, and playfulness are the expectations."[150] This promotion of play led to the integration of "health, nutrition, and physical fitness into school activities and the curriculum," with parents and caregivers also encouraged to participate in a Families in Training (FIT) after-school program that established "monthly challenges" pegged to "Healthy Fitness Zone Standards."[151] In another case, Butterfield Trail Middle School in Arkansas promotes its students' well-being by cultivating a sustainable garden and by revising its curriculum so that it now "incorporates science and nutrition into instruction while promoting long-term health education."[152]

In Ontario, we will see, the province's commitments to well-being alongside broad excellence (not just in mathematics, literacy, and science) and equity (interpreted as inclusion of all students and their identities) led teachers, principals, and school district leaders to address all the aspects of young people's learning and development. In due course, we will present examples of many ways in which this integrated, interdisciplinary approach has manifested itself.

The province's well-being strategy is not just about dealing with bullying, post-traumatic stresses, or mental health problems. It is about bringing educators together to work toward the learning and well-being of the whole child in an integrated and collective way. It's about the whole school and sometimes the whole community working to support the whole child. The traditional African proverb is right. It really does take a village to raise a child.

None of this means that a whole child approach is faultless. Even the most promising methodologies have bad versions. A lecture from the front of the room can be brilliant and inspiring, but it can also descend into teachers reading from the textbook or from the text of a PowerPoint presentation.

Whole child approaches are no different. For this reason, one of the pioneers of child-centered education in the UK in the 1950s and 1960s, Chief Education Officer Sir Alec Clegg, actually asked one of his experienced leaders to write down what a bad version of everything she supported would look like. "A wet playtime [recess] all day," she observed, along with "work that is . . . badly displayed . . . noisiness that comes from lack of purpose . . . groups working side-by-side on incompatible activities and, of course, work of a low standard."[153]

In the same school where Andy's son was writing and editing in a group with the assistance of a computer, his 5-year-old sister spent hours during the first week of school sitting in a lavatory stall worrying about what she should choose to work on. Over the rest of the year, she chose mathematics as little as possible and subsequently struggled with the subject until she was in high school.

As this example shows, educating the whole child should not be about abandoning structure, focus, and direction. It should be about rethinking how all those things are accomplished together. To do this, we need consummate professionals in our schools, not rookies who sometimes misconstrue being a gentle facilitator as leaving children to fend for themselves when they actually need expert support.

In the end, whole child approaches seek to integrate academic learning with student well-being by getting teachers and other educators to work together on all of the child's needs and by developing the child's potential for learning within a structured, integrated whole. If this work is undertaken ad hoc, individually, or without proper training and support, it can be interpreted and implemented as badly as any other strategy. But done well, by multidisciplinary teams of teachers, it has a great chance of success.

Conclusion

This chapter has outlined six social-psychological theories of well-being that are widely used in schools today. There are others we have not addressed, many of them equally popular and influential, such as theories of resiliency and grit. It's impossible to provide comprehensive coverage, but we want to show some of the major ideas that are influencing well-being initiatives in schools, some of the assumptions and claims that underpin these theories, and the general orientation of positive psychology that underpins most of them.

In Chapters 4 and 5, we will set out a complementary perspective that plays a strong role in our own understandings of and recommendations about well-being in society. This perspective is rooted more in theories of organizations and society than in small-group psychological research.

First, however, in Chapter 3, we want to raise some questions about aspects of well-being that psychologists may have misinterpreted or missed altogether. These questions will establish a firmer foundation for understanding why well-being has assumed such importance today and what particular forms it takes in the dynamic and diverse societies in which we live.

3

Questioning Well-Being:
The Quest to Do Better

Teachers don't always agree—even among themselves—with the things they are asked to implement. Testing and performance targets are anathema to most of them, of course. But disagreements about the best ways to teach literacy and "wars" over what kind of mathematics students should learn or whether technology is more of a good thing than a bad thing are very familiar to most teachers.

It's hard to imagine teachers fighting over the value of well-being, though. They might feel they should have more resources or stronger support, but who could possibly be against well-being itself? Indeed, in our interviews with more than 200 educators, attention to well-being was ubiquitous. Everyone viewed it as a welcome relief from the relentless overdrive of tested performance in the basics. As we have just seen, there are lots of available research studies, professional learning, and guidebooks to back them up.

So it seems a bit perverse to question well-being. In education, it's sometimes tempting to embrace popular new ideas and practices a bit too whole-heartedly. Concepts such as *resilience, grit,* or *growth mindsets,* for example, sound so inherently positive, it can be easy to love them a bit too much and overlook their drawbacks. Like the message in pop singer Kelly Clarkson's song "Dark Side," though, sometimes we have to love ideas, like people, in full knowledge of their dark sides too.[154]

Scrutinizing ideas such as well-being for their weaknesses and imperfections is a bit like resistance training in physical development.

We must generate a bit of our own resistance if our basic ideas are to become even stronger. To do any less is to risk our ideas collapsing when they meet their first big test.

For this reason, we engaged participants from the 10 districts in questioning a number of key ideas to which they were attached. At one point we asked, "What's wrong with growth mindsets?" They looked at us like we had lost our minds. Did we really think it was better to have *fixed mindsets*—to believe that people who struggled with their learning were unable to improve and that we couldn't help them? Why wouldn't anyone want to believe that if children struggle with something, it's not evidence that they'll never do it, but simply that they can't do it *yet?*

Yet once we asked these educators to question growth mindsets, in minutes they came up with all kinds of critiques. Did growth mindsets mean that anybody could become equally good at anything? That seemed improbable, they concluded. Did having a growth mindset deny the existence of special talents that some people had more than others? If so, it was obviously wrong. Dennis swims almost every day, and Andy was once in a band. But however hard we try, we'll never be world champion swimmers or inductees into the Rock & Roll Hall of Fame—not yet, not ever. Even more seriously, participants asked themselves: Have growth mindsets ignored the influence of poverty or of bad policies on students' ability to learn and attributed failure to students or their teachers because they just have the wrong mindset?

At the end of this reflective process, educators didn't abandon growth mindsets. They actually seemed a bit relieved that they weren't expected to be superhumans who could turn every child into an Albert Einstein or a Michelle Obama if they just put the right amount of effort and positive thinking into it. While holding on to the basic concept and intent of growth mindsets—that human potential is more malleable than many people think—they were now approaching the concept more realistically.

It's the same with well-being. It, too, is not beyond reproach. This chapter raises four questions about the ways in which it can be and sometimes is misunderstood and misused in schools today.

These questions are as much about what's missing from our data and from what we've seen in schools as it is about what is problematic. This means that we don't just report what educators have told us, but we also probe deeply into things they left unsaid that may matter a great deal. The four questions are

1. Does the well-being agenda wrongly claim to be able to solve massive social problems with individualistic, psychological solutions?
2. Might well-being advocates unintentionally end up producing a generation of self-absorbed narcissists?
3. What's the point of having initiatives in well-being if other parts of the school system are perpetrating ill-being?
4. Are our ideas about well-being culturally biased?

The Limitations of Positive Psychology

Positive psychology focuses on people's states of mind and their relationships. These approaches, however, also need to be addressed in relation to the times, circumstances, reasons, and interests that can suddenly bring small-scale perspectives to the fore.

In the 1930s, following the stock market crash in the United States and a historical moment when capitalism reached obscene levels of excess, a brand of management theory emerged that sought to counteract these forces. Initiated by Elton Mayo, a US-based and Australian-trained psychologist who had studied the effects of battlefield "shell shock" (now known as post-traumatic stress disorder) in his earlier career, a new "human relations" school of management explored the motivational factors in workplaces that enhanced productivity.[155]

Until this point, the dominant approach in US management theory had been that of Frederick W. Taylor.[156] Taylor had believed that productivity and efficiency were best increased by breaking down tasks into subcomponents, standardizing them, and monitoring them through time-and-motion studies of worker performance.

Faced with disillusionment about Taylor-like industrial practices, the human relations school emphasized the importance of how well workers could be treated by management and how this could contribute to efforts to increase their productivity. In *Management and the Worker,* Fritz Roethlisberger (a graduate student of Mayo's) and William Dickson investigated the effects on productivity of attempts to alter the physical environments of workers at the Western Electric Company's Hawthorne Works in Chicago.[157] What surprised the researchers was that the physical environment turned out to be less important in determining productivity than the social relations among the workers. Even when experimenters made the room in which workers spent their days colder and turned down the lights so it was almost impossible to see anything, productivity still went up because the workers appreciated that someone was actually taking an interest in them. This phenomenon of improved results being an effect of research interest itself became known as the "Hawthorne effect" before social scientists renamed it as the "halo effect."[158]

In 2007, the worst economic crisis since the Great Depression gave rise to a new kind of human relations tradition. Positive psychology, and its associated interventions, such as cognitive behavioral therapy (CBT), flourished in the aftermath of financial devastation, in which 63 percent of Americans experienced declines of their total wealth and the UK economy shrank for five quarters in a row.[159] Lacking the power or the will to attack the root causes of the Great Recession, happiness studies and initiatives took off among CEOs. Businesses appointed chief happiness officers. Cognitive behavioral therapy was embraced as a way to help employees and others accept that although they might not be able to change their circumstances, they could at least change how they *thought* about those circumstances as a basis for self-improvement. Companies subsidized their employees' gym memberships. Some entities— including the city of Chicago, following bargaining agreements with the teachers union—even linked real-time biometric data collected from employees' wristbands to performance bonuses. If unions once had a "chip on their shoulder" about top-down employer control, workers now had "chips on their wrists" that enabled employers to exercise digital surveillance over them, not just at work, but all the time.[160]

After the global economic collapse, many Americans lost their homes, millions of workers across Europe became unemployed, the growing gig economy saw more and more workers get hired on zero-hour contracts, UK local authority budgets were cut in half, teachers across Europe had their salaries frozen or reduced, and rates of homelessness in the UK doubled. Yet UK Prime Minister David Cameron's answer was to approach Martin Seligman about the benefits of positive psychology. He wanted to find solutions for the poor that didn't entail financial sacrifices by the wealthy. Indeed, Cameron's government made eligibility for unemployment benefits contingent on attending courses on CBT.[161]

The result has been a tendency to overrely on individual psychological or exclusively educational solutions for solving systemic social and economic problems. It is what William Davies, author of *The Happiness Industry,* calls "critique turned inwards."[162] In *The Wellness Syndrome,* Stockholm University professor Carl Ceder-ström and his City University of London colleague André Spicer sum up what this means. "As authorities lose interest in structural reforms," they say, "they become more interested in small-scale behavioral interventions. In place of politics, we are left with . . . increasingly invasive lifestyle tweaks." "As a result," they conclude, "we abandon political demands."[163]

Although we have to believe we can promote any child's well-being, whatever the circumstances, we must not give up attacking the existence and persistence of poverty and other causes of ill-being outside the school. In the United States and the UK, 70 to 80 percent of the explanation for student achievement resides in families or societies and not in schools.[164] There's no point expecting educators to protect and promote children's well-being all on their own when there is insufficient investment in other public services. When teachers are forced to take on more and more social work responsibilities, their ability to focus on their students' learning and well-being is diminished. Ontario educators in high-poverty communities, and in schools serving Indigenous families, felt this reality very strongly when their students were unable to access mental health supports and suicide-prevention counseling because social services were underfunded.

One director of a district serving a high proportion of Indigenous students that had "one of the highest suicide rate areas in all of Canada" was disconsolate that his district lost five students in five months. One was a 10-year-old who "was deemed high suicide risk" and had been on a waiting list for mental health services for eight months without being seen by a therapist. A teacher lamented losing two students to suicide over the course of the school year because of long waiting lists for mental health services. Some students waited up to three years to be seen. The director explained:

> We've got one public school—they've lost two students since January. How does that impact the class for the rest of the year? How does that impact the teacher? One of the children up there last year was deemed high suicide risk, was on a waiting list for eight months, didn't even get seen. High risk! Ended up taking their own life, except the kid was 10 years old. How does that impact the classroom? Why are we waiting? If you're deemed high risk suicide and you don't go to the top of the list as a 10-year old, then what gets you to the top of the list? Does that impact the classroom? I think it does.

Notwithstanding the benefits of movements such as mindfulness and resilience, overinvesting our hopes in them can mean we stop looking outward at what's causing problems in the first place. It's admirably heroic to pull drowning people from a river. It's just as important to go upstream to stop whoever is pushing them in. This issue concerns not only the *prevalence* of positive psychology interventions but also how the *content and substance* of these movements and interventions have been defined.

Daniel Goleman's popular idea of *emotional intelligence,* for example, has been criticized for concentrating on emotions that are easily regulated and trainable through commercially run, profitable programs, rather than on ones that are not so easily addressed, such as disgust, one of the basic emotions of racism, or disengagement (a common problem caused by many workplaces themselves).[165] The school programs of emotional self-regulation we have described are vulnerable to the same criticisms. They are mainly there to calm down anger and alleviate anxiety, not to identify and release the creative expression of exhilaration or surprise that can induce thriving within innovative classroom environments, for example. Members of one anti-racist teachers' network draw attention to how "most SEL standards are rooted in Eurocentric norms, not to empower, love, affirm, or free Black, Brown, or Indigenous children."[166] Instead of many standard processes of emotional self-regulation, they argue for "SEL rituals and routines that welcome the full range of emotions and provide tools to support students in processing and asking for support."[167]

What might a culturally appropriate response look like when young people of color find themselves in emotional turmoil? Monique Morris, author of *Sing a Rhythm, Dance a Blues,* tells the story of a girl who was overwhelmed by intense anxiety before she had to deliver remarks on her experiences in the US criminal justice system to a national conference. At that moment, a friend simply began braiding her hair. This immediately calmed her down. Instead of employing a standardized routine of emotional self-regulation, this wordless act of interpersonal care, sustained by Hispanic girls and women since time out of mind, enabled the girl to pull herself together.

Not all definitions and interpretations of SEL are as exclusively psychological or purportedly neutral as those that have widespread currency in the United States. For example, in its 2019 statement for Social and Emotional Learning, the Salzburg Global Seminar, made up of educators from all over the world, included social cohesion as one of its five key concerns that called for SEL initiatives. "How can we help young people feel confident in their own identities, and be vested in community from local to global levels?" the statement asked. One of the guiding principles of the Salzburg Alliance that followed from the seminar is a "human rights" approach in which "SEL and Life Skills are not value-neutral and need to recognize that education promotes human rights-based values and fosters human dignity."[168]

Alfie Kohn takes issue with how people have sometimes used Carol Dweck's growth mindsets—a project priority in many of the Ontario districts—to turn teachers and schools away from acknowledging the overwhelming external impact of poverty, lack of public funding for schools, and poor curriculum or pedagogy.[169] Dweck herself has decried what she views as a "false growth mindset" after seeing how her ideas have been used to blame students themselves for having "a fixed mindset, without understanding instead that, as educators, it is our responsibility to create a context in which a growth mindset can flourish."[170]

In the United States, the controversial network of more than 200 KIPP charter schools teaches zest, social regulation, and Angela Duckworth's "grit" among six signature character strengths. But these are pursued within a framework of rather traditional pedagogies and rigid discipline that has been heavily criticized for limiting students' capacities for self-determination. Approaches like these that can drive up tested achievement might simultaneously be damaging students' well-being and broader engagement in ways that students then have to overcome by developing grit and stoicism.[171]

Mindfulness, too, can be misused. Its intention to turn people inward has never been to leave them there—but that isn't always clear from how it is offered. Hundreds of teachers in one of our Ontario districts took online courses in mindfulness when they were working under conditions of multiple initiatives that seemed to be creating much of the teacher stress that the courses were responding to in the first place.

Then there is the curious case of why US educational leaders and researchers have set aside the broad ideal of and aspiration for well-being (which, ironically, was invented in the United States by the World Health Organization in the 1940s) in favor of a much narrower psychological approach to SEL. The CASEL framework for social and emotional learning does not include spirituality, for example. This omission may be necessary given the separation of church and state in the First Amendment to the US Constitution, but it is still a striking exception to other frameworks, such as Ontario's, that have found ways to recognize and address young people's spiritual needs without attaching them to any specific system of religious belief.

A second consequence of narrowing down well-being to SEL is that there is no reference to physical health. In the litigious and big-business environment of the United States, criticisms of physical ill-being, especially in the form of childhood obesity (where the United States has some of the worst statistics in the world), risk accusations of fat shaming in a culture that now celebrates many shapes and sizes (even though some of these represent serious threats to health and mortality).[172] Promotion of physical well-being and healthy eating also runs counter to the commercial interests of the billion-dollar agri-business that markets cheap, unhealthy fast food to predominantly low-income consumers, including children.[173]

In both these cases, CASEL's origins in Daniel Goleman's work on emotional intelligence help explain its social and emotional focus and its absence of attention to young people's needs for physical development and spiritual growth. Couching well-being as a kind of learning is also part of the trend toward the "learnification" we discussed in Chapter 1, in which improvement efforts are judged by their impact on test scores. The learnification in SEL is evident in its claimed benefits for cognitive outcomes and achievement gains rather than personal health or societal well-being. It is time for Americans to reclaim the concept of well-being—not to replace SEL but to expand and enrich it in a way that can respond to the needs of all their students.

Immense social and political problems shouldn't be reduced to individualistic psychological solutions—positive or otherwise. Psychological responses to problems shouldn't be a substitute for dealing with the compelling social, political, and educational injustices of our time, such as racism, extreme inequality, threats to democracy, or the devastation of the earth. Injustices such as these should not make educators and students feel powerless. Rather, through initiatives such as Roots of Empathy and Facing History and Ourselves, they can be occasions for critical thinking, political empowerment, and resilience directed toward changing the world, not just toward managing ourselves.

Take the case of Colombia, for example, where Vicky Colbert has spent more than 40 years building a network of more than 25,000 schools located mainly in poor rural communities throughout the country. The Escuela Nueva network outperforms other schools and systems with similar demographic characteristics. Its success is confirmed in research conducted by the World Bank and in Colbert's receipt of the world's two largest prizes in education, totaling $5 million.[174] In their quest to build peace and democracy in a country that had been torn apart by drugs and violence, and to give students a voice in their own learning, Escuela Nueva's educators have used the forest, and nature in general, as assets. They use pedagogies rooted in the classic ideas of John Dewey, Maria Montessori, and Paulo Freire to help students become active participants in and sometimes leaders of their learning. As a result of its successes, the Escuela Nueva model has now been disseminated to 19 other countries.

Psychological and sociological understandings and strategies of well-being within and outside education must now come together. We must improve support for vulnerable populations outside schools as well as within them. We also have to ensure that young people don't only turn inward to focus on themselves and their relationships but also look outward to their world through learning that has meaning and purpose. And in general, if we want to help individuals to be well, we need to do what we can to prevent our societies, communities, and schools from getting sick. We have a lot more to say about these issues in the next two chapters.

The Excesses of Narcissism

The modern well-being agenda is not the first to address young people's social and emotional development. It has a number of analogous movements in the past. One of them is the popular but ultimately ill-fated self-esteem movement that began in the 1970s. Research on self-esteem programs and practices of that period showed that bolstering students' opinions of themselves had no effect on their learning outcomes.[175] Even worse, the movement actively exacerbated antisocial attitudes by generating "narcissistic, defensive, and conceited" students who believed that they were just as awesome as their well-meaning but misguided educators told them they were.[176] This is a history that advocates of well-being definitely don't need to repeat!

Echoing concerns about the excesses of self-esteem initiatives in the 1970s, Cederström and Spicer worry about how the "wellness syndrome" "seeps into all aspects of our lives" today, exacerbating the very problems it is meant to solve:

> The frantic search for the perfect diet; the paranoid pursuit of happiness; the forced workplace workout; the endless life-coaching sessions; the detailed tracking of our bodily functions . . . these desperate attempts to increase productivity through wellness create their own problems. They encourage an infectious narcissism which pushes us to take the great turn inwards, making our body into our first and last concern. They generate a creeping sense of anxiety that comes with the ever-present responsibility of monitoring every lifestyle choice. They feed a sense of guilt that comes from the inevitable slip-ups when we don't follow our diet or fail to live up to our life goals. People whose life has been seized by wellness are not just healthier, happier and more productive. They are also narcissistic, anxious and guilty.[177]

Narcissism originates in the Greek legend of Narcissus, who was fatally entranced by his own reflection that he saw in the water. Sigmund Freud first wrote about the psychiatry of narcissism in 1915.[178] The American Psychiatric Association lists narcissism as an official "personality disorder." It is defined as "a pervasive pattern of grandiosity, need for admiration, and lack of empathy."[179]

For Christopher Lasch, in his 1979 book *The Culture of Narcissism,* the narcissist uses other people as instruments of gratification even while craving their love and approval.[180] Jeffrey Kluger, who satirically dedicates his book *The Narcissist Next Door* to himself, tells us how narcissists are "afflicted with a bottomless appetite" for "recognition, attention, glory, rewards."[181] If you're dating a narcissist, he warns his readers, it takes an average of 15 months to find out that all the attention they initially shower on you is just an act that is really all about them. So beware of whirlwind romances!

In his book *Selfie: How We Became So Self-Obsessed and What It's Doing to Us,* Will Storr tells us that, contrary to popular belief, narcissism mainly results not from having too little self-esteem but from having too much.[182] It can commence early on in school, through offering children unconditional praise simply for showing up or merely being who they are. This outpouring gives children an inflated sense of self-importance. They would be better off if they were to learn that they have to earn others' respect.

Obsessions with self-esteem are often thought to be the purview of overgrown "flower children" of the 1960s and left-wing progressives who are not interested in standards and rigor, but only in their children's happiness and their right to play, uninterrupted, forever. This perception is, indeed, a part of the story. The case also can be made, however, that too much self-absorbed self-esteem is actually a cause and consequence of ruthlessly competitive and highly individualistic free-market societies.

Enter Alan Greenspan, chairman of the US Federal Reserve, one of the most powerful financial positions in the world, from 1987 to 2006, and one of the key founders of economic neoliberalism. As a young man, Greenspan entered politics and became an advisor to President Richard Nixon at the behest of the bestselling author and cult-like figurehead of unfettered individualism, Ayn Rand. Sitting with other acolytes at the feet of Rand, Greenspan picked up her message of "virtuous selfishness," in which small government, free markets, minimal taxation, and deregulation would prevail.[183]

Rand's lover and younger follower was Nathaniel Branden, who went on to write *The Psychology of Self-Esteem* in 1969.[184] Like Rand, Branden wanted to free people from excessive social conformity. He thought this was best done by promoting their intrinsic sense of self-worth.

From the very start, critics worried that Rand and Branden were undermining the social ties that make life worth living. But their ideas resonated with many Americans. In the 1980s and 1990s, California Assemblyman John Vasconcellos drew together an expert panel called the California Task Force to Promote Self-Esteem and Personal and Social Responsibility. Despite the task force's uneven and ambivalent findings, its overall conclusion was interpreted as a highly positive endorsement of the power of self-esteem. Soon more than 80 percent of California school districts were implementing self-esteem programs. Students were being told they were all spe-cial, and in schools across the world, grades soared improbably upward, as red marking pens were consigned to the trash bin.

In 2003, a comprehensive review of the research literature on self-esteem by Roy Baumeister and his colleagues showed a correla-tion between high self-esteem and high grades.[185] Closer inspection, however, revealed that the grades preceded self-esteem, not vice versa. High self-esteem didn't accurately predict positive educa-tional outcomes. Moreover, many unethical—and even evil—indi-viduals had high self-esteem, Baumeister and his team found. Narcissists were an extreme example of inflated self-esteem. They had an "addiction to esteem," believing that they deserved to be treated differently from other people because they were special.[186]

Most researchers on narcissism agree that the phenomenon is not wholly bad and can bring positive things—such as charm, humor, drama, confidence, and glamor—to an organization. In moderate proportions, it's unfair to regard these qualities as a disorder or even to call them narcissism at all. Few actors could take to the stage and few politicians would run for high office without a bit of narcissism. Lacking a few of the qualities just listed, organizations would become dreary communities of emotionally repressed, supplicating piety.

The problems only set in when qualities associated with individ-ual narcissists who are flamboyant exceptions start to overtake entire organizations. Jean Twenge, whose work on adolescent anxi-ety and digital technology we will encounter later, was mentored by Baumeister. In 2009, she coauthored her own book on narcissism.[187] In *The Narcissism Epidemic: Living in the Age of Entitlement*, Twenge and her coauthor, W. Keith Campbell, found that narcissism and self-esteem have grown and spread exponentially in the last few decades and have now reached epidemic proportions. Twenge and Campbell are most concerned about people exuding a kind of self-admiration that "does not distinguish between a healthy sense of self-worth and the unhealthy narcissism that can instead result."[188]

To check if manifestations of self-admiration were changing over time, they studied 85 samples of US college students from 31 campuses who had filled out the *Narcissistic Personality Inventory* between 1979 and 2006. What they found was that students in the

2000s were "significantly more narcissistic" than ones in the previous three decades and that the rate of increases in narcissism had
become steeper between 2000 and 2006.[189] The narcissism epidemic,
they concluded, had reached the same proportions as the obesity
epidemic, and parenting and school practices were among the factors responsible.

We shouldn't feel sorry for narcissists, but we should be concerned about the impact they have on others. A research team led
by Kostas Papageorgiou at Queens University, Belfast, has deter-
mined that narcissists tend to be happier than other people but are
often unlikable and unethical in their relations with others.[190] They
seem to live in an impenetrable bubble of excessive self-regard.

So we must beware of equating well-being with happiness or
with having people celebrate unconditionally who they are and
what they do. If we do this, we risk communicating that a life of
meaning and purpose should not also sometimes involve struggle.
The timeless virtues of selflessness, sacrifice, humility, and even suffering in the pursuit of a noble cause should still serve to inspire
our young people.

Teachers who recall their beginning years of learning to teach
will remember times when they were stuck, moments when they
failed, and critical feedback that was hard to take. This is what Saint
John of the Cross called "the dark night of the soul."[191] Yet they
might also recall how they went on to feel exhilarated when the
suffering was over, the obstacle had been overcome, and the hard
work had been endured to yield a better result. Becoming fulfilled
and successful as a professional, then, does not involve boundless
happiness and unending praise. It involves sacrifice and steadfast-
ness, honest introspection, and the moral courage to question one's
own actions and decisions from time to time.

It's much the same for our students. Our efforts to promote well-
being should treat every student as unique, but not as someone
who is "special," with its overtones of implied superiority. The
emphasis on well-being must not degenerate into a quest for happiness alone. It must retain its association with effort, sacrifice, fulfillment, and accomplishment. We must help our students discover the
dignity that comes from working hard, making a social contribution,

and growing in wisdom and insight. In the end, they will appreciate this approach far more than if we just try to make them feel happy and special all the time.

Teachers and young people must never lose sight of the value of hard-earned accomplishment as part of and sometimes as a precursor to well-being. Otherwise, well-being will be cast too easily as the next form of self-indulgent narcissism that produces what people in Singapore have labeled as "strawberry generations" of often spoiled and easily bruised young people who are "needy, fragile, and lethargic."[192] A backlash will then set in, and a narrow curriculum of standardized basics will be back before we know it.

The Perpetration of Ill-Being

Organizations have no business promoting well-being when they unnecessarily perpetrate ill-being. Of course, threats to people's well-being are in the nature of some jobs. If you are a first responder, if you work in palliative care, or if you teach in an environment that is impoverished or isolated, stress comes with the job. Some jobs will always need to provide well-being supports, to help staff carry out their difficult missions without suffering overwhelming personal consequences.

A lot of modern workplace environments create avoidable stress, though. Fast, flexible economies demand that their workers on zero-hour contracts come in any time, as required; that they will be available on their smartphones 24/7; and that they will forego absenteeism by coming into work when they are sick, out of fear of losing their jobs. A few workouts and deep-breathing sessions aren't what these workplaces require. The jobs need to be restructured to treat their employees with decency and dignity.

Educational institutions also have avoidable stresses in addition to their inherent ones. As we will see later, misuse and overuse of digital technology is one of these. Another concerns testing—especially what are known as high-stakes tests.

High-stakes tests were introduced for accountability purposes to monitor and report on the performance of whole institutions and systems, as well as their teachers. The tests have high stakes because failure to meet agreed-upon performance levels or targets in a school or a district—or even in the case of individual teachers—can lead to educators losing their jobs. These tests have also traumatized communities when they have led to schools being closed down after they have been subjected to huge pressures to turn things around.

Critiques of high-stakes testing have been extensive.[193] They refer to what Donald Campbell called the "perverse incentives" of high-stakes testing to meet expectations by any means possible, even cynical and fraudulent ones.[194]

Ontario, however, has "mid-stakes tests." These are administered to check how schools are performing and to determine whether intervention is required. The consequences are not as severe and life-changing as in a high-stakes system.[195] Australia's NAPLAN test is similar, in terms of where the stakes are pitched.[196]

In Ontario, the presence of mid-stakes in the provincial test known as the EQAO (short for Educational Quality and Accountability Office) is evident in the fact that test results have been made known to the public as a basis for parents' choice of school.[197] Results are given to district directors and superintendents who can then use them to inform and justify interventions. Data examined by educators through six-week teaching-learning cycles of performance review involving interim assessments have identified students who were "yellow" (at risk of not achieving proficiency targets) or "red" (performing far below proficiency) rather than "green" (at or above proficiency) so that just-in-time strategies could be used to raise performance.

Ontario's mid-stakes tests do not possess the high stakes of more punitive systems. Testing does not take place in every grade, but only in grades 3, 6, and 9 for reading, writing, and mathematics, and then close to graduation. Principals and teachers are not hastily replaced. Schools are not closed down. There are no semi-private systems of English academies or US charter schools waiting in the wings to take over from traditional public schools when results fall short.

The mid-stakes tests in Ontario were meant to ensure accountability and transparency and systemwide improvement while avoiding the negative effects and perverse incentives of their high-stakes counterparts. Instead of negative pressure, there was positive pressure and support. Instead of being punished, struggling schools or districts received assistance in an environment of "non-punitive accountability."[198]

However, our research revealed that the mid-stakes testing process has not avoided most of the perverse consequences that have afflicted schools in high-stakes environments elsewhere. Even in the 10 districts that invited us to study their reform work, we found teaching to the test, movement of desks into rows for test-prep classes, and so on. In addition, the tests had a negative impact on efforts at innovation. Innovations mainly avoided the grades in which students were tested, and even the grades before.[199] Two other consequences of mid-stakes testing had particular implications for students' well-being.

First, educators were concerned about students, such as recently arrived immigrants with language or trauma issues, or ones with autism spectrum disorders, who had no chance of succeeding on the test, yet whose scores would be counted in the school's final profile. A coordinator explained, "They don't report on the participating students. They report on *all* students. The kids with developmental disabilities who do not write are still in the denominator. Students who don't write the test and who are exempt are then given a zero." One teacher was exasperated about unfairness and inequity in relation to students who had to take the tests even though they were autistic, nonverbal, living in motels due to extreme poverty, and so on. "It's very stressful for them," she said.

Second, there were concerns that the EQAO was actively harming students' well-being. "I have kids that suffer from anxiety, so putting them into a testing situation like this seems totally wrong," one teacher said. Another recalled, "I spent so much time all year long trying to build the confidence of these children, that they were learners, that they were good at what they were able to do, and then this test would roll around and I would have to then give these kids things that they weren't able to do. I couldn't support them." A principal concurred: "Kids feel a lot of stress about it. Even though they're not going to be punished for it, they feel a lot of stress and anxiety about writing it." One educator described the test anxiety her own family had experienced:

My son is in grade 3. Two nights ago (when he went to bed) it was, "What if I put a comma in the wrong place?" I was like, "It doesn't matter." I've never said anything one way or the other, or anti-whatever. I'm like, "So you put a comma in the wrong place." He's like, "But the teacher is saying . . ." And I get it, because the teachers feel badly when it's ranked in the paper and the school is going to be reflected poorly.

Student reactions such as these led Ontario's educators to question the necessity of the EQAO altogether. "There's a lot of pressure," one principal remarked. "I can picture one of my grade 3 teachers. She's carrying the weight of things she can't control." This teacher had a student with ADHD who spent hours each day "spinning in his chair." She needed the time and space to support the student, but she also "knows this [the EQAO] is coming." She found herself preparing students for the test rather than creating an environment that would promote learning and well-being.

Our evidence on EQAO assessments led us to report back to the Ontario government and its premier that the testing system they had inherited was actively creating ill-being, even though their new policies were meant to promote well-being. The government then set up a review team of its six advisors—including Andy—that, among other measures, proposed abolishing all standardized testing before grade 6.[200] This recommendation was accepted. A new era seemed to be dawning for Ontario's schools.

In 2018, however, a new government was elected. It retained grade 3 and other testing, and it took the report and any reference to the *Achieving Excellence* agenda off its website. However, the EQAO has nonetheless made some incremental improvements, such as loosening the criteria for exemptions and changing test-taking times and conditions to relieve student stress.

A 21st century movement toward deeper learning and stronger well-being that is embracing a range of innovative practices has been rapidly outpacing the 20th century system of large-scale mid-stakes and high-stakes assessment. In Ontario and elsewhere, if testing and selection processes are creating unnecessary levels of ill-being, it is important to review and revise current assessment processes. Simply introducing well-being measures to compensate for the ill-being caused by the tests makes no sense at all.

More and more people are fed up with the whole system of large-scale testing and everything that has come with it. The *Washington Post's* education editor, Valerie Strauss, has observed that the political and bureaucratic appetite for standardized testing in the United States is waning—and not just as a way to cope with the pandemic.[201] She reports remarks by Georgia's Republican governor, Brian Kemp, that the "current high-stakes testing regime is excessive."[202] Ohio passed legislation in 2020 to reduce standardized testing.[203] Universities such as those that make up the entire California state system are eliminating SAT scores as a college entry requirement, on the grounds that they are unfair to minority students.[204]

Even before COVID-19, the former assistant secretary of education under President George H. W. Bush, Diane Ravitch, detected a growing tendency in the United States to pull away from high-stakes tests.[205] Wales and Scotland, which had already diverged from England by abandoning high-stakes testing, suspended all school-leaving examinations through 2021.

Yet defenders of testing are digging in. Marc Tucker, Distinguished Senior Fellow at the National Center for Education and the Economy, has warned that when "schools suspend testing, this will mean that there will be no way of knowing how badly these kids have been damaged by COVID-19."[206] In November 2020, the *Washington Post* published an article by Chester Finn, a policy analyst and former US assistant secretary of education, proposing to reintroduce statewide tests after the pandemic because, he claimed, they provide the best way to identify gaps and guide interventions. "How will parents and teachers know which students need the most catch-up in which subjects? Who has the greatest need for summer school or tutoring? And how will district and state leaders know which schools coped better and worse?" he asked.[207] The *Post* followed this up with an editorial board opinion article in January 2021 titled "Why We Shouldn't Abandon Student Testing This Spring."[208] The editorial repeated tried but rather tired arguments about identifying inequities and enabling parents to know whether their children were achieving or not. It also added concerns about needing to assess the impact of COVD-19. It urged the incoming US education secretary, Miguel Cardona, to resist the temptation to abandon the tests.

Laura Jimenez, director of standards and accountability at the US Center for American Progress, argued that in state-level terms, despite COVID-19—and perhaps even because of it—"the annual assessment requirement should not be waived."[209] Jimenez conceded that end-of-year, one-time standardized tests are the least useful of all state assessments but expressed the belief that they should be retained to help identify learning gaps that occurred during the pandemic and to guide funding allocations afterward.

In March 2021, despite a letter from 500 US researchers, including Dennis, requesting that testing be suspended during the pandemic, Secretary Cardona insisted that the testing would persist because "student data obtained from the tests was important to help education officials create policy and target resources where they are most needed."[210]

Outside the United States, a September 2020 review of Australia's national NAPLAN test proposed only minor alterations in the grades being tested, changing the time of year for administering the test, revising the content of writing assessments, and extending the number of subjects to be tested, for example.[211] The federal minister for education swiftly responded that even these changes were unnecessary.[212] University of New South Wales professor Pasi Sahlberg is one of many critics who have targeted NAPLAN and its supporters. "Those who advocate the necessity of national standardised testing regimes back their views by positive consequences of high-stakes testing," he noted, "while ignoring the associated risks that research has exposed: narrowing curriculum, teaching to the tests, and declining student motivation, just to mention some."[213]

The negative side effects that continued use of high-stakes and mid-stakes testing incur, especially among the most disadvantaged students, are well documented, including in our own research. Post-COVID, we must not turn back to high-stakes or even mid-stakes testing. Testing will use up precious resources that will be needed to support the most vulnerable after their many weeks away from their schools, teachers, counselors, and special education staff. It will also exacerbate the anxieties and vulnerabilities of the most disadvantaged students as yet more pressure is placed on them to raise results that provide them with no direct benefit.

We don't have to cling to a bad thing because we fear there may be nothing to replace it. Tests can be administered to samples rather than to everyone, as in Finland or on the United States' *National Assessment of Educational Progress.*[214] They can be provided to individual teachers to *inform* their professional judgments, as in Scotland, rather than *replace* those judgments. They can maintain accountability without having negative consequences for students and their well-being.

Technological transformations are heralding the end of the industrial-age testing practices that have incurred excessive student anxiety for generations. With digital technology, assessment can now be continuous rather than episodic. Students can indicate their levels of understanding of online curriculum content in real time and display digital portfolios of work that can be shared with their teachers. Teachers can share their ongoing assessments with parents and with colleagues in other subjects more easily than in old analog testing systems.

Even examinations at the end of high school, long thought to be untouchable in the UK and East Asia, now have credible alternatives. There may still need to be components of sit-down exams, but if these are based on ever-changing, problem-based questions, they can be taken and retaken as needed. Students can prepare for them like driving tests, at any time throughout the year, rather than in a one-time, high-stress, win/lose environment. The systemic ill-being that comes with large-scale testing need no longer persist even as a necessary evil in our education systems. Better assessment alternatives already exist, and more are on the way.

Cultural Bias

What do you do when you are faced with a significant problem? The typical North American response, with positive psychology written all over it, is to look on the bright side, be hopeful, and believe it will all work out in the end. But UK newspaper columnist Oliver Burkeman, in his mischievously titled book *The Antidote: Happiness for People Who Can't Stand Positive Thinking,* adopts another approach.[215] He proposes imagining the worst-case scenario where it could all end badly—and then deciding whether you can live with it. If you can, he says, everything after that looks better.

The clever thing about Burkeman's book is the way it contrasts American ways of feeling happy with other cultural ways of finding fulfillment. William Davies, whose book, *The Happiness Industry,* we discussed earlier, points out that Americans score high on happiness partly because they like to talk about it so much.[216] The French, by contrast, score low because they feel that showcasing their own happiness is vulgar.

Burkeman says that the Stoics of ancient Greece and Rome "emphasized the benefits of always contemplating how badly things might go" and that Buddhists recommend equanimity in the face of life's many uncertainties.[217] Other writers have pointed out that Maslow's developmental ideal of self-actualization may not fit with Asian and Indigenous cultures.[218] In these cultures, it's the well-being of the family or the group that is paramount and not the autonomous individual of the West. By the end of Burkeman's book, it's clear that there are many ways to be well, not just one.

Wellness, for some, like Dennis, means mindfulness, understood as calming the body and mind in order to think clearly and with greater compassion for all living beings. For others, like US President Theodore Roosevelt, or Andy to a lesser extent, along with many other lovers of the wilderness, it's about outdoor adventure. In East Asian cultures, wellness may be defined by duty, filial piety, or making sacrifices in the present for well-being in the future—what Western psychologists call delayed gratification.[219] These issues of cultural variation raise questions for how educators understand well-being and its relationship to learning.

Emotional self-regulation programs, for example, emphasize calmness. But is calmness always the best way to be? Or is its appeal that it makes teachers' classrooms more manageable? There are important cultural differences in emotionality, and children in diverse classrooms bring these varied ways of being to school with them. Periods of calmness can have value for children from all cultures, but imposed self-regulation can sometimes be a source of inequity, exclusion, and even racism for children from communities of color. Similarly, the joyous and aggressive emotions expressed in outdoor play may not always make young people so amenable in a traditional classroom. The learning environment needs to adjust to this wider range of emotions rather than always trying to fit children's diverse emotions into conventional classrooms.

A diverse and inclusive curriculum must not just encompass the content of literature or science, or even just the different ways that students learn best. It must also be sensitive and responsive to cultural differences in students' emotionality—including being talkative or quiet, physically outgoing or inscrutably restrained, calm and deferential or assertive and bold. For teachers to be empathetic with the range of students' diverse emotions, they also need to become aware of their own emotionality—that it is not neutral or universal or superior, but specific to their own identities.

There are times for emotional self-regulation and also for emotional expression and release. In both cases, social and emotional learning programs should address a wide span of emotions, not just those that make children easier to teach.

Conclusion

If well-being is perceived as being unconnected to learning or achievement, if it is seen as self-indulgence, if it is undermined by other policies that actually create ill-being, or if the approved ways of being well do not fit with some of the cultures to which children belong, it will attract criticism and undermine public confidence. Well-being is a part of our cultures and societies that in turn help define who we are. Well-being, in this respect, is affected by changes and variations in our cultures. These are the issues we address in the next two chapters. In the following chapter, we examine two social changes that have brought the well-being agenda into prominence, and in the chapter after that, we look at three ways in which that agenda can and should unfold in the near future.

4

The Rise of Well-Being:
Between GERM and VUCA

We are now in the third decade of the 21st century. When we look at things such as school testing and examination systems, though, it sometimes seems like we're trapped in the last century—or even the one before that. At the same time, during the COVID-19 pandemic, most of us experienced moments when we felt like we were rushing headlong toward the world's end. Even before the pandemic, many young people were already getting bored and frustrated with out-dated elements of public education that seemed indifferent to their needs. Yet they have also become increasingly anxious and appre-hensive about the onrushing future. Young people and their well-being are being squeezed between and thrust upward by two great tectonic movements of social and educational change. Like an Alpine mountain range emerging in great geological folds as tec-tonic plates press upon it from either side, the quest for well-being is rising up from under the surface. It is a prominent new feature of the educational landscape.

One tectonic plate is pressing from those parts of the past that have had no patience with whole child education and that, like Charles Dickens's character Thomas Gradgrind, have held fast to the stance that "facts alone are wanted in life."[220] This movement has pushed standardization, testing, and a relentless drive to improve performance numbers in everything from Gross Domestic Product (GDP) in the economy to national test score gains in education—often at the cost of people's well-being. The other tectonic plate is an outgrowth of the present and the future. It is defined by extreme uncertainty and magnified by the influence and impact of digital technologies. These two tectonic movements have already been assigned acronyms: GERM and VUCA.

GERM

For at least 30 years, nation after nation pushed whole child education to the margins of their policies. A burgeoning movement put data and measurement at the center of school reform. It was obsessed with maximizing economic growth and improving performance numbers in everything from industrial assembly lines to health targets and flight times. Inevitably, raising students' test scores got caught up in the same surge.

Kate Raworth, inventor of the acclaimed theory of "donut economics," amplifies a growing critique of conventional economics by saying there is more to human existence than GDP.[221] Taxing more income and cutting government services such as public education to build up a bigger GDP, she says, is not the answer. The greatest source of inequality, she points out, is not income, but wealth. Just 1 percent of the world's population—including tech billionaires such as Bill Gates, Tim Cook, Mark Zuckerberg, and Jeff Bezos—owns more than 50 percent of the world's wealth. In the United States, just 0.1 percent owns a fifth of it.[222]

Mariana Mazzucato, prize-winning author of *The Value of Everything: Making and Taking in the Global Economy,* concurs.[223] In the midst of the pandemic, she warned against "renewed austerity to reduce the enormous debt-to-GDP ratios" that would arise from government borrowing.[224] Obsessions with growth and insistence on austerity when growth goes awry are two sides of the same coin. Economic inequality is the rough edge of injustice that welds growth and austerity together.

Richard Wilkinson and Kate Pickett have used epidemiological data to show that across nations, and in state-by-state comparisons in the United States, the strongest predictor of ill-being is economic inequality.[225] With the concentration of wealth in fewer and fewer hands, inequality and poverty have wreaked havoc on people's quality of life. In 2018, UN Poverty Envoy Philip Alston described cuts in UK local authority budgets (including budgets for schools) of 50 percent as "callous."[226] Under Prime Minister David Cameron's austerity-driven government, rates of homelessness doubled—often among young people.[227]

Alston reported that in the United States, a country with more than 25 percent of the world's billionaires, "40 million live in poverty, 18.5 million in extreme poverty, and 5.3 million live in Third World conditions of absolute poverty." Spelling out the implications for quality of life, Alston noted that the United States "has the highest youth poverty rate in the Organization for Economic Cooperation and Development, and the highest infant mortality rates among comparable OECD States. Its citizens live shorter and sicker lives compared to those living in all other rich democracies."[228]

Even in comparatively high-achieving Canadian school systems, failures to fund sufficient mental health support for young people in the community outside the school led to avoidable youth suicides in the 10 districts we studied. Educators found these stories heartbreaking. In manufacturing towns, schools struggled to keep students learning, even as their parents battled with unemployment or held jobs that failed to pay a living wage.

This economic age—oriented to growth and interspersed with austerity, and stretching from the 1980s to the present—has been accompanied by educational policies that have been focused on performance numbers and on delegating the problems of inequality to schools. This has been the era of what Finnish education reform specialist and University of New South Wales professor Pasi Sahlberg calls the "Global Education Reform Movement," or GERM. Educational systems under GERM became fixated on top-down accountability, education for economic competitiveness, standardized teaching and learning, and relentless high-stakes testing in the pursuit of constantly improving performance results.[229]

GERM began in the late 1980s and early 1990s in the UK and in a few US states, including Arkansas, New York, Tennessee, and Texas. It was not until the passage of George W. Bush's No Child

Left Behind Act of 2002 and Barack Obama's Race to the Top legislation of 2009, however, that the US variant of GERM became pervasive throughout the land.[230]

As we saw in the previous chapter, large-scale testing was also introduced in Australian states and in Canadian provinces including Ontario and Alberta. Other nations also made efforts to follow in the footsteps of these English-speaking systems with their emphases on literacy and mathematics, test scores, and targets.[231] Globally, the World Bank imposed conditions for lending that required less developed countries to create national standards, establish databases to compare school performance, and introduce systems of standardized testing.[232] Meanwhile, after the OECD published its first set of PISA test results in 2001 and produced comparative rankings of national performance, governments started to concentrate their educational efforts on how they could raise their scores in literacy, mathematics, and science.[233]

The characteristics of this performance-driven movement had adverse consequences for students' well-being. The curriculum became a shadow of what it should have been. Arts, social studies, and physical play ceded place to an interminable focus on narrow versions of literacy, mathematics, and science. Students became disengaged. They got more and more anxious about examinations and tests. They stopped playing outside, and childhood obesity rates rocketed. As the late Sir Ken Robinson observed, the reductions in recess time that made way for test preparation meant that elementary school students got less opportunity to exercise outdoors than maximum security prisoners in the United States.[234]

Under the heavy burden of bread-and-butter basics, young people became less likely to see the point of what they were doing or to develop a sense of purpose in school and in life. Even when students succeeded, their success didn't mean they were physically or psychologically well. Indeed, competitive, high-performing, test-driven nations in East Asia, along with the UK, had some of the worst records in child well-being anywhere in the world.[235] More and more students are experiencing what Korean-German philosopher Byun-Chul Han calls "the burnout society," in which traditional forms of social solidarity have withered and everyone is expected to be "entrepreneurs of themselves."[236]

Still, GERM has lingered, like a stubborn virus that has not yet met up with a vaccine or a cure, in spite of growing evidence of its incalculable damage. Meanwhile, another age has now started to surface alongside it: one that business and policy specialists call "VUCA."

VUCA

Arising from business management theory in the 1980s but increasingly used in military strategy, business, politics, and organizational studies since the early 2000s, VUCA is an acronym for four new states of social and political life:[237]

- *Volatility* of change that occurs at accelerating speed in shifting directions.
- *Uncertainty* of evidence, information, and capacity to predict the future.
- *Complexity* of intersecting forces.
- *Ambiguity* regarding what events and circumstances actually mean to people of different identities and perspectives.

A VUCA world results from the rapid expansion of digital communication, the increasing global movement and mixing of cultures, and the proliferation of intersecting identities. It is characterized by the growth of a flexible and insecure gig economy of temporary, part-time, low-paid, and constantly changing work, at the expense of predictable and secure employment. In education, it is evident in the profusion of semiprivate US charter schools, Swedish "free schools," and chains of "academies" (analogous to charter schools) in England. It can be seen in the growth and spread of online, hybrid, and blended learning options, and in escalating demands from anxious parents with competing interests, agendas, and identities.

If GERM boxes everybody into standardized and dehumanizing bureaucracies, VUCA blurs the boundaries of schooling and identities and confronts people with constant uncertainty. Even the apparent upside of VUCA, with its borderless implications, dangerously communicates that, like the title of a Bon Jovi song, human aspirations and accomplishments are *limitless.*[238] The convergence of GERM and VUCA in education traps young people in a world that is controlling, competitive, and constraining on one side, while being unpredictable, unrestrained, and insecure on the other.

Not surprisingly, this convergence of forces has created a mental health crisis among young people of global proportions. It has manifested itself in countless ways. Rising rates of anxiety, depression, and even suicide are occurring in places as far apart as the Indigenous communities of northern Canada and the United States, and the super-competitive nations of East Asia. The UK's Children and Young People's Mental Health Coalition found that in an average class of 30 15-year-old pupils,

- 3 could have a mental disorder,
- 10 are likely to have witnessed their parents separate,
- 1 could have experienced the death of a parent,
- 7 are likely to have been bullied, and
- 6 may be self-harming.[239]

The greatest refugee crisis in 70 years has brought children from dislocated families and war-torn countries into more and more teachers' classrooms. In addition to years of missed schooling, many refugee children have also been exposed to multiple incidents of post-traumatic stress involving family deaths, violence, and dislocation. In 2015, a report from the Migration Policy Institute on *The Educational and Mental Health Needs of Syrian Refugee Children* found that 79 percent of such children were grieving a death, and half of them were suffering from post-traumatic stress disorder.[240] This amounted to an average of having experienced seven incidents of post-traumatic stress for some groups. And yet these same immigrants have too often been expected to submit to inflexible requirements accompanying a standardized curriculum and high-stakes tests.

Alongside all the issues accompanying the arrival of refugee newcomers in many school systems, there has also been overdue reckoning with the historic injustices that have been inflicted on marginalized and oppressed groups such as Indigenous, Black, Asian, disabled, and LGBTQ communities, placing heightened demands on teachers to be responsive to everyone they teach. The Black Lives Matter movement, expanding in the United States in 2020 after the killings by law enforcement officers of African Americans including Willie McCoy, George Floyd, and Breonna Taylor, has spread across the world in a multiracial movement of outrage and protest.[241] The UK, for example, has seen prominent coverage of Black celebrities and community leaders being pulled over and handcuffed by police when no clear offense has been committed.[242]

The white working class, meanwhile, has also been beset with problems, including an epidemic of what have been called "deaths of despair" related to opioid addiction and suicide.[243] Many supporters of Donald Trump in the United States and Brexit in Britain have felt ignored, left out, and left behind by liberal elites.[244]

The downsides of digital technology and virtual identities are adding fuel to this fire. Over the last decade, on-screen, hand-held technology has created an Instagram and TikTok youth culture that has become preoccupied with superficial entertainment and self-indulgence, and plagued by cyberbullying as well as adolescent anxiety about image and appearance. A 2020 UK research study of more than 2,000 girls on young women's use of technology reported that a third of the sample would not post selfies online without digitally enhancing their appearance.[245]

In her book *iGen,* Jean Twenge attributes a spike in anxiety levels among teenagers since 2012 to the widespread ownership and use of smartphones. Since 2012, adolescents' increasing engagement with their devices has ironically made them less vulnerable to face-to-face risks such as alcohol abuse and physical violence.[246] Teenagers are going to fewer parties and prefer to spend time in their rooms on Friday or Saturday nights. But sleepless, alone, and on their smartphones far into the night, checking out what everyone else thinks of them and their images, girls, especially, become increasingly anxious and depressed.

This trend, Twenge notes, has occurred across all socioeconomic groups. During COVID-19, children's screen time more than doubled and even tripled to levels far in excess of those recommended by pediatricians.[247] Even before the pandemic, excess screen time among children was raising widespread concerns about direct neurological damage and the loss of children's interest and ability to read deeply for meaning rather than rapidly for recall.[248] A 2018 report by Nature Canada found that 76 percent of preschoolers exceeded the recommended maximum screen time of one hour daily advised by the Canadian Pediatric Association, with negative consequences for sleep, eating habits, physical activity, cognitive functioning, and mental health.[249] Other research findings have also pointed to negative effects of excess screen time on childhood obesity levels and on opportunities for outdoor play.[250]

Young people also seem to be increasingly vulnerable to feelings of isolation and lack of purpose in life. Perpetrators of school shootings in the United States are highly likely to be isolated, to be bullied, and to lack a sense of belonging in school.[251] A UK survey points out that 27 percent of young people believe that life has no meaning or purpose.[252] All this has contributed to distrust of leaders, withdrawal from citizenship, and loss of belief in democracy itself as people have turned to strongman demagogues, reality TV stars, comedians, and clowns for easy answers or *any* answers to their plight.

Then, on top of all this, in the midst of the greatest pandemic in 100 years and during the aftermath of the worst global recession since the 1930s, everything that many of us took for granted—good health, secure employment, effectively functioning democracy, and just being able to send our children to school—was thrown up in the air. As the Swedish climate change activist Greta Thunberg explains, and as those who possess Indigenous knowledge have understood for millennia, these multiple crises are not an unfortunate coincidence.[253] We live on an interconnected planet. The crises are all part of the same thing. As a species, we have lost our way. The world is falling off its axis, and it's time for us to put it back on.

The Eruption of Well-Being

Between the two tectonic movements of GERM and VUCA, a new feature is emerging on the educational landscape—a movement toward addressing people's concerns about well-being, identity, and quality of life. Even before COVID-19, there were more than a few signs that the prevalence of ill-being and the need for well-being were beginning to grab people's attention. The emergence of positive psychology gave prominence to wellness and ways to achieve it in everyday interactions. These included mindfulness meditation, building resilience, developing growth mindsets rather than fixed mindsets, and training people to manage their emotions. Spas, wellness retreats, and yoga classes became booming business propositions. Epidemiologists and transnational organizations such as UNICEF produced evidence and indicators spotlighting countries with the highest levels of well-being. They identified social and economic policies in those countries that others could emulate. Last, the growth of a social media culture in which sports and entertainment celebrities began to disclose mental health problems such as depression, addictions, or having once been victims of bullying made it easier for many other people to face their psychological struggles and assign higher priority to wellness in their education and their lives.

In the midst of the global pandemic, we are getting even more insights into how to put the world right. Public sector employees who, only a short time ago, were depicted as costs to the economy, are now appreciated as the essential workers who risked their lives every day to keep us healthy, fed, and safe. From the balconies of Italy to the doorsteps of Japan, entire populations applauded the sacrifices made by their healthcare workers. More and more citizens now see self-important, quasi-totalitarian national leaders who couldn't deal with the pandemic as "emperors with no clothes." In a number of countries, these citizens are showing signs of seeking political leadership that is more empathetic, inclusive, collaborative, and respectful of science and expertise instead.

Ordinary people everywhere stepped up to help their neighbors, support the vulnerable, and simply greet each other as they passed at a physical distance in new relationships of civility. As traffic on the streets and in the skies subsided, many people also started to reconnect with the natural world. They could hear the birds sing again. Educators assembled innovative high- and low-tech solutions to the necessity of learning at home with incredible ingenuity and alacrity. The Black Lives Matter movement has seen people of many races and religions joining together across the world to seek justice for groups that have been marginalized and oppressed for generations.

The world is waking up. We are stirring from our slumber. Now, instead of greater economic growth and higher educational performance for their own sake, more and more people and their governments are addressing how schools and other organizations can enrich and enhance our collective quality of life. Economic performance is one reason to have good public schools, but it is by no means the only or even the main one. There is more to life than being economically productive or being able to perform well on tests.

How do schools help young people develop a sense of purpose in life, treat others with dignity, form friendships, build positive identities, become responsible citizens, live healthy and fulfilling lives, experience enjoyment, exercise leadership, feel senses of awe in spirituality or nature, stand up to injustice, and so on? How can our schools treat childhood as something that has value in its own right and not just as a waiting room for jobs or other aspects of adulthood? Rather than teaching kids only how to *perform* or *produce,* why can't we also teach them how to *be* and how to *live together,* as human beings? How do we develop children as whole people rather than allocating disproportionate effort to increasing their ability to perform well on tests and examinations? These are the questions that must define the educational agenda in the next part of the 21st century. They don't just add well-being to our educational improvement priorities. They move well-being to the very center of them.

Well-Being and the Pandemic

If any self-respecting educator or politician ever thought that well-being had a place in schools but was secondary to real learning, achievement, and test results, the COVID-19 pandemic disabused them of that notion.

In the early months of 2020, a great sickness spread across the world. It was the most virulent and far-reaching pandemic in more than a century. The novel coronavirus swept through country after country. It infected millions. It especially struck down the elderly and the vulnerable. It was a physical health pandemic of unprecedented proportions.

If this crisis was not enough, in its wake, a second pandemic of mental and emotional health problems among adults and young people swiftly followed. In almost 200 countries, COVID-19 closed down schools for months on end. More than a billion children were confined at home, trying to learn with help from their families or on digital devices, away from the support of their teachers and their schools.[254]

Suddenly we got to witness what the world was like without schools and teachers. This was a world where working parents had to become uncertified substitute teachers, where children became isolated from their friends and peers, and where the good and bad sides of technology and teaching online were exposed for all to see.

As teachers and school systems scrambled to respond, many of the immediate concerns were about learning losses, about unequal access to technology for learning at home, and, later, about having to suspend the end-of-school examinations that provided certification for work or university entrance. Transnational organizations, including the World Bank and the OECD, estimated that the global economy would sustain massive shortfalls due to lost learning and undeveloped skills.[255] More serious still were the widening learning gaps between children in wealthier and poorer families during COVID-19.[256]

Even worse than all this, though, was what was happening to vulnerable students. Young people were now completely at the mercy of their home environments, with no compensatory public protection and provision for those in chaotic and sometimes abusive household circumstances. Not only did many of these children have families that had been plunged into poverty by COVID-19; they were often already living in overcrowded and highly stressful environments before the pandemic. These students were learning less than their more privileged peers. Unprecedented numbers of them became uncontactable and fell off their schools' radar altogether.[257]

University of Ottawa professor Jess Whitley and her colleagues surveyed 265 parents who had children with identified special needs and conducted interviews with 25 of them about their experiences of emergency online learning during the pandemic. Not surprisingly, they found that the pandemic exaggerated the effects of the presence or the absence of inclusive approaches that had existed before it. "Those who had financial, work, or health challenges, or who had fewer resources to draw upon, described an abrupt end to services" and therapies, the authors noted.[258] Whereas some parents welcomed "regular, personalized check-ins, by email, phone, or video chat" from their child's education assistant or teacher, not everyone was offered these kinds of connections. Moreover, "very little attention was being paid to connecting peers with each other during at-home learning," and parents felt that this oversight affected their children's mental health. In sad commentaries on the problematic nature of "normal" schooling before the pandemic, some parents observed "their child grow calmer, happier, and more rested away from the stresses of school schedules and social anxieties" during at-home learning, and even considered moving their children out of the public system once it was over.

Elsewhere, Whitley drew attention to how the families of some students with special needs couldn't fathom how to use the assistive technologies that the schools had been using to help their kids to access and express their learning. Meanwhile, she noted, other parents were distraught that they couldn't explain to their children with severe disabilities why they just couldn't go to school, be with their friends, and enjoy their regular routines anymore.[259]

After weeks or months at home, almost all students lost their teachers' face-to-face support. Many young people experienced poverty and stress. They saw family members become ill, or worse, and had little chance to play outside. Rates of domestic abuse and fights over custody arrangements rose dramatically during the COVID-19 pandemic.[260] More than a few students found themselves being forcibly sheltered in place with parents who actually posed a threat to their mental health. LGBTQ students, for example, described the serious mental health costs of being locked down with homophobic parents.[261] In more mundane terms, many children simply lost the habits that schools teach them—sitting in a circle, waiting their turn, or knowing how to listen and cooperate.

Surveys of teachers' experiences during COVID-19 in multiple countries revealed that vulnerable students were at the top of teachers' priorities and concerns. The realization dawned on educators everywhere that Abraham Maslow's hierarchy of needs should come before Benjamin Bloom's taxonomy of learning objectives—certainly during the pandemic and perhaps all of the time.[262] Basic shelter, food, and security now took precedence over traditional academic preoccupations and all their modern manifestations, such as global competencies and 21st century skills.

Teachers contacted their most vulnerable students and their families as soon as they could—within a couple of days after school closures where possible. But many systems feared litigation from parents protesting about unequal treatment of some children ahead of others. Or they were wary of child protection and safeguarding issues in which unsupervised teachers might be calling children who were undressed or in inappropriate surroundings. Or they continued to operate as the unwieldy and unyielding bureaucracies of top-down regulation they had always been.[263] These sorts of systems made despairing teachers wait two or even four weeks before they were allowed to use their professional judgment and establish contact with parents. Teachers wanted to be the trained, expert, and collaborative first responders to their students who were in crisis. But when they tried to reach out to families, too many systems didn't trust them as professionals and simply stopped them in their tracks.

All these issues surrounding children's physical and mental health were further amplified when it came to deciding whether and how children should return to school while the coronavirus was still out there. Following a period of near-unanimous commitment to keeping children at home to protect them and because initially it was thought that they might be super-spreaders of the virus to vulnerable adults, the tide of opinion and expertise began to move in the other direction.

As Northern Hemisphere summer vacations approached and decisions had to be made about plans for schools reopening (or not) in the fall of 2020, the pediatric associations of the United States and the UK, along with pediatricians from the children's hospital in Toronto, Canada, advised that the physical risks posed by COVID-19 were now being superseded by the mental health problems that more and more young people were experiencing by enduring protracted isolation at home.[264] In Canada, elementary-age children were spending upward of five hours per day on screen time—more than double the limit recommended by Canadian Pediatric Association guidelines.[265] During the pandemic, a UK research team conducted a rapid review of 83 articles on the impact of loneliness and isolation "on the mental health of previously healthy children and adolescents." The researchers concluded that "children and adolescents are probably more likely to experience high rates of depression and most likely anxiety during and after enforced isolation ends."[266] Even before COVID-19, one-third of US teenagers said they were depressed or overwhelmed by stress and that the biggest stressor in their lives was their schools.[267] A 2017 survey of more than 5,000 secondary school students in England found similar results, especially with regard to the mental health effects of social media.[268] Teenagers have been the age group most prone to experience mental health problems during COVID-19.[269]

Tying together pre- and post-pandemic realities for adolescents' well-being, a UK survey of more than 1,000 teenagers found that rates of depression during the pandemic were up 2 percent, but rates of anxiety had actually fallen by 10 percent.[270] A number of students, such as those with autism spectrum disorder, others who had been victims of bullying in schools, or students who were negatively affected by high school pressures, actually experienced some relief from stress when they moved to learning at home.

Even though teenagers like these welcomed the escape from high school stresses, on balance, a powerful case developed for children to return to school. It was important that this return be done safely and with all the right safeguards and supports. An interesting point is that many of the countries that did this most successfully were ones in Northern Europe that already had a strong commitment to and positive record on well-being. Nations such as Norway and Denmark reopened schools early, used strict sanitizing procedures, spaced desks apart, bunched children into smaller classes and pods that could interact internally but were shielded from each other, and conducted classes in the outdoors wherever they could.[271]

Despite all the excitement among technology companies—and among some politicians and educational systems—about a new dawn for blended or hybrid learning beyond school walls after COVID-19, the physical necessity for schools as places that support healthy child development and as places for children to be so their parents can get back to work is unassailable. The big question would now be about the conditions under which children should return to school during and after a pandemic.

Alongside the mental health case for children being back in school was an additional economic argument. Most parents can only work as long as their children are cared for outside the home. *The Economist* magazine was among the first to recognize this simple truth and to advance this position publicly.[272] A number of governments started to line up behind this argument but were unwilling to commit resources or additional personnel to provide conditions in public schools that were safe, secure, and sufficient for children's mental health and learning.

Former US President Donald Trump and his Secretary of Education, Betsy DeVos, threatened states that would not require parents to send their children back to school with withdrawal of federal funds for education, even when coronavirus infection levels in those states ranked among the highest in the world.[273] After considerable indecision in trying to coordinate a response that accommodated a national patchwork of academies similar to US charter schools, England's education minister summarily announced that parents who did not return their children to school in September 2020 would face being fined.[274]

In Ontario, the Conservative government that had succeeded Kathleen Wynne's Liberal Party administration initially offered varying solutions that school districts could adopt at their discretion. These included blended options of part-time at school and part-time at home with online learning. Eventually the government mandated choosing between full-time learning at school, part-time learning in high school operating every other day with smaller classes, or required synchronous online learning at home, delivered by different sets of teachers, for several hours a day.[275]

This combination of back-to-school options that were also adopted in many other places was parodied in a US satire of a school district message to parents. The parody was as funny as it was frighteningly close to the truth. One fake question and its optional responses looked like this:

> This fall, you favor:
> 1. In-person learning, and constant fear
> 2. Hybrid learning, mixing constant fear with a dollop of logistical chaos
> 3. Remote learning, marrying logistical chaos with the cold cloak of devastating isolation
> 4. Moving to Maine and launching your own homeschool.[276]

Conclusion

Beyond COVID-19, young people's well-being will depend on more investment, not less, because many of them will be in particular need of extra counseling and support. Children need to be in school for economic, educational, and mental health reasons. But given all we have learned about the primacy of child well-being, the economic consideration should not ignore, override, or undermine the other two. We must find a better way to connect the big picture of social and economic change before, during, and after the pandemic to the protection and promotion of young people's day-to-day well-being and quality of life.

How should we do this? Answering this question is the purpose of the next three chapters. These address three forces that we will need to harness in order to fully achieve well-being for all of our students in the years to come. They are prosperity rather than austerity in economic and social policy; ethical rather than overly exuberant uses of digital learning technologies; and engaging with restorative nature rather than condemning children to the nature-deficit disorder that results from too much time being devoted to additional instruction and test preparation indoors.

5

Prosperity for All:
The Social Economics of Well-Being

Many of the skills and dispositions that are identified with and influenced by social psychology serve a valuable purpose in schools and are tools that teachers can use to help their kids to be healthy and to thrive. Teachers can take care of basic needs for security and safety. They can help students build themselves up to become resilient and bounce back from setbacks and adversity. We can have classrooms and schools where children develop an irrepressible, Dolly Parton–like sense of buoyancy, so they are hard to push down in the first place. Schools can teach kids language and strategies to be calm and quiet when their emotions run out of control. They can provide opportunities for exercise, breathing, and stretching, so that children's bodies are not at odds with their minds. Schools can also cultivate growth mindsets, so that students do not become downcast or feel defeated when they cannot understand or accomplish something at first. All these are invaluable things to teach everyone—especially those who are most vulnerable.

Research in social psychology provides teachers with evidence-informed approaches to enhance their students' well-being. It has given teachers tools and insights that go far beyond the old adage of setting high expectations. Now there is a body of research and practice that shows exactly how those high expectations can be acted upon to improve learning and well-being.

Yet well-being still comes down to more than individual behaviors in individual classes and schools. States of well-being vary across social groups. The coronavirus crisis affected practically everyone's mental health, but teenagers were more vulnerable than most. Suicide is always a personal tragedy, but in 1897 the French sociologist Émile Durkheim was the first to point out that suicide rates varied depending on how socially integrated or not the societies were in which suicides occurred.[277] Today, youth suicide rates are much higher among vulnerable groups in Indigenous communities, among students who are LGBTQ, or in countries where school examination pressures operate at extreme levels and create cultures of anxiety and perfectionism, for example.[278]

A comprehensive approach to student and teacher well-being must therefore consider social as well as psychological dimensions. We have to take an interdisciplinary stance and address the social, economic, and political conditions in the societies and communities in which students are educated and how they optimize or interfere with young people's prospects of being well. And we have to engage our students with learning how to contribute to their communities and societies, now and in the future, in ways that support their own and others' physical and mental health, alongside academic success.

Students and educators are whole human beings. Their lives and their work are part of the world and are not set apart from it. They are all affected by the bigger picture of social, economic, and environmental change. We believe they should also be responsible for contributing to and helping to shape that big picture in a conscious and deliberate way, through how students learn, what educators teach, and how they all live their lives.

Like a movie, these chapters therefore pan out to address three of these inescapable wider issues that are affecting everyone's well-being and that will do so for the foreseeable future. We then zoom back in to address what these mean for the protagonists who define the everyday narratives of teaching and learning. We begin with the threat of economic austerity and the promise of its opposite—social prosperity.

Inequality

Most of us are drawn to international rankings. Whether it's Olympic medals or educational performance, we want to know where we stand and who is the best. Even those who say they are opposed to competitive rankings are often among the first to declare the results when their institutions or nations are near the top.

Rankings of well-being attract the same fascination. Who are the happiest people in the world? Which are the healthiest nations? Where are the best places to live? Most people are intrigued. They really want to know.

When we scan the countries that score high on various indicators of well-being, the same nations or type of nations head the list. As of 2020, the UN's five happiest countries were Finland, Denmark, Switzerland, Iceland, and Norway (the UK ranks 13th, and the United States, 18th).[279] On *Transparency International's* index of corruption perception, Denmark, New Zealand, Finland, Singapore, and Sweden were the least corrupt countries.[280] According to *The Economist Intelligence Unit*, the world's "full" democracies were Norway, Iceland, Sweden, New Zealand, and Finland.[281]

In 2020, UNICEF published a report card titled *Worlds of Influence: Understanding What Shapes Child Well-Being in Rich Countries.* It ranks 38 countries on indicators related to well-being goals as they relate to children. The top five countries are the Netherlands, Denmark, Norway, Switzerland, and Finland. The UK ranks 27th; the United States ranks 36th; and Canada, Australia, and New Zealand are all down in the 30s. [282]

What explains these rank positions and the repeated appearance of several of the same countries from Northern Europe near the top? Two researchers who have been fascinated with what explains the variations in well-being among different countries and also among US states are the British epidemiologists Richard Wilkinson and Kate Pickett.

Epidemiologists came into the spotlight during the COVID-19 pandemic. Night after night, on news broadcasts, they explained how and why the virus and its effects varied among different demographic groups, and how and where it spread. In their bestselling 2009 book, *The Spirit Level,* Wilkinson and Pickett used epidemiological methods to identify the factor that, in statistical terms, explained differences in well-being between nations and states more than any other.[283]

Wilkinson and Pickett conclude that well-being and its opposite, ill-being, are the result not of absolute wealth and poverty, or economic growth or recession, but of relative levels of economic inequality in income and wealth. Above basic survival levels, it's not how much money you have, or how little, that affects your well-being. It's your economic standing and your status compared to others that affect your well-being as an individual and everyone as a society. Whether it's mental health, alcohol dependency, drug addiction, obesity, teenage pregnancy, rates of imprisonment, incidences of violence, levels of distrust, bullying in schools, or educational underachievement—the patterns are the same. Economic inequality is the major cause of ill-being.

Figure 5.1 shows what the overall patterns look like. The horizontal axis shows increasing income inequality as you move from left to right. The vertical axis displays increasing health and social

FIGURE 5.1

Relationship Between Income Inequality and Health and Social Problems in Nations

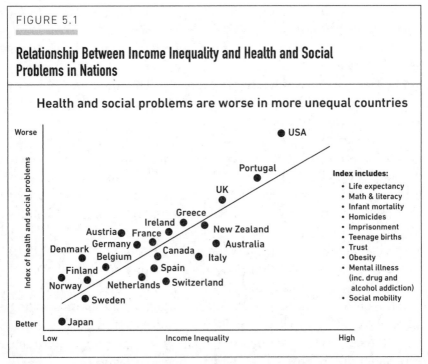

Source: From *The Spirit Level: Why Greater Equality Makes Societies Stronger* (p. 20), by R. Wilkinson and K. Pickett, 2009, Bloomsbury Publishing.

problems as you ascend the chart. The countries in the bottom left-hand corner—Japan, along with the usual Nordic candidates of Norway, Sweden, and Finland—have better performance in health and social issues and low economic inequality. In the top right-hand corner are their opposites—the United States, the UK, and Portugal. These are countries with high inequality and more pervasive health and social problems.

The same patterns apply in comparisons among US states, as Figure 5.2 illustrates. The US states with greater economic inequality, including Alabama, Mississippi, and Louisiana, are also the ones with the worst performance in health and social problems. In both US and international terms, these differences are also evident in the relationship between economic inequality and child well-being, as is evident in terms of country-by-country comparisons in Figure 5.3, with the Netherlands, Finland, Sweden, Norway, and Denmark being the top performers.

FIGURE 5.2

Relationship Between Income Inequality and Health and Social Problems in US States

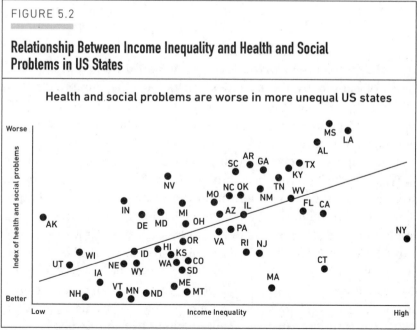

Source: From *The Spirit Level: Why Greater Equality Makes Societies Stronger* (p. 22), by R. Wilkinson and K. Pickett, 2009, Bloomsbury Publishing.

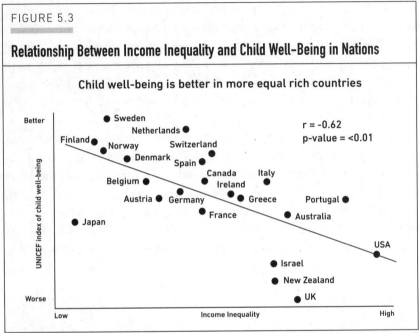

FIGURE 5.3

Relationship Between Income Inequality and Child Well-Being in Nations

Child well-being is better in more equal rich countries

Source: From *The Spirit Level: Why Greater Equality Makes Societies Stronger* (p. 23), by R. Wilkinson and K. Pickett, 2009, Bloomsbury Publishing.

"The problems in rich countries," Wilkinson and Pickett state, "are not caused by the societies not being rich enough." Rather, what matters is that "the scale of material differences between people" at one point simply becomes "too big. What matters is where we stand in relation to others in our own society."[284]

The impact of social inequality was excruciatingly evident during COVID-19. The groups most prone to infection, illness, and death were not just the old and infirm. In the United States, according to an article published by National Public Radio, "Communities of color are being hit disproportionately hard by COVID-19." African American deaths were "nearly two times greater than would be expected based on their share of the population," and the risks of being a confirmed case were up to "four times greater" among Hispanics.[285] In the UK, the risk of death among people of Bangladeshi background was "double that seen among white British people." "People of Chinese, Indian, Pakistani, other Asian, Caribbean, and other black backgrounds also face . . . a higher risk of death of between 10% and 50% the risk of death compared with white Britons."[286]

Public Health England, an executive agency within the UK's Department of Health and Social Care, attributed some of the problem to historic racism and discrimination that discouraged minority communities from seeking help or demanding better protective equipment from official agencies or work supervisors. It also identified the crowded and unsafe occupational and living conditions of the working poor, among whom many ethno-racial minorities are concentrated, as being at the heart of the issue.[287] After international travelers had introduced the coronavirus to a new country, it spread more quickly among poorer communities than in others.

Societies characterized by high levels of economic inequality typically provide limited protections for, insufficient inclusion of, and minimal opportunities for their weakest and most vulnerable members. This situation was palpably obvious during the COVID-19 pandemic, but it was already widespread well before that point. Anne Case, the Alexander Stewart 1886 Professor of Economics and Public Affairs Emeritus at Princeton University, and fellow Princeton professor and 2015 Nobel Prize winner in economics Angus Deaton have documented the devastating effects of economic inequality on the health and well-being of Americans in their grimly titled text, *Deaths of Despair and the Future of Capitalism.*[288]

Case and Deaton collected data on rising rates of "deaths of despair" among different populations. They studied deaths due to suicide or to slow poisonings resulting from opioid addiction or alcoholic liver disease. These deaths of despair were also mirrored in diminished quality of health in the same vulnerable populations, in terms of pain, mental distress, and loneliness.

In the 1970s and 1980s, they report, it was African Americans who were the greatest casualties of deaths of despair. Their jobs in the central city were the first to be hit by the first wave of globalization, as William Julius Wilson had documented in *When Work Disappears.*[289] For the past 20 years, though, the white working class—especially those without a bachelor's degree—have, in the most ominous sense, been catching up. While Black mortality rates have been declining slightly, "those of working-class whites were rising."[290] The most recent wave of globalization has been drawing this second demographic into its deadly embrace. After this, Case and Deaton warn, America's white-collar, suburban middle classes will be next, unless something is done to stop the trend.

A widening wealth gap in the United States has brought with it a loss of traditional working-class manufacturing jobs. Poverty for many has often ensued, but there is even more to the situation than that. Replacement jobs that have often been trumpeted as contributing to lower unemployment rates have been nonunionized, without benefits, and often insufficient to secure a living wage. Like the long-term care-home (nursing home) workers we just discussed, people who have to work multiple jobs lose a sense of belonging to any one of them in particular. Promotion prospects and hopes for improvement are slim, and US workplaces suffer from an epidemic of what's called "presenteeism."[291] People show up for work when they are sick, underperforming, and even at risk of infecting others, because they can't afford to lose their jobs and health benefits. As Case and Deaton warn, "Destroy work, and in the end, working-class life cannot survive. It is the loss of meaning, of dignity, of pride, and of self-respect . . . that brings on despair, not just or even primarily the loss of money."[292]

In *The Inner Level,* the sequel to Wilkinson and Pickett's earlier book, the authors present data that connect income inequality to status anxiety—whether, and how much, people feel others look down on them because of their financial position. Status anxiety, along with all the associated stress, they found, increases with income inequality.[293] The greater the gaps, the more other people are able to look down on you. British journalist Owen Jones and Harvard University philosopher Michael Sandel both bemoan how the working class and the non–college educated, respectively, have been targets of the "last acceptable prejudice" of liberal elites.[294] In his *New York Times* article titled "The Resentment That Never Sleeps," published just after the 2020 US presidential election, Thomas Edsall notes how "diminished status has become a source of rage on both the left and right" and points to "the anger of white non–college voters over their disparagement by liberal elites."[295]

The same issues are apparent in post-Brexit Britain. Deborah Mattinson, in her book *Beyond the Red Wall,* conducted interviews in three strongly pro-Brexit, Boris Johnson–supporting, working-class communities in Northern England. One of them is the Northwest mill town of Accrington, where Andy grew up and the place that he focused on in his memoir about education and working-class life.[296] The people in Accrington and communities like it now, Mattinson reports, believe that Britain's Labour Party has abandoned them and become the party of the middle-class South instead.[297] In a heartbreaking BBC News item about Christmas food banks in nearby Burnley, the BBC recorded the anguished and outraged words of a woman dying of cancer who felt "angry because people aren't listening."[298]

Yet ironically, as University of Berkeley sociologist Arlie Hochschild found when she went to live among Donald Trump supporters in Louisiana, it's not the spectacularly rich that incur the greatest resentment among the "have-nots." It's those who seem to have a little bit more and appear to be getting it by unfair means such as positive discrimination, union protection, or unearned welfare benefits that become the target of anger and frustration.[299] Why is this?

There is no denying that in the United States a significant part of the answer has to do with race and systemic racism. When physician and author Jonathan Metzl traveled across America's heartland states to interview right-wing, white, working-class voters, he found a "chop off your nose to spite your face" mentality. Interviewees for his book, *Dying of Whiteness,* would readily vote for policies that would harm them—and in health terms, even kill them—as long as there was someone standing up for them in the White House, or the state house, who wouldn't let undocumented immigrants or Black "welfare queens" pick up benefits in education, health, or welfare at their expense.[300]

It is not simply the case, Metzl argues, that the white working class possesses a deep-seated racist bias that is somehow mysteriously ascribed to their DNA. Rather, policies promoted by those enjoying extreme economic privilege exploit *all* of the working class. They lower taxes for the wealthy and cut back healthcare and funding for public schools, undermining public trust and confidence in the legitimacy of democratic procedures. They mollify the white working class by appealing to, and amplifying, their long-standing fall-back position, in social status terms, that whatever else happens to them, at least, as sociologist and civil rights activist W.E.B. Du Bois once put it, they are "not black."[301]

An old African proverb reminds us that "as the waterhole shrinks, the animals look at each other differently." When wealth becomes concentrated in fewer hands, there are diminished rewards and opportunities for everyone else. As inequalities deepen, opportunities for upward social mobility decline. Competition for the few slots that remain becomes more intense as the middle classes try to protect their privilege against upwardly mobile aspirants. Pressures related to school examinations intensify. Private tutoring services become booming businesses. "Curling parents," as the Danes and the Dutch call them, sweep every obstacle out of their children's paths. Parents pass on their anxieties to their kids because of objectively worsening economic realities.

Amid all this sifting and sorting, students in the poorest zip codes come off the worst of all. David Lammy, the UK's shadow secretary of state for justice, despairs that "a child in one of England's most deprived areas is ten times more likely to go to a secondary school that 'requires improvement' or is 'inadequate' than a child in one of the least deprived areas." He concludes, "Poorer children receive a poorer education," which is manifestly unjust.[302] Part of the reason, he continues, is school competition and choice, in which higher-performing schools "off-roll" or push out lower-performing students, many of whom have special needs, just before examination results factor in.[303]

The situation is the same in the United States. Children in poverty go to school in districts that, compared to wealthier districts, have less funding. These schools have higher concentrations of students from racial minorities. Their teachers are, as an aggregate, less qualified and less well paid.[304] In schools with fewer financial resources, students have lower likelihood of access to digital technology as well.[305]

With the possible exception of Cuba, all societies—even Scandinavian nations—are characterized by some measure of inequality. What leads to social problems of ill-being is not the coexistence of people who are richer and poorer, but of ones who are filthy rich and dirt poor. These are societies where CEOs' salaries and bonuses are hundreds of times greater than those of their lowest-paid employees. "If governments understood the consequences of widening income differences, they would be keener to prevent them," Wilkinson and Pickett argue.[306]

Greater Equality

Societies that have less economic inequality already exist in nations with strong records of well-being among children and adults. They hold out lessons for the rest of us. Differentials of income and wealth are smaller. Governments' support for vulnerable citizens that become sick, unemployed, or just old is stronger. Norway's Government Pension Fund Global (GPFG), for example, protects all its citizens for at least two generations "by investing the proceeds from Norway's supplies of North Sea oil."[307] In societies characterized by high levels of well-being, organizations, including businesses, are operated more cooperatively—with government, executives, and workers engaged together in building their companies and sharing in the rewards. Quality of life is valued, and health services are available for everyone.

Finally, these nations' public education systems are strong. Teachers in all schools are well-trained and highly qualified. Most parents send their children to their local public school because they have confidence that their local school is also the best school for them. School systems are built on cooperation and trust in democracy and professionalism rather than on externally imposed accountability and marketplace models of competition. With the singular exception of the Netherlands, where school choice is associated with historic religious freedoms, private education sectors are small, as are quasi-private provisions in the form of charter schools and academies.[308]

Does a strong public education system actually improve well-being, and does the absence of one truly cause ill-being? Sweden offers an important lesson here. Unique among Scandinavian countries, Sweden in the past 20 years moved toward embracing US-style charter schools in the form of what were called "free schools" that were often owned and managed by hedge fund companies. In the aftermath of these reforms, Sweden's achievement scores on the OECD's international PISA tests plummeted faster than those of any other country.[309] In addition, its UNICEF ranking on child well-being fell. The country declined from being in the top 5 to being in 10th place overall by 2020. Within this overall metric, Sweden actually ranks a lowly 22nd place in young people's mental health. It is now by far the lowest placed of all of the Scandinavian countries.[310]

If we want more well-being for many families and students in schools and societies—not just for a few in this school or that class, here or there—we will need to create societies that are more equal. We will need to reduce income and wealth gaps and not just educational achievement gaps. Following on from the pandemic, US President Biden has spearheaded a move to set minimum corporate taxes globally so that those with extreme wealth will pay fair taxes where they trade. His administration has also committed substantial resources to reduce economic inequality, address inequalities in school funding, and halve the rates of child poverty. It is time for all leaders to heed Nelson Mandela's sage observation that "there can be no keener revelation of a society's soul than the way in which it treats its children."[311] This assertion should be evident in policies that provide sufficient support for early childcare, properly paid parental leave, and strong public school systems that work for all children everywhere. While we certainly need more optimistic and positive interactions in all our institutions, we also need to build decent, inclusive, and more equitable societies and school systems too.

Austerity

Inequality is closely intertwined with economic austerity. As the COVID-19 pandemic deepened, education secretaries and ministers around the world became increasingly concerned that, as the debt incurred by people being put out of work ratcheted upward, their finance secretaries and ministers might plunge public education and all government expenditures into years of austerity. This development would hurt the poor—and the children of the poor—the most, they feared. Austerity was the main strategy for achieving financial recovery after the global economic collapse of 2008. Why should it be any different this time?

Austerity, though, is neither inevitable nor desirable. Writing in 2014, after the global economic crisis, President Bill Clinton's former secretary of labor, Robert Reich, insisted that austerity economics was "dangerous nonsense," a "false snake oil" for "saving the economy by killing it." Austerity, he demonstrated, had only exacerbated poverty and suffering and increased inequality, because "95% of the economic gains since the recovery began in 2009 have gone to the top 1%."[312] The Trump administration's weak response to the coronavirus, which made it the global leader in COVID-19 mortalities in spite of comprising only 4 percent of the global population, was itself a consequence of years of austerity in public health funding.[313]

Leading economists agree with Reich. Mariana Mazzucato points out that it is government, not the private sector, that will mainly generate new value by creating jobs, expanding public health and other public services, and ending the digital divide.[314] Indeed, strong, well-funded governments made the most decisive, collaborative, transparent, and coherent responses to the pandemic crisis. This is the approach that post-pandemic education strategies will require too.

Kate Raworth points a finger at tech companies who depended on government funding to start up their innovations. It's time for them to give back what is the government's due, she argues.[315] Doing so will enable political leaders to switch their focus from higher and higher GDP in order to generate more taxable income of the 99 percent in ways that also shield the wealth of the super-rich to taxing extreme wealth to improve everyone's quality of life, she says. Raworth is part of a gathering chorus of critics of conventional economists who say there is more to human existence than increasing GDP.

Robert Reich points to the rise of the big-tech billionaires as the emergence of a new oligarchy—a small group of the super-rich that control everything that matters. In *The System: Who Rigged It, How We Fix It,* he explains that the widening gap between the 1 percent—or even the 0.1 percent—and everyone else is not primarily the result of impersonal forces such as technology and globalization. It is the consequence of deliberate concentrations of wealth and power.[316]

In Reich's view, the oligarchs are not committed to public good. They reward short-term shareholdings in their companies rather than provide long-term benefit for the economy. They increase executive pay to astronomical levels that are not justified by performance. They often pay zero federal taxes because of exemptions, loopholes, or strategic relocations of company headquarters out of state or offshore. And, after economic collapses that their actions cause, they press for austerity in education, health, and other areas. These practices negatively affect the weaker or just plain ordinary members of society, in order to release resources for the super-rich. Neither Democrats nor Republicans, Reich concludes, have been "committed to challenging the increasing concentration of wealth and power in America."[317]

In *Plutocrats: The Rise of the New Global Super-Rich and the Fall of Everyone Else,* Canada's finance minister and deputy prime minister, Chrystia Freeland, claims that the world is now a *plutocracy* of rule by the wealthy.[318] In addition to all the strategies listed by Reich, Freeland shows how super-elite families buy their children places in top universities by making sizeable "legacy" donations to those institutions. They build not-for-profit foundations where they can shelter their wealth and champion their own causes with tax-subsidized dollars. They also hijack the global agenda of social change while schmoozing at invitation-only events in Davos and Aspen.

In *Winners Take All: The Elite Charade of Changing the World,* journalist Anand Giridharadas describes how certain themes are included or excluded from these conferences and from popular TED Talks. Directed at a business, technology, and policy audience, TED Talks may showcase brain science, positive psychology, or innovative technology. They sometimes raise issues of diversity. But one thing they won't go near is economic inequality.

Why not? Giriharadas quotes a TED Talks organizer who says, "Poverty is essentially a question that you can address via charity. Inequality," however, "is about how you make your money that you're giving back in the first place." "To fight inequality means to change the system." That means having "to look into one's own [wealth] privilege."[319]

Prosperity for All

The alternative to austerity is prosperity. We usually understand *prosperity* to mean great fortune, especially in financial terms. But the Latin origin of *prosperus* is, simply, "doing well." Prosperity is, at root, about "a successful, flourishing, or thriving condition."[320] The preoccupation with economic growth is about increasing the *wealth of nations*. The prosperity alternative, or what we think of as a "Prosperity Doctrine," is about improving the *health of nations*.

Some of the world's most inspiring women leaders, such as Jacinda Ardern of New Zealand and Katrin Jacobsdottir of Iceland, are following the lead of female economists including Raworth and Mazzucato in giving primacy to quality of life alongside, and even ahead of, economic growth. First Minister (equivalent to prime minister) Nicola Sturgeon of Scotland spoke for all of them when she said, "The goal and objective of all economic policy should be collective well-being" or, as she further explained, "to create a world that considers the quality of a person's life to be as precious an asset as financial success."[321]

After all the sacrifices that everyday citizens and essential workers made during the pandemic all over the world, this is a time to build everyone back better through pursuing a bold new Prosperity Doctrine. Doing so will establish greater security in everyone's quality of life, invest in more jobs, and provide more sources of support in public education everywhere. We can accomplish this if we do the following:

- *Invest in the public sector, including public education, to help rebuild the economy.* The public sector is not a drain on GDP but an active contributor to it, not least through the jobs and income it provides, which have a multiplier effect in generating spending that boosts sales.

- *Provide help for vulnerable students* who have been returning to school with mental health issues due to social isolation and being confined for long periods with their families when there have been increases in child custody battles, escalating rates of domestic violence, and problems of poverty and basic food security.

- *Increase equality and opportunity.* This outcome can be achieved, in part, by expanding state employment, which is often the first step up for young people from disadvantaged families. Upwardly mobile youth typically don't have access to the insider networks of privileged families in the private sector. Strong public sectors increase rates of upward social mobility by offering middle-class jobs based on merit.[322]

- *Create high-level vocational training programs.* This undertaking will raise the status of working-class jobs and decrease resentment. One consequence of the pandemic is that some manufacturing facilities will return from overseas. The availability of essential goods can no longer depend on vulnerable global supply chains. These new, working-class manufacturing jobs require sophisticated training.[323]

- *Teach young people about the existence and the ethics of wealth tax, tax avoidance, and tax evasion.* This effort should occur in addition to teaching them financial literacy and income tax management. Young people need to leave school with socially responsible opinions about other people's wealth management as well as their own. It's time to face up to *wealth privilege* in addition to *white privilege.*

Conclusion

Our suggestions are not pipedreams. During the pandemic, Heather Boushey, economic advisor to US President Biden, advocated for government policies such as unemployment support because, among other things, these generate consumer demand to keep the economy going.[324] In *Unbound: How Inequality Constricts Our Economy and What We Can Do About It,* she points out that when the wealthy protect their own advantage and block further upward mobility, their action is not only unjust; it is also inefficient. "Economic inequality," she says, "hinders productivity and growth by blocking the flow of people, ideas and new capital."[325] In other words, inequality and austerity undermine prosperity in people's quality of life as well as in terms of material improvement.

Quality of life and economic improvement can and should go together. If prosperity for all is our goal, then growth must not be a perpetual obsession. Austerity that decimates the public good; strips libraries, schools, and other vital public services of resources; and rewards the already affluent cannot be the answer.

The Prosperity Doctrine is about building everyone back better. It is about creating the economic, social, and educational conditions for equity and inclusion that will improve all young people's opportunities and quality of life. It must be about making well-being a priority, as a foundation for a healthy society in which all young people can flourish.

6

Ethical Technology Use:
The Moral Side of Screen Life

Before the pandemic, one of the issues that most divided opinion among teachers and parents was the use of technology in schools. Enthusiasts embraced and advanced the idea of digital learning taking place anytime, anywhere. Digital technology, they believed, would engage students, ignite innovation, and put an end to the "factory schools" that belonged to a bygone era. Opponents, meanwhile, regarded digital devices as instruments that trivialized learning, undermined the professionalism of teachers, distracted students, and threatened their well-being. Although some systems provided laptops and other devices for every child, others imposed total bans on smartphones on school premises.

Digital Potential

On the positive side of the issue of technology use in schools, our research in Canada and five US states revealed many benefits, even before the pandemic. In Ontario, students used online resources to advance innovative and engaging projects. Teachers tracked and recorded students' learning with smartphones and digital tablets, to provide formative feedback in real time. High school students developed an app to alert teachers when one of their peers was experiencing a mental health issue. Students with special needs used devices and programs to convert text to sound, and vice versa, to overcome barriers to literacy and improve their writing achievement.

Hundreds of teachers in one district registered for a highly valued online course in mindfulness. Other teachers in our US project planned curriculum together across isolated rural locations. All these uses of technology had undeniable value.

Teachers are rarely the digital dinosaurs that some critics allege. Data from the OECD reveal that in 2018, 15 countries reported that 60 percent or more of teachers already used digital technology in their teaching, extending above 80 percent in Denmark and New Zealand.[326] Many countries had significantly increased their technology use over the five years preceding this report.

During the pandemic, digital technology was a lifesaver for many young people and their parents. In many cases, it defined the difference between learning remotely and not learning at all. Learning at home with digital support benefited some students with ADHD who could get out of their seats, lay prostrate on the dining room table when they needed to, clutch a cuddly toy for comfort sometimes, and generally move around more, in ways that were just not permissible in school.[327] Shy students, who were afraid of speaking up in regular classes, sometimes found new confidence when they could express their opinions at their own pace on a device. Many students, including Andy's own 6- and 8-year-old grandchildren, took great delight in photographing their work and sending it to their teacher, uploading and downloading material, making videos for in-class presentations, listening to text as well as reading it, self-assessing their progress, feeling proud about directing their own learning, pressing buttons and tabs to organize material, coaching their own teachers on digital skills when they got stuck, and handing in their ticket-out-the-door at the end of the day's classes.

All across the world, teachers who had never taught an online class suddenly found themselves in charge of some form of virtual learning. Over time, teachers reported significant improvements in their digital competences. Australian journalist Sophie Black noted that after a while, "the tech worked more smoothly, teachers became more comfortable in front of the camera, and principals incorporated parent feedback."[328] An OECD survey of senior educational administrators reported that efforts to maintain some kind of educational continuity for students were "designed in a collaborative manner including teachers" in 75 percent of cases.[329]

With help, teachers and professors started to master even some of the more daunting challenges of online remote teaching, including building relationships. Dennis and some of his Boston College colleagues, for example, have reported getting the best student evaluations ever. This was because, during their flexible workdays at home, these professors could check in with individual students more effectively than during "normal," on-campus days, stacked with classes, meetings, and research project commitments.

Online resource guides also started to reach teachers. These sometimes took on the most difficult problems, such as the emotional aspects of online interaction. For example, two of Andy's University of Ottawa colleagues, Michelle Hagerman and Hugh Kellam, produced a module about how to develop relationships with students in a virtual space.[330] It included ideas from an online teacher based in a Detroit public school with whom Hagerman had worked on a 2017 research study. This teacher had posted personal pictures of herself and her students on the school's home page. She hosted and moderated discussion forums that enabled students to reflect on the course, their own learning, and the development of their digital skills. The teacher continuously solicited feedback from students, which she used to improve her online teaching. Throughout the school year, she engaged with students in their own language codes, dialects, and colloquial expressions, not only to encourage cultural diversity but also to keep them focused on their learning.[331]

Hagerman and Kellam added further suggestions on how to build emotional connections. These include using GIFs and memes to lighten up the feedback process and scheduling the kind of one-to-one interactions that students highly value. They also provided clear procedures and opportunities for students to contact their teachers when they experienced difficulties.

Digital Dangers

Even with all these improvements and adjustments, though, teachers, students, and parents remained concerned that online teaching was ineffective and undesirable. In the pandemic, everyone was forced to make the best of a bad job. Over the long term, however, millions did not regard online learning as a viable option.

In a survey conducted by the Alberta Teachers Association in June 2020, with about 2,500 teachers and administrators, one teacher reported "feeling unmotivated to teach through a distance when more than 50 percent of my class is not participating and parents are taking out their frustrations on me. It makes me feel like I am not good at my job when I am trying my best and battling my own feelings of depression and anxiety from this situation."[332] Something was happening that had never happened in the history of public education. Every day, parents were watching teachers teach. But teachers often didn't like the way they had to teach now. They didn't feel especially good at it.

Some parents interrupted online classes when they weren't happy with what they were seeing. One Canadian school district leader had to send a letter to all parents asking them not to criticize teachers online when they didn't approve of what was going on or heard teenagers swearing, for example.[333] Of course, there's always backchat, secret messages, and profane comments in regular classes. Online, though, these everyday occurrences in regular school become visible and audible to everyone, including the parents. When everyone is watching, it's a teacher's nightmare.

Australian high school teacher Amra Pajalic complained that remote teaching was "all of the bad parts of the job—the corrections, the administration follow-up, creating digital lessons that weren't executed due to internet issues—with none of the good— the feeling of satisfaction when a lesson was executed well, helping a student with a problem, and the look on my students' faces when they achieve an outcome." By contrast, in the regular classroom, she said, it was possible to "see from their notebooks, as I walk around the classroom, who is struggling."[334]

In an online survey completed for the US publication *Education Week,* 82 percent of educators said that student engagement dropped after remote learning was instituted.[335] A survey of remote learning in Australia found that 68 percent of primary school teachers felt it was having a negative impact on students' well-being.[336]

A heartbreaking commentary on the emotional impact of learning at home during the pandemic, published in the *Washington Post,* presented extracts from 60 stories and pieces of artwork from students.[337] One 5th grader drew a depiction of how he was worried that in a race among his emotions, anger was catching up to sadness, with happiness positioning dead last. A kindergarten student showed herself screaming "No! No! No!" in front of her computer. "Children are losing interest in food," the authors of the article reported. "They are complaining of back pain and burning eyes. They are developing feelings of depression." Matthew Biel, chief of the child and adolescent psychiatry division at Georgetown University School of Medicine, was quoted as saying, "Your 7-year-old wants to be recognized when they raise their hand. Oftentimes [that] doesn't happen on Zoom. They want to be able to make a comment, make a joke with a peer—can't do that, no chatting allowed. Wants to be able to get up and walk around the classroom and move—can't do that, we need to see your face on screen."[338]

Reflecting on his observations at the end of 2020, New York City journalist Ross Barkan concluded that remote learning "is still a lackluster substitute for the socialization that comes with education in a physical classroom." He continued, "Students make friends, learn from each other, and form crucial bonds with their teachers. Young children are in particular need of in-person learning. Adequate mental and emotional development can't happen in isolation."[339]

Ironically, although remote learning through digital technology was one of the greatest sources of educational frustration during COVID-19, it became the center of a global campaign for a new, high-tech normal after the pandemic. Critics were not impressed. Taking on all the overblown enthusiasm among policymakers and philanthropists about "reimagining" the basic idea of school through technology, Daniel Willingham and Benjamin Riley, two distinguished policy experts and advisors, argued in the *Washington Post* that "we need fewer dreams of transformative systems and technological revolutions."[340] Instead, they said, we need *"greater emphasis on the humans involved in education"* (their emphasis). Writing in *The Atlantic,* early childhood specialist Erika Christakis complained that the pandemic has not been the first moment where "we seem ever more invested in technological quick fixes—'self-monitored' math lessons on iPads and the like—that take young children away from the adults charged with teaching them" and from the emotional and face-to-face connections that are essential in early brain development.[341]

The Issue of Screen Time

The back-and-forth character of discussions about technology benefits and risks is particularly intense in debates about the time that children and teenagers spend in front of screens. During the pandemic, millions of young children experienced close to 200 minutes per day of government-mandated, real-time instruction—far in excess of recommended pediatric guidelines for screen time. In Canada, for example, during COVID-19 restrictions, children from 5 to 11 years old were spending about five hours a day on screens—exceeding the maximum of two hours a day recommended by the Canadian Pediatric Society (which is double the amount recommended by their US counterparts).[342] Mark Tremblay, director of healthy active living and obesity research at the Children's Hospital of Eastern Ontario, expressed alarm over the immense amounts of time during the pandemic that children were spending on screen-based activities. He warned that "all of these temptations are associated with an increased risk of all the things we're afraid of: physical-health problems, mental-health problems, emotional-health problems."[343]

Excessive screen use can indeed be damaging. In the documentary *The Social Dilemma*, Tristan Harris, a former Google employee responsible for digital ethics, describes how prompts for addictive behaviors, such as ones used in the online gambling industry, are built into the design features of online programs. He refers to his former employers as nothing less than "digital Frankensteins." Study after study shows how these digitally induced behavior patterns are linked to increases in depression among almost 40 percent of users, whereas rates of depression and anxiety drop when use of social media is limited to no more than 10 minutes per day.[344]

In line with this burgeoning literature denouncing the quantity of time that today's youth spend with screens, some of the mental health consultants in our study in Ontario had concerns that their colleagues who were implementing technological innovation in their classrooms were not paying attention to the downsides of their efforts. One consultant worried that "we're living in a time right now, there has been so much transformation as a result of technology" that has led to "kids just not sitting down and not coping well." A colleague was concerned about the "huge impacts that we're seeing on mental health and well-being." A third noted that "when we're staring at screens so much it's changing the way that our biology is working."

Against this body of opinion and research are dissonant voices that challenge whether it's true that all screens are like drugs, with negative effects on well-being that need to be limited. It's not just about *quantity* of screen time, they argue, but also about the *quality* of what's offered and how it's used. Writing in the "Consumer Tech" section of the *Washington Post,* Geoffrey Fowler and Heather Kelly point out that for many young people, interacting on screens via Skype, Zoom, or other means protected them from isolation. The World Health Organization actually encouraged young people to play video games to encourage them to stay at home. The US Centers for Disease Control and Prevention, they point out, recommended that people "call, video chat, or stay connected using social media."[345] In times of a pandemic, screens can be better for well-being than the alternatives—which often include little or nothing at all. Of course, they say, spending endless hours on devices is not a good thing. Keeping them out of the bedroom at night protects young people's sleep. Other than that, the consequences depend on what screens are used for. A video message to a grandparent is not the same thing as indulging an hours-long addiction to and obsession with reaching escalating levels on a violent video game. This deceptively simple example of screen time highlights how the pros and cons of technology use for learning cannot be decided simply by counting up hours. They also need to address quality of use and the relationships between technology use and other learning activities.

Digital Decisions

What can we conclude from this collection of divergent research and opinion about digitally based learning and its relationship to student well-being before, during, and after the pandemic? What deliberations and decisions should teachers and schools make about the use of technology in relation to learning and well-being? Here are some thoughts on these questions.

Pandemic-Proof Learning

In 2018, the World Health Organization warned that "epidemics of infectious diseases are occurring more often, and spreading faster and further than ever in many different regions of the world." They added, "The background factors of this threat are biological, environmental and lifestyle changes, among others."[346] Like hurricanes, fires, and floods, the probability of pandemics will increase due to climate change, deforestation, greater proximity of exotic species to human populations, and quantity of international travel. In his 1940s novel *The Plague*, Nobel Prize–winning author Albert Camus wrote, "There have been as many plagues as wars in history, yet always plagues and wars take people equally by surprise."[347]

The risk that future pandemics will arise within a generation is not trivial. The WHO has warned us to be prepared in health terms. We must also be prepared in educational terms. We must ask: *How can our educational systems be designed so that they operate in a pandemic as effectively, or almost as effectively, as in other circumstances?*

Part of the answer must be through the increased availability of technology. Some countries were able to respond swiftly and nimbly to the pandemic because of their prior stance on technology. PISA's highest performer outside Asia—Estonia—designated internet access to be a human right in 2001. Estonia has its curriculum available online, as a matter of public provision.[348] Uruguay instituted one laptop per child in 2007 and has a national innovation agency that provides curriculum and innovation materials online. It saw a massive uptick in use of its platform within days of moving to learning at home.[349] South Korea had near-universal access to Wi-Fi and devices before the pandemic hit, and one teacher per school was designated to participate in a national network to develop online teaching and learning.[350] Singapore also has a national platform, called the *Student Learning Space* (SLS).[351]

The point is not just that a national digital learning platform exists but that it is publicly accessible, has the capacity to be personalized by every teacher for every student, and is interactive rather than one-directional in nature. Digital learning has many imperfections and should not be a driver of educational change. But it should be an integral part of what our educational systems offer, with the ability to expand or contract as circumstances require.

For all this to happen, access to digital technology for learning must be public, universal, inclusive, and free. As in Estonia, access to the internet, and to devices, should be a human right that is available to everyone on an interactive curriculum platform. This accessibility will reduce the scale of the digital divide that is an increasing source of inequity in children's education. It will enable a large system to be managed and mobilized in an agile and flexible way to benefit all learners.

Ethical and Seamless Technology

The revelations and proposed revolutions organized around digital learning inside and outside schools are both understated and overstated. They promise learning that can be available anytime, anywhere—which implies that digital learning will be everywhere, all the time. Or they propose blended or hybrid arrangements that imply some kind of half-and-half compromise. Both positions are flawed.

The first argument implies that because so much depends on digital technology during the pandemic, learning should be digitally based all the time. At the extreme, its advocates say that technology should replace teachers, and feedback algorithms can and should substitute for human judgment. Some argue that school buildings should come down altogether in favor of loosely defined online networks.

This argument is flat-out wrong. When they get back to school, during and after the pandemic, children do not need yet more *anytime, anywhere* learning. They mainly need more face-to-face support in the *here and now*. Teenagers, for example, need to go to school to be with their friends, develop their senses of who they are, become responsible and well-informed citizens, learn about how to deal with racism and prejudice (especially if they live with parents who are racist and prejudiced!), and so on. They need less time on screens, not more.

Physical schools populated by real, three-dimensional educators rather than avatars and holograms are and will always be essential for most students—and not only so their parents can go to work. *Enough, but not too much,* of digital technology and a lot more face-to-face support for the large numbers of vulnerable students after the pandemic—that's what our reimagined new normal for schools needs to encompass.

Regardless of its many strengths, digital technology will never replace great, inspirational teaching. Nor will it make weaker teachers more inspiring, caring, or empathetic. On its own, it will not produce teachers who are more able to understand and develop global learning competencies such as collaboration or citizenship, more equipped to deal with prejudice and bullying, or more ready to help their children learn and play outdoors. Only effective selection, training, development, proper remuneration of, and effective collaboration among high-quality teachers will do that.

The second argument, proposing hybrid or blended technology, is also flawed. It suggests there are only two kinds of learning and teaching—ones that are digitally based, and everything else. It puts digitally based learning on a level and equal playing field with all other kinds of learning combined. This is a silly proposition. It would be just as preposterous to propose hybrid or blended formats for all outdoor or arts-based or book-based learning.

The term *hybrid* has an unfortunate etymology. Deriving from the Latin *hybrida,* it refers to "the offspring of two dissimilar animals, specifically a tame sow and a wild boar."[352] In educational innovation, hybrid learning crossbreeds the male-dominated digital technology (wild boar?) industry with in-person learning that is led by a predominantly female (tame sow?) teaching force. We need to get past this characterization, and not just for metaphorical reasons.

In a post-pandemic world, digital learning can and should become as routine, effortless, and seamless as all other learning resources—no more *and* no less. Digital resources must be available to everyone who has the skills to use them, alongside and with equivalent status as other tools. These include books, pens, whiteboards, graph paper, paint, sports resources, outdoor environments, manipulative materials, science equipment, glue, and scissors—not forgetting the sheer power and presence of human interaction on which everyone's well-being ultimately depends.

We should not become overly exuberant about hybrid learning, learning without walls, digital learning becoming ubiquitous, and so on. It's time for learning related to digital technology in our schools to become ethically seamless and seamlessly ethical; to be used in a prudent way so that it will make a difference, not in a profligate manner that displaces higher-value activities.

Risk Assessment and Management

Digital technology in education should not be used without careful calculation of gains and losses, or opportunities and threats. We need to determine the *unique value proposition,* or UVP, of any use of digital technology compared to other learning alternatives, to be confident that it will improve learning and well-being.

At the same time, teachers, schools, school districts, big tech companies, and the government also need to avoid harm resulting from things such as excessive screen time, online addiction, reinforcement and amplification of in-group prejudices and conspiracy theories, and digital perfectionism among adolescent girls who become anxious about their online appearance and the "likes" that they do and don't attract.

One engaging example of how to address risks and ways to deal with them is the 2018 Disney children's animated movie *Ralph Breaks the Internet.*[353] Its plot involves two protagonists in a video arcade driving game. When the game no longer works because of a broken steering wheel and the characters face extinction, they migrate to the new world of the internet in search of solutions to their plight. As the protagonists whiz around the internet, the movie introduces children to examples of digital risks. These include the seductive power of collecting digital hearts and likes over the development of real-world relationships, the distracting appeal of pop-up ads that can divert the characters from their goals, and the addictive excitement of staying in the gaming world rather than going back to real life, which feels too slow by comparison.

Apple, Google, and other social media providers and platforms do, of course, now have apps to enable users to monitor their screen time, though these don't always distinguish between different kinds of screen use. They also put the onus on the users to manage their habits, rather than taking responsibility for making their own designs less deliberately addictive. Part of the mounting global pressure for big tech to be more socially responsible should include regulating products to ensure they avoid doing harm to children's well-being.

Writing in the social media section of the *Guardian,* Belinda Parmar complains about the impact on her children of "junk tech" packed with "digital 'snacks' that require no cognitive effort," comprising "mindless drivel about what people had for breakfast, [and] the insatiable checking for likes, comments, and forms of approval that make us hungry for further validation."[354] She proposes that every school should have a tech officer who focuses not just on kids' uses and misuses of tech but also on the addictive algorithms and designs that are built into the tech itself.

We can go one step further. There should be a digital watchdog committee or working group in every school, school system, and tech company, made up of enthusiasts and skeptics (from a standpoint of digital knowledge and expertise), who can address the threats and the opportunities of digital tech in equal measure. We all need to embrace the significant opportunities that exist in technology-based learning, but none of us should be afraid to dip into its digital dark side too.

Conclusion

The future of digital technology will have a huge societal influence on student well-being. How far schools and school systems are willing to take an evidence-informed and *ethically seamless* approach to its use will determine whether that influence turns out to be positive or negative. An ethical and seamless approach to digital technology use urges all of us to address equity and inclusion of access. It enhances quality of use in terms of benefits for learning and well-being rather than just expanding delivery through hybrids and blends. Last, it supports strategies for combating risks related to addiction and screen use. Technology should not be presented as a *shining knight* that comes to rescue students and teachers from the (so-called) "dark ages" of schooling. Rather, technology should be a *shining light* that brightens up teaching and learning practices that are already pedagogically strong.

7

Restorative Nature:
For People and the Planet

After learning at home during the first wave of the pandemic, students across the world returned to school under conditions involving health protocols. Physical distancing requirements raised questions about their impact on children's emotional development, mental health, teacher-student relations, and the nature of the school as a community. One response that many countries took was to increase students' time outdoors, where risks of transmission are significantly reduced. Being outdoors in nature with others has benefits for well-being, not only during a pandemic but also as a general rule.

Outside-In

Learning outdoors is a long tradition in Nordic countries, and it can and should be expanded in all places, not just during a pandemic. In Norway, they say, there is no such thing as bad weather—there is only bad clothing! In a country that routinely ranks among the highest in the world on many indicators, children are not sheltered from long, dark, and freezing cold winters. They are taught to thrive in all weather conditions. Resilience is not just a psychological aptitude. It is also a physiological trait that can be nurtured by a culture that prioritizes optimum health and wants its young people to embrace the natural world.

The solution to the problem of creating a pandemic-proof educational system, then, is paradoxical. We need to develop more virtual learning *and* more learning outdoors. Denmark makes more use of digital technology for young people's projects than any other country, yet it was also a leader in learning outdoors during the pandemic.[355] High-quality learning can be more digital *and* more natural. Although many educators oppose pitting virtual versus physical learning against each other, in a pandemic, and as a whole, learning needs to get more digital *and* more physical.

For several years we were visiting professors at the University of Stavanger in Norway. We went there every year to work with the university and local schools. When we went to one elementary school in June, we were greeted by a group of grade 2 children. They stood on the stone steps of their outdoor theater, singing their school song with joyful voices, including lyrics about belonging and togetherness. This activity unified three integral elements of well-being: singing, being outside, and emphasizing belonging.

On another occasion, we visited a district at the end of a long fjord. We toured one of the schools, had lunch with the mayor and her staff, and then met the superintendent and her colleagues in the district office. At the end of the meeting, the superintendent said, "You must see more of the community." We could not understand their schools without experiencing the community, she felt. She and some of her team took us to the opposite side of the fjord, where we went behind some bushes to change into swimsuits and all plunged into the icy water together. In Norway, this kind of thing builds relationships and connects people to their communities. In US schools, and in the education systems of many other countries, it would likely get you fired!

Using the outdoors sounds like an easy and attractive option on sunny summer days. But the outdoor environment is a resource for Nordic educators all year round. Andy conducted research in another Norwegian elementary school that regularly holds assemblies or gatherings of the whole school outside, even when it is freezing cold. Children and their teachers pick blueberries in the fall and take walks in the woods in winter. When a soccer ball was kicked into a nearby stream, the children left the playground and scrambled across the rocks and stream banks to retrieve it. The school teaches children "to love how to move, to get around and be with your friends, to learn to talk," the principal pointed out. When they are engaged in play, nature, and conversation, she believed, children and adults alike learn about and come to appreciate different sides to their personalities than just those that are revealed in a walled-in classroom.

Perhaps this kind of Norwegian school is just an idyllic exception to the general rule—one that is peculiar to a country that is one of the world's most affluent and that has a distinctively collectivist way of life. Certainly, US educators who are worried about lawsuits might feel apprehensive about allowing the kind of rough-and-tumble outdoor activities that Norwegian educators encourage. But there is no real *educational* reason why learning outside cannot be integrated into school life, even in countries that have far fewer resources than Norway.

In one of the Escuela Nueva schools in Colombia that was part of our research, children recorded observations of migrating birds. They grew and sold vegetables for family and school meals that they also sold in the community. They created a map of the school and its surroundings to help visitors find their way around. Learning came alive through nature.[356]

We have seen similar kinds of engagement with nature in our work with more than 30 remote rural schools in the US Pacific Northwest. Rural communities in the United States and many other countries are often places of poverty, lack of opportunity, and geographic isolation. Yet they also possess spectacular natural beauty. In trying to engage students with their learning and their communities, many of the schools and their teachers drew upon these rich resources of natural capital.

In some cases, students compiled time-lapse videos of their local environment to strengthen senses of local pride and build awareness of communities elsewhere. Teachers in a school in Oregon used environmental protests about exploitation of resources in a national wildlife refuge to get students engaged with arguments between environmentalists and business groups.[357] Other teachers got students involved in researching the use of drones in local agriculture. In Healy, Alaska, in the midst of awe-inspiring wilderness on the edge of Denali National Park, teachers work to address the differences between and commonalities among local coal miners and national park rangers.

The town of Wishram, in Washington State, lost employment when its rail yards closed down; it was cut off from the world when a new highway passed it by. The town stands above the banks of the Columbia River, on the traditional lands of the Wishram Native American tribe, whose cultural heritage includes salmon fishing. So studying and dissecting salmon under the supervision of a local park ranger was a way to connect Indigenous natural heritage to future tourism opportunities and the jobs they provide.

The school in the small town of Cusick, also in Washington State, counts members of the Kalispel Indian Reservation among its students. Alongside employment in the local casino, hunting and fishing continue to sustain many Kalispel families. A teacher in the town's high school described how one of her students had "shot his first deer last week. He is trying to figure how the traditional customs and practices of the Kalispel merge with the 21st century." She pointed out how he showed her pictures on his smartphone of gutting and skinning the deer, as well as "preparing the hide to be tanned and the meat to be preserved." This is a prime example of how learning can be more physical *and* more digital, simultaneously.

One of our 10 Ontario districts in the far north of the province, where 50 percent of the students were from Indigenous communities, started an outdoor education program involving canoeing, dog sledding, fishing, and building fires and shelters in wilderness settings, tapping into the children's traditions, culture, skills, and strengths.

A coach in the district's nationally renowned hockey program got Indigenous students to improve their learning and attendance records by having them connect their outdoor hockey strengths to other areas of learning. He did this by setting up a professional learning community with regular subject teachers to link hockey-based knowledge and skills to cross-curricular learning objectives. For instance, in grade 8 mathematics classes that were also environments of caring and support, students linked their experiences using sticks and pucks to make mathematical calculations of things that mattered to them.[358]

For this coach and his colleagues, traditional outdoors learning skills and strengths were not an alternative to or an escape from other kinds of instruction in literacy or mathematics, for example. They were powerful cultural resources that could motivate Indigenous students to experience many kinds of success. The coach noted how "there are kids in there and you can't get them to do stuff like writing and reading. Then you take them outside and they are the first ones to know how to build a fire and shelter."

There are four things of value that we can take from these many examples of learning outdoors, before and beyond a pandemic, as well as within it. These are (1) connecting with Indigenous heritages, (2) developing environmental responsibility, (3) combating "nature-deficit disorder," and (4) promoting healthy physical movement.

Indigenous Heritages

Ancient Indigenous traditions all over the world teach us that our place in the world as humans is not to dominate nature, or to set ourselves aside from or above it. Rather, it is to understand that we are part of nature and that by understanding nature, we can also develop a deeper understanding of ourselves. The education that is essential for Indigenous students and that reconnects them with nature is, in this respect, good for all students.

In spite of centuries of devastation from colonization and cultural invasion, the world still has 350 million Indigenous people who are dispersed across many countries. Educators must have the capacity and commitment to work collaboratively and respectfully with Indigenous peoples to undertake the arduous work of recovering lost traditions and languages. This undertaking must go beyond what Natalie St. Denis, an Indigenous educator of Mohawk, Maliseet, and Mi'kmaq background in Quebec, describes as "simply exploring." Instead, it must enable students to grow toward "adopting Indigenous ways of knowing, being, and doing."[359]

Here, the understanding of well-being is anything but purely psychological. As expressed in the First People's Principles of Learning developed by the First Nations Education Steering Committee in British Columbia, "Learning ultimately supports the well-being of the self, the family, the community, the land, the spirits, and the ances-tors."[360] Nature and culture are interconnected. Humans are part of nature, and nature is part of humanity. Nature is a spiritual entity, bound up with a sense of meaning and value in the whole of life.

Environmental Responsibility

Primatologist Jane Goodall has reiterated the concerns of the WHO that modern environmental changes are creating dangerous disruptions in our relationship with nature by bringing people and exotic species together in unhealthy ways. Our exploitative approach to nature can be reversed, she says, by getting children out into nature as early as possible, to appreciate its wonders and develop stewardship of its future. "It is only when you care for nature that you protect it," she stresses.[361]

A systematic review of 119 peer-reviewed articles conducted by a team at Stanford University found that environmental education not only helped students' critical thinking skills but also had a num-ber of "social-skill related benefits." These included "self-esteem, autonomy, character development, maturity, empowerment, verbal communication, leadership, poise, and the ability to communicate with others."[362]

This kind of evidence has led some countries, including Scot-land, to make daily outdoor play a significant part of the early child-hood curriculum, with plans to extend it upward into the elementary years.[363] Likewise, a global movement of *forest schools* that started in Denmark involves learning while getting dirty and wet, falling over, and climbing trees. Forest schools mushroomed in popularity during the pandemic, when learning outdoors was embraced as a healthy option to virtual schooling.[364] In April 2021, Nova Scotia took key lessons from the pandemic seriously and allocated budget funds so that every school in the province could design outdoor spaces (not just more playground equipment) for teaching and learning.[365] Many countries now link these kinds of initiatives with Education for Sus-tainable Development (ESD) so that students learn to take environ-mental responsibility for protecting the planet and reversing the climate change that threatens all our futures.[366]

"Nature-Deficit Disorder"

In *Last Child in the Woods,* American author Richard Louv warns that loss of contact with natural environments—due to urban living, too many school hours devoted to testing, and excess screen time that keeps many young children indoors for long periods of time— has led to what he calls "nature-deficit disorder."[367] This condition leaves the young bereft of any sense of belonging to an actual physical space and has a negative impact on learning and well-being, he claims. Straying from the inherent Indigenous connection between human beings and the rest of nature, it seems, has not only been bad for children in Indigenous communities; it has been bad for all of us.

The popular Netflix documentary *The Beginning of Life 2: Outside* draws together global experts from a range of disciplines who are concerned that children in urban environments are being deprived of the mental health and social benefits that result from being closely connected to the natural world. Children are calmer when they work and play outdoors, the documentary notes.[368] The more natural the outdoor environment, the more positive the impact is. For instance, children diagnosed with ADHD who are taken out for walks benefit more from walking in a park than in a built-up environment. Contributors to the documentary emphasize how being connected to and participating in unstructured outdoor play is not just physically and psychologically beneficial; it also helps us make a spiritual connection with our humanity as part of nature. Children report that once they are involved with nature, they take more responsibility for it and care about it more.

There is risk, of course—a scraped knee, bruised elbow, or sprained ankle, perhaps. But children recover from these injuries and learn, by experience, how to avoid them. Such risks are of less concern than the risk of long-term damage to mental health that comes from being deprived of access to natural environments. Writing in the *New York Times,* Ellen Barry describes how educators in Canada, Australia, and the UK are finally responding to the litigious culture of padded playgrounds, flat surfaces, and helmets for everything by "bringing in risk," "sharp-edged" implements, and "spiky" bushes into playground environments.[369] These elements build resilience by including more risk in environments that are not only outdoors but also less manicured and artificially protected than many outside spaces have become in schools.

Healthy Physical Movement

It's beneficial to *be* in outdoor environments. It's an even bigger boost to well-being to *move* in those environments. This is what our Norwegian colleagues were expressing when they described how their conversations with children changed when they walked in the woods together. Physical movement significantly enhances well-being in and of itself. In *The Joy of Movement,* Stanford University psychology lecturer Kelly McGonigal reviews and reaffirms all the traditional claims in favor of sustained physical activity—the release of endorphins, increased fitness, altering neural pathways, and so on. But there is even more to it than this, she says.[370] Sustained physical activity, especially outdoor activity such as running or hiking, reconnects us, in sociobiological terms, with our primitive nature as hunter-gatherers searching for food. How much more preferable to be trail running over rocky terrain in a forest than pounding out the miles on treadmills in our local gyms!

Some years ago, the British travel writer Bruce Chatwin wrote a book about the nature of Aboriginal "songlines" across Australia that Indigenous peoples walked not just as geographic pathways but also as spiritual journeys that defined and retold narratives of their own histories and spiritual lives.[371] Many of humankind's problems, Chatwin speculated, started when we made too drastic a switch from being nomads to becoming settlers. Walking is not only good for the body; it's uplifting for the spirit and the mind.

One memorable quote that stays with both of us as avid long-distance hikers is that of Danish philosopher Søren Kierkegaard. "I know of no thought so burdensome that one cannot walk away from it," he said.[372] However great or seemingly insoluble an intellectual, professional, or personal problem seems to us before we set out on a long walk, by the end of it, the problem has become much smaller and sometimes has even disappeared altogether.

Physical activity—especially outside—builds fitness, reduces obesity, helps to ward off mental health problems including depression and anxiety, and is often a more desirable alternative for dealing with attention deficit disorders than overprescribed medications or even self-regulated calming routines. Outdoor physical activity uplifts the spirit, increases happiness, and boosts intellectual creativity as well as results on conventional measurements of achievement.

Getting Outside the Box

Despite the overwhelming evidence and insight about the benefits of nature, many of our poorest children continue to live in crowded apartment blocks. They are not only deprived of the benefits of financial and other resources; they are also deprived of access to the natural world. They are transported to school in motorized metal boxes. When they get there, they spend all day in another box, cut off from the outside, inundated with standardized tests and an overcrowded curriculum, with less and less time to play outside. Even then, their only option is to do it on artificial surfaces.

Why are there massive movements by technology corporations and philanthropies to make digital learning available ubiquitously—anytime, anywhere—and barely any such movement to make nature and physical activity accessible in the same way? The evidence about the benefits of nature for learning and well-being is much more consistent and compelling than the evidence in support of digital technologies. Irrespective of the research, the big-tech fix keeps pushing us toward the virtual more than the natural world. It's time to get the virtual and the natural worlds back in balance.

The substitution of social and emotional learning for child well-being in the United States only adds to these problems. Unlike the well-being agendas of other nations, SEL in the United States mostly neglects physical and spiritual well-being. Given that the United States has one of the highest rates of childhood obesity in the world, this is a disturbing act of collective national neglect. It is as if children are viewed in the way that Ken Robinson once parodied university professors—people whose bodies have the sole purpose of being transportation devices for their heads.[373]

If we are to get children out of their concrete and metal boxes, we must think outside the box ourselves. We need to do a lot more than add a few outdoor camping trips or field excursions to the regular curriculum. Children need to be in touch with nature every day, not just as an add-on or a special treat.

We can start by adopting the common practice in Nordic countries to get children outside for some playing time every 50 minutes or so—not just a choreographed body-break in class, but free play in the open air, outdoors. Then we can learn from what many teachers and schools did during the pandemic (and what many teachers in less developed countries have been doing forever) and teach parts of the curriculum outside—as in Hamilton and Butterfield schools in the ASCD's Whole Child network that we described in Chapter 2. This practice is incredibly valuable in and after a pandemic. It's also an important way to approach teaching and learning as a matter of routine.

The capacity to teach one's subject or curriculum in an outdoor environment should become part of all teachers' training and ongoing professional development. Outdoor learning options should also be included in online curriculum guides for potential activities across the curriculum. Natural, physical, and environmental competences should be accorded as high a priority as digital competence. People's lives and the future of the planet may well depend on it.

If this sounds unrealistic, consider how the Shetland school district responded to the pandemic in Scotland. It created 10 *Nature Nudge* videos—one a week—with accompanying activity sheets to "'nudge' pupils outdoors to learn in nature . . . The project connected all ages with their local landscape and wildlife, provided a sense of community and increased the chances of a good engagement with education." As one parent reflected, it "was a great reason to do things together and outside. We learnt so much, as a family."[374]

The capacity to do this in all kinds of environments, not just on remote Scottish islands, will require redesigning and adapting school spaces for regular learning use, including gardens, wild areas, sheltered outdoor areas for learning in good and bad weather, and so on. Schools and school systems spent a fortune on wiring up schools for connection to the internet before the advent of Wi-Fi, then on purchasing devices for every child for digital learning purposes. We should now also be prepared to invest to the same degree to enable all our students to learn and our teachers to teach in a natural environment as a routine and regular part of school life. Like learning through digital technology, learning naturally should assume no greater or lesser importance than any other aspect of learning. But every child should be able to learn and play outdoors, in nature every day.[375]

Last, we can initiate and support educational and social movements that make education more physical and more natural. We can advocate and act in response to global climate change, as demonstrated in the wave of school strikes around the world inspired by Greta Thunberg.[376] We can support and expand more diffuse networks such as the forest schools that promote learning in and through nature; or the thousands of schools using the Escuela Nueva model developed in Colombia by Vicky Colbert that promote peace, democracy, and student voice in ways that are rooted in nature. We can initiate local movements such as the hockey program for Indigenous students in our Northern Ontario school district, or the 40-year-old Roots and Shoots program in Lambeth and Southwark in London, England, that caters to young people with social, emotional, and learning problems by providing them with vocational training in an outdoor environment.[377]

We can even be like the inspirational high school teacher whom Andy interviewed some years back who countered the pervasive negativity of a government intent on demeaning its public school teachers and inflicting unworkable reforms on them by doing something positive every day. He simply surrounded the big box of the school's red brick building with a garden that his students created as part of their curriculum.

Conclusion

Maslow's hierarchy of needs, positive psychology, emotional intelligence, growth mindsets, mindfulness, and the concept of the whole child are some of the most prominent frameworks that schools and their teachers have been drawing upon when they consider how to improve their children's well-being. Approaches such as these have great strengths and make positive contributions, as we have already seen. Improving well-being is indeed partly about initiating positive practices and changing small habits in mindset or capacity to self-regulate, for example.

However, emotions and well-being also happen at a large scale. There is a big picture of well-being, and it doesn't just belong to big decision makers in policy and government. It belongs to all of us. It is our collective responsibility. The social, political, and economic environments can either support people's well-being or undermine it.

This chapter and the previous two have explored how we can harness three uplifting forces in this wider context in a way that will lead to better well-being outcomes in our schools. What big-picture alternatives stand before us in this moment of immense opportunity? We can let ourselves be defeated by the outdated movement of GERM and become overwhelmed by the chaotic influences of VUCA. Or we can seize the opportunity to choose the higher ground between and beyond GERM and VUCA and recommit to, as well as reinvent, public education in ways that will increase well-being and learning for all young people. Instead of well-being problems *erupting* as a result of the pressures from GERM and VUCA, well-being solutions can get *uplift* from these movements, like a rugged young mountain range.

In figuring out how to pay off the great deficits incurred by the costs of the pandemic, we can turn back to the failed GERM-ridden policies of economic austerity. We can slash school budgets, increase educational inequities, and remove funding for the counselors and mental health supports that will be needed even more as a consequence of the pandemic. Or we can activate a Prosperity Doctrine that invests in public education and other public services. This option increases equality and protects the well-being of the vulnerable by providing more support for them. It enhances opportunity and social mobility by creating more middle-class, public-sector jobs, and it increases economic growth by putting living wages in people's pockets.

The VUCA-like force of technology in education should not be a tool of digital zealotry that provides learning anywhere, anytime, for anyone, no matter how variable the quality is. Nor should we over-value technology as a blended or hybrid solution that wrongly implies that digital technology should have half-and-half status with everything else combined. If there is one thing we have learned from the pandemic, it is how much we need in-person schools in the here and now—to care for the vulnerable, provide inclusive opportunity, build community, prepare young people for democracy, and serve as places for children to go to so their parents can go to work.

We should insist on an ethical and seamless approach to digital technologies that makes them neither more nor less a part of school life than all the other tools and media at teachers' and students' disposal. Teachers should be as proficient in the use of these media as they are with respect to all others, because the best and most appropriate uses of digital technology, as with all other media, should come down to teachers' professional judgment. All this should be based on a national platform of resources and access that is public, universal, and free, as a basic human right.

Last, we can allow ourselves to keep on disregarding the importance of nature, play, and physical activity. We can persist with the ill-designed boxes of brick and cement in which many of our children are condemned to learn. We can perpetuate the industrial-era, GERM-ridden practices of standardized testing and one-time competitive examinations that eat up our children's time with indoor preparation and practice activities at the expense of more embodied, exploratory, and creative engagements with the world around them. And we can ignore, overlook, or just whine about the negative impact of screen use and screen time on children's learning and well-being, and on their freedom and willingness to engage in relationships with one another and with the natural world around them.

Alternatively, we can restore young people's connection to nature and to learning outside as a healthy way to live and learn that also develops everyone's sense of responsibility for the planet and its future. Young people's engagement with climate change and its future can be aroused by interdisciplinary projects and scientific curriculum content. But all this intellectual input will make little difference unless children also develop an emotional, physical, and spiritual attachment to nature early on, in their everyday life. Deliberately designing schools, classes, and learning so that nature is as ubiquitously available as technology corporations and philanthropies claim digital learning should be, must be one of our highest well-being priorities in the coming years.

In the third decade of the 21st century, governments, corporations, and philanthropies are rushing headlong into adopting and expanding digital technology as a basis for a post-pandemic educational future. Yet just over a century ago, it was access to nature that animated government leaders. In 1916, US President Woodrow Wilson signed the act that created the National Park Service, bringing together 35 national parks and monuments "to conserve the scenery and the natural and historic objects and the wild life therein and to provide for the enjoyment of the same . . . as will leave them unimpaired for the enjoyment of future generations."[378] Engagement with nature was regarded as a foundation of a healthy society. Alongside the contemporary enthusiasm for digital transformation, therefore, we need to restore and retain this historic appreciation of natural restoration.

Together, the three uplifting forces of *prosperity for all, ethical technology use,* and *restorative nature* explain why the Prosperity Doctrine in education is needed to overcome the twin pressures of GERM and VUCA in our post-pandemic world. We've already seen what the alternatives to these three forces lead to, and the consequences for children and the world are unacceptable and unsustainable. It's time to revisit and rethink what schools are for. Doing so means figuring out once and for all what the best relationship is between achievement and well-being, which is the subject of our next chapter.

8

Well-Being and Success: Opposites That Can Attract

The relationship between well-being and achievement is not straightforward, doesn't happen automatically, and isn't always easily understood. In an ideal world, students at school will achieve a lot and also be well, feel fulfilled, and positively thrive. But students and systems can have academic success without well-being and even at the expense of well-being. Conversely, well-being can also exist without and even at the cost of success.

The research on the relationship between well-being and achievement has been the subject of a 2020 review by Tania Clarke at Cambridge University. Clarke challenges the notion that there is such a thing as an "achievement-well-being trade-off in education" in which "well-being is regarded as opposed to, or in tension with, children's academic achievement."[379] She finds that although the relationship "is not straightforward and calls for nuance," overall, "children's well-being and achievement are positively associated."[380]

Clarke's review responds to widespread concerns that, in the eyes of their advocates, well-being and achievement can easily lose sight of each other. When is well-being a touchy-feely distraction from the basics of rigorous learning? Conversely, is it being used to compensate for the ill-being that is created by some aspects of schooling today, such as standardized testing and outdated methods of teaching? Do achievement and well-being occupy separate silos that have little or no connection with each other?

Get the well-being agenda wrong and opponents will ignore important evidence and insights from social psychology and research on emotional intelligence and mindfulness. They will readily portray it as emotional self-indulgence that distracts from academic basics. Budgets for addressing well-being will be cut, and GERM will come roaring back with a vengeance.

Get the well-being agenda right and it will support and be supported by effective learning, so that all our students can be successful *and* well. This outcome is the gold standard to which we should aspire. Here we agree with the OECD's 2017 report on student achievement and well-being or life satisfaction, which argued that

> most educators and parents would agree that a successful student not only performs well academically but is also happy at school. Indeed, schools are not only places where students acquire academic skills; they are also social environments where children can develop the social and emotional competencies they need to thrive.[381]

Success Without Well-Being

In the OECD's 2017 comparison of nations on measures of tested student achievement and average life satisfaction, the sharpest contrasts were between nations that performed badly on both sets of indicators (see the bottom-left quadrant in Figure 8.1) and countries that performed exceptionally well in both areas—mainly countries in Northern Europe.

Arguably, the most interesting cells on the OECD's scatter diagram are what appear to be inverse relationships between well-being and success. In the bottom-right corner are a range of systems, mainly located in East Asia and Southeast Asia, where high academic performance occurs alongside low levels of average life satisfaction. In these countries, students *test* well but do not *feel* well.

As we noted in Chapter 4, Richard Wilkinson and Kate Pickett point to one explanation for these patterns.[382] Health and well-being, they show, are consistently worse in countries with greater economic inequality. For example, Hong Kong, one of the 10 most economically unequal systems in the world (a situation that has

FIGURE 8.1

OECD Chart Comparing Life Satisfaction with Mean Science Scores

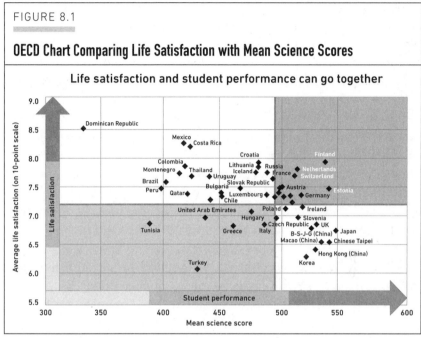

Source: OECD, *PISA 2015 Results: Students' Well-Being* (p. 232).

worsened over the past half-century), also registers a lowly 76th place on the World Happiness Index.[383]

The OECD's report on well-being or average life satisfaction introduces another key factor, though. Scoring second worst on life satisfaction among all countries is South Korea. Along with a range of other East Asian and Southeast Asian countries, as well as the UK, it occupies a worrying quadrant of high academic achievement combined with low average life satisfaction, even though its level of economic inequality is not particularly extreme.

The other countries in this quadrant (Japan, for instance) don't all have high economic inequality either, but they do have one characteristic in common: a culture of testing that equates educational success with performance on competitive examinations. UNICEF's periodic survey findings on child well-being in developed economies reveal that the nations with low rankings on well-being are typically also the most competitive academically.

The academic success of a number of Asian educational systems—including Singapore; South Korea; Shanghai, China; Japan; and Hong Kong—has often been attributed to factors such as strong teaching professions and societal commitments to public education.[384] But the high performance of these systems also comes with a shadow system of private after-school tutoring and cramming for traditional examinations.[385] In our school observations in East Asia, we have seen the human costs of cram schooling in the evening, among students who are visibly exhausted when they arrive at school the next morning. This situation has led to consequences that range from students indulging in an "escape from learning" in Japan once they get to university after competitive examinations have been passed, to serious mental health issues and high levels of suicide among young people in Hong Kong and South Korea.[386]

In South Korea, the cutthroat competition to get into the most prestigious, top three universities—known by their initials as the SKY universities—plunges high school students into "examination hell."[387] This state of mind is a Dante's inferno of academic competitiveness, with students trapped in seemingly endless spirals of school, homework, after-school test preparation, and sleeplessness. Here, and in other countries in East Asia, rising rates of depression, anxiety, and suicide among young people have reached crisis proportions.

In *Little Soldiers: An American Boy, a Chinese School, and the Global Race to Achieve,* journalist Lenora Chu describes her experience of moving to Shanghai from the United States with her husband and managing to place her 3-year-old son in the most competitive kindergarten in the city. Just getting him accepted was an ordeal. Repeated efforts got no acknowledgment from the principal. Only when Chinese American Chu involved her manifestly "foreign" US husband and only after the school conducted a searching interview with the parents and the child did the principal finally change her mind.[388]

The pressures of global assessments only intensify matters. When every announcement of the PISA results is pending, government ministers all over the world prepare announcements based on two scenarios—one if the results go up, another if they go down. Why do they need one test of 15-year-olds to tell them how their students are doing? Why don't they know this information anyway?

In *Let the Children Play,* Pasi Sahlberg and William Doyle discuss a new PISA test that measures the literacy and numeracy skills of 5-year-old children. The test has been labeled "Baby PISA." This metric, the authors warn, will launch a new "movement to start age-inappropriate academic instruction in reading and mathematics—and squeeze out play."[389] Baby PISA will make things worse as pressures to prepare for tests go down to 3-year-old toddlers. Already, teachers in Ontario have told us about kindergartners being taught how to shade in test bubbles to prepare them for their first tests at age 7.

One of Singapore's leading school reform experts, Pak Tee Ng, reports that parents there go to extreme lengths to get their children into the best schools. When the government introduced new measures requiring residency in a school's neighborhood, as well as a record of volunteering in the school, as criteria for acceptance, parents moved into desirable neighborhoods two years before their children were ready for school. They began volunteering in the school of their choice in order to win favor with the administrators and to give their children a strategic advantage for the battles that lay ahead.[390]

Back in Shanghai, at roughly the same time that the National Center on Education and the Economy (NCEE) in the United States was praising the city's students as the best performers in the world, Lenora Chu's son found himself in an environment driven by the twin imperatives of achievement and obedience.[391] For instance, the boy hated eggs and never ate them at home. But his teacher warned him, "If you don't eat the egg, then your Mom won't come to get you today."[392] Talking was forbidden during lining up and lunchtime, reluctance to take his nap was met with threats to demote him to the class for 2-year-olds, and at one point, failure to comply was met with threats to have him taken away by the police! The parents also purchased the services of tutors, even in kindergarten, and breakfast time was often taken up with tests.

Chu denounces these extreme actions but ultimately concedes that this kind of discipline isn't so bad if it is balanced with more freedom and creativity at home. Chinese American professor Yong Zhao, author of *What Works Can Hurt* and *Who's Afraid of the Big Bad Dragon? Why China Has the Best and Worst Education in the World,* couldn't disagree more. In a review of Chu's book, Zhao describes Chu's son's educational experience and ones like it as "an out-dated education model that does serious and significant damage" because it promotes "rigid, authoritarian, and unhealthy competition." According to Zhao, "Fear induced good behaviors are fake. They are lies made to evade punishment or receive award."[393] Zhao quotes a meta-analysis of 1,400 studies that showed these patterns of control lead to behavior problems, social and emotional difficulties, high anxiety, and, ultimately, higher mortality. In the end, he says, these ways of treating children are cruel. Asking Western educators to emulate the schools of China is a sure-fire way to increase student ill-being.

The expansion of after-school classes and tutoring in Asia has been startling. But the trend is not an exclusively Asian one. About a quarter of Ontario's families purchase tutors for their children.[394] In the UK, Lee Elliott Major and Stephen Machin note that after-school tutoring grew by more than a third over a decade from 2005. In the UK and elsewhere, they say, this trend is all part of a new global educational "arms race" for opportunity and success.[395]

Canadian writer and parent Carl Honoré worries that "parenthood is at risk of becoming a rat race of panic, guilt, and disappointment." Children "grow up terrified of failure" and yet expect "everything on a silver platter." "Does all this pushing, testing and benchmarking actually work?" he wonders rhetorically. "Does it make children happier, healthier and smarter? Does it create better workers and citizens?"[396] For many students, parents, and teachers, the constant quest for higher achievement leads straight to misery.

Gabriel Heller Sahlgren, a lead economist for the Centre for Education Economics in London, acknowledges that "pupils' happiness is lowest when they are in the classroom and when they do school and homework."[397] On the other hand, he notes that some "research shows that spending more time in school, more instructional hours, and more homework raise pupil achievement."[398] If we care about high achievement, he contends, we have to accept that some effective pedagogies may be "neither fun nor inspiring."[399] Indeed, Heller Sahlgren continues, "effective learning is often not enjoyable at all."[400]

Ontario-based educators David Tranter and colleagues argue that there is a "third path" between and beyond academic success and student well-being that advances young people's development through positive relationships.[401] It reaches into the social issues that affect well-being and success, like racism, Indigenous oppression, and developing positive diverse identities. Sacrificing quality of life for academic achievement gains is not justifiable.

There is no reason, however, why academic success should continue to be pursued and achieved at the expense of student well-being. Ever since the late 1980s, education policy in England has prioritized achievement above all else. But in Chapter 2, we also saw how, even in the midst of unrelenting pressure to drive up academic standards, whole child educational networks still managed to evolve. Moreover, the COVID-19 pandemic has put preoccupations with student well-being far ahead of traditional requirements for standardized testing. Even in traditionally competitive South Korea, a movement that began with 13 schools at the beginning of this century has spread to more than 1,000 locations, or approximately 9 percent of the schools in the country. These schools are committed to developing dignity, peace, and social justice. The movement has pushed the country's Ministry of Education to promote "exam-free" semesters to improve student well-being.[402] Increasingly, sacrificing quality of life for academic achievement gains is regarded as neither acceptable nor sustainable.

Well-Being Without Success

Just as it is possible to have academic success without well-being, well-being can also be achieved at the price of academic success. Let's look at the remarkable story of Iceland. People all over the world have become fascinated by how this tiny island nation, with a population of just over 340,000, could give rise to one of the most successful soccer teams on earth—quarterfinalists in the European Championships and then the World Cup.

In 2016, Andy met the then–minister of education, science, and culture, Illugi Gunnarsson, and asked him how it was that Iceland excelled at sports. Proudly showing his photograph taken with former England soccer coach Kevin Keegan, the minister explained that Iceland's success was the result of a deliberate 15-year-old strategy.

Iceland, he explained, had been experiencing serious problems with drug and alcohol abuse, as well as school dropout, among its young people.[403] After inquiring into the problem, the Icelandic government concluded that young people just did not have enough to do.

In response, the government then built leisure centers all over the country. It constructed more than 100 soccer fields and hired 600 highly trained sports coaches to work with young people. Teenagers found themselves training alongside professional players at public expense.[404]

Everybody worked hard and mixed together. Nobody was special. The Icelandic team that resulted had no great stars, just well-trained, hardworking players who were deeply proud of their country and who functioned well together as a highly collaborative team.

Substance-abuse problems dropped dramatically. The *Huffington Post* reported that "from 1998 to 2016, the percentage of 15-16 year-old Icelandic youth drunk in the past 30 days declined from 42% to 5%; daily cigarette smoking dropped from 23% to 3%; and having used cannabis one or more times fell from 17% to 5%."[405] These are the extraordinary results of a consistently pursued policy to improve well-being that was informed by rigorous and empirical social scientific research.

One side effect of all this was world-class men's and women's teams in soccer and handball. When Andy visited Iceland again in 2018 to work with the mayor of Reykjavik on developing a new educational vision for the city, the 30 or so partners involved in the exercise consisted equally of school leaders and teachers on the one hand, and leisure center workers on the other.[406] Again, all programs were paid for with public money, so everyone could join in the effort to improve young people's lives.

However, by late 2019, when Andy met with Iceland's new minister of education, science, and culture, Lilja Dögg Alfreðsdóttir, her country was facing the prospect of posting its worst-ever PISA results for student achievement, despite being a small, homogenous nation with a strong economy, high rates of employment, and good economic equity. The greatest drop in PISA achievement, compared to previous assessment cycles, occurred in the top 10 percent or so of the country's students.[407]

What was going on with Iceland's combination of strong improvements in well-being but relatively disappointing performance in terms of academic success? Was Iceland becoming a nation of people who were emotionally content but intellectually complacent?

The minister then sought to combine academic success and well-being by learning from different education systems around the world, with a specific focus on the performance of vulnerable groups and the importance of teachers and school leaders. Iceland's teachers and schools needed to build on their prior successes to develop a shared understanding of how they could collaborate to bring well-being and academic success closer together.

Following an extensive stakeholder consultation beginning in 2018 and cooperation with the OECD and the ARC Education Collaboratory of nations that Andy leads, the minister presented a new education policy for 2020–30. With the long-standing problem of early departure from school as a concern, the policy emphasized perseverance as a core value, along with courage, knowledge, and happiness. In the five pillars that supported the vision, Iceland retained rather than diminished its strength in well-being and therefore identified one of the pillars as that of putting well-being first.[408] Quality, superior teaching and skills for the future were among the remaining pillars, in a drive to assign high priority to greater success alongside the country's existing record on well-being. Iceland's policy, in other words, is a commitment to achieving both success and well-being. If we look at Iceland's policy like a hand of cards, it has held on to well-being as its ace, while adding kings and queens in areas such as academic success and quality teaching, to produce a winning hand.

In Chapter 4, we drew attention to a group of national leaders, including Icelandic Prime Minister Katrin Jakobsdóttir, who have argued that well-being, or quality of life, is as important as GDP in determining what counts as success on a national and global scale. Ideally, of course, it would be best if all communities and societies could be stellar performers in terms of well-being as well as economic success. But would it necessarily be all that bad if well-being is exceptional while educational achievement is merely very good? Might it just be an indicator of life having some kind of balance? An Olympic gold medalist in the heptathlon or decathlon, for example, will be the top performer in a number disciplines that make up the cumulative event, but not all of them. Moreover, the medalist will almost never outperform all athletes in the world in any one of those events, whether it's a sprint, a pole vault, or a hurdle race. Wanting to be top or almost top in everything will lead to national perfectionism and, when the unrealistic targets cannot be met, eventual disappointment and despair. This goal, indeed, was the design flaw with the United States' No Child Left Behind legislation, which expected all categories of students in every school to be proficient in reading and mathematics by 2014.

Well-Being with Success

The key moment when Ontario moved from its focus on raising tested achievement in literacy and numeracy to advancing a wider agenda of broad excellence, equity defined as inclusion, and well-being, was also in 2014. At that point, Premier Kathleen Wynne acknowledged and responded to the crisis of youth well-being in the province as one of four new policy pillars or priorities.

The government did not, however, then develop a top-down strategy to implement improvements in well-being. Instead, it announced the priority, provided a clear sense of direction, assigned well-being to the portfolio of one of the assistant deputy ministers, and set up a ministerial committee to manage well-being initiatives. Within these parameters, school districts were asked to develop their own understandings and strategies to improve well-being. Our interviews with Ontario's educators pointed to the emergence of three distinctive approaches:

1. *Improved well-being is a prerequisite for achievement.* Most children cannot achieve if they are mentally or emotionally unwell, bullied, anxious, sleep-deprived, enraged, hungry, or depressed.
2. *Academic achievement is essential for well-being.* Failure destroys dignity and leads to ill-being. Focus and accomplishment provide the purpose and direction that allay anxiety in children and adults alike.

3. *Well-being has its own value.* It is a complement to academic achievement. It helps develop well-rounded people who are also happy and fulfilled. It is a form of success in its own right.

Let's take a closer look at each of these approaches.

1. Improved Well-Being Is a Prerequisite for Achievement

According to the *2016 Report Card on Child and Family Poverty in Ontario,* more than one in six children grows up in poverty, and the number is increasing. Student ill-being emanates from "unfavorable socio-economic and family circumstances" that lead to "a low sense of personal competence, a feeling that one cannot control and plan one's life."[409] Teachers see the consequences of children's ill-being for their learning. In one district, a teacher remarked:

> We know right from the beginning that the students were ready to learn if they were well fed. A lot of them weren't coming to school well fed, so we had the breakfast program and we had fresh fruit available in the class all day long for the kids to snack on.

A principal described how her staff went out of their way to make sure that their students' needs were being met. "They bring in clothes and make sure they're fed, and they do all those extra little things so that they're ready to learn. These teachers make breakfast for the kids. They're putting butter on the toast. If we want them to be able to learn to read and to write, they have to do these things." A colleague explained that for "one child in grade 2 or 3, his glasses kept breaking. The teacher called an optometrist and explained the situation. The optometrist donated glasses. The optometrist even came to school for the fitting for the child."

Given the needs of Indigenous parents, one school created a new position: the Aboriginal Family Support Worker. An elementary school principal explained that

> It's a new position that we designed to support our families. Really, it's a pseudo-parent for our kids. She's parenting the parents, helping them get organized so that their children are up and coming to school or working with the agencies to support their families and get them the services that they require. She

takes families to the food bank. She really just is there for whatever we need her to do. She does lice checks with the kids—all
of those kinds of things that are really helpful.

Wherever possible, schools in this district try to draw on the
assets that parents offer in their communities. One principal
explained how "the parents that come to our school are advocates
for all of our kids and do a lot of activities. They are quite great at
being advocates for *all* kids." The parents raise funds to provide
"free lunches for kids," and they work with foundations and government agencies to "help support the large amount of food that we
have available to the kids."

In other districts, schools made special efforts to address a new
"high immigrant population and Syrian refugees." One teacher
noted how "numbers are going up, up, up with English language
learners. Some of them are coming from pretty horrible situations."
These students carry with them the effects of post-traumatic stress
after having seen family members killed, homes destroyed, and constant violence all around them—as well as having received little or
no formal education previously. "I think about some of these students. There are going to be lifelong mental health issues," the
teacher said. One district's response was to appoint a new superintendent with responsibility for mental health and to fund new community youth workers, speech pathologists, and ELL staff to work
with refugee students.

Another district was located in and around a working-class city
where local employment opportunities and associated incidences of
poverty rise and fall with the fortunes of the core industry. In 2011,
the region had a 24.2 percent youth poverty rate compared to a
provincial rate of 17.3 percent.[410] One in four young people live in
low-income families, many of whom are working several jobs to
make ends meet. Educators were grateful for the commitment of
trade unions and philanthropies to this community. "It's a part of
the culture here," one said. "There's huge care in this district,"
another colleague observed. "There's huge care around mental
health, huge care around the partnerships, huge care around poverty. When I came here, philanthropy is a cultural value in this community, and so people help."

The sense of civic responsibility in this community is evident among charities, community groups such as City Pride, unionized labor, and partnerships with United Way, with the local community college, and with industries and apprenticeship placements. They fund mental health seminars on topics including student anxiety, as well as a "Run for Well-Being" event to educate teachers around student mental health.

Ill-being does not only manifest itself at the lowest levels of Maslow's needs hierarchy. It can be psychological as well as physical, and it can affect the affluent as well as the poor, through societal and surrounding pressures that create anxiety and stress, for example. "Some of their anxiety is related to parental pressure," one teacher observed of her students. "Some of the anxiety is perfectionism." As we saw in Figure 2.6, one way that schools supported students was by providing a calming space that helped them to gather themselves and settle down when they were stressed or upset. "Kids had the option of going there when it was needed," one teacher stated. It provided a valuable respite from academic pressures, "where you could just go and relax."

Notwithstanding all these developments, the research on well-being indicates that caring for students who are at risk of experiencing ill-being is often insufficient. Promoting well-being involves more than avoiding ill-being. How, for example, do we prepare students to thrive in classrooms with challenging academic material, complex social environments, and digital technologies? Learning requires discipline and zest, the ability to focus, the capacity to explore topics from different points of view, the social skills to interact with others, and the stamina or grit to persevere through difficulties and bounce back from disappointment. Enhance positive well-being, this argument goes, and you will also improve achievement.

In the words of one of Ontario's system leaders in our project, "Doing what we need to do to leverage that wellness that we are trying to engender across the entire system, into increased student achievement—that's one of the goals now."

2. Academic Achievement Is Essential for Well-Being

The relationship between well-being and academic achievement runs in both directions. Well-being can support achievement, and achievement can also be a catalyst for well-being. For example, one principal wanted to raise mathematics results on the province's standardized test, even though "the children do well" already and they "mark high." "Pushing that thinking and pushing the question" of how to raise mathematics results was a central component of reforms in another district. Increased expectations were meant to enable students "to boost their confidence" and to "make them feel good about being learners." Clarity of purpose and direction was also important. The director of this district stated, "I think it's stressful to waste time and not know where you're going." "In the absence of direction, people do what they want. It isn't always the most purposeful thing."

In between and cutting across achievement and well-being is Carol Dweck's concept of growth mindsets, to which many schools and districts were committed, as we saw in Chapter 2. Growth mindsets promote the simple but compelling idea that "your basic qualities are things you can cultivate through your own efforts."[411] The growth mindset "makes you concerned with improving," with not being able to do or know something *yet.*[412] Growth mindsets are related to "the love of challenge, the belief in effort, resilience in the face of setbacks, and greater success."[413] They are the bridge between well-being and academic success.

Having a sense of achievement isn't or shouldn't be all about getting good test scores, though. Even though it was unknown by many of Ontario's educators, Maslow's zenith in his hierarchy of needs, self-transcendence, was behind many learning innovations across the 10 districts. For example, these included comparing water quality on First Nations Reserves with that in neighboring communities and learning about, as well as raising funds to adopt and accommodate, Syrian refugee families. In cases such as these, students deepened their own learning and sense of accomplishment by addressing the well-being of others.

Incorporating students' identities into the curriculum can also lead to higher academic achievement and increased well-being. Success in activities that have value in terms of one's culture leads to senses of pride that restore people's dignity. Indigenous students in northern Canada now have a curriculum that engages with their knowledge and experience of the wilderness. Students with learning disabilities learn about their disability, about accomplished and famous figures who also have that disability, and about how to advocate for themselves with their teachers and through their individual educational plans so they can become successful and also more self-confident as young people.

The complex but close interrelationship between well-being and achievement is also evident in other times and places. For several years Andy has served as an advisor to the government of Scotland on its education strategy. One of Scotland's four curriculum priorities is developing "confident learners."[414] Visits to schools confirm that across the country, many students are able to express with confidence what they are learning and why they are learning it.

A fundamental and inalienable aspect of well-being is human dignity. The first principle of the United Nations Declaration of Human Rights is that "all human beings are born free and equal in dignity and rights."[415] According to the *Oxford English Dictionary, dignity* comes from the Latin *dignitas* and means "the state or quality of being worthy of honor or respect."[416] Dignity can be taken away from people through violation, abuse, or humiliation. In schools, the most common source of loss of dignity for students involves being labeled as a failure. One of the chief arguments against holding students back a grade relates to their intense experiences of social shame as a consequence.

Extreme inequality damages people's sense of human worth and dignity. In 1973, Richard Sennett and Jonathan Cobb wrote a book titled *The Hidden Injuries of Class,* based on interviews with 150 working-class adults in Boston, Massachusetts, about their lives. Their interviewees struggled to achieve many things, but what they craved was dignity and respect. However, what they repeatedly experienced was a denial of their dignity through experiences of failure at school. One interviewee felt "stupid" in school and "came to think that his power to understand was undercut by his defects of character, his lack of perseverance, of willpower to perform well."[417] Sennett and Cobb concluded, "The terrible thing about class in our society is that it sets up a contest for dignity."[418]

Success can bolster well-being. Failure can destroy it. Narrowing what counts as success to test scores in two or three basic subjects increases the frequency of failure. On the other hand, widening what counts as success to include the arts or outdoor learning, for example, reduces the frequency of failure. Helping students be more successful is not only about focus, outcomes, and accomplishments. It is also about widening and deepening the many ways in which their aspirations of a hard-won sense of real accomplishment can be possible.

3. Well-Being Has Its Own Value

Earlier we pointed out how several Ontario districts adopted social and emotional learning programs for students in the belief that they complement academic achievement. The work of Stuart Shanker, author of *Calm, Alert, and Learning,* has been influential in many of them.[419] Teachers who have taken workshops on Shanker's research have been encouraged to make inventive use of classroom materials as ways to help their students to regulate their behavior.

On the advice of an occupational therapist, one classroom erected a climbing wall for students with fetal alcohol spectrum disorder to use when they were restless. Other classrooms provided spinning devices in the form of cones and egg-capsule chairs where students could sit, spin, and close themselves in for security. Another school in the same district had self-regulating spaces for meditation and classrooms with calming devices, where students were able to decompress until they were calm enough to pay attention to instruction. All of these are ways that teachers adapted their learning environments to promote student well-being.

Teachers and administrators remarked how there had been significant improvements in students' ability to self-regulate since these materials had been provided. It took far less time to calm students down before they could rejoin a class. Half the students were being sent away half as often to calm down, and for less than half the time compared to past situations, teachers said. It was better to give students the time and space they needed to get in the right frame of mind to focus on learning, teachers believed, than to punish them when their minds were racing or their bodies were restless.

In another district, "there was hitting" and "there wasn't a lot of communication" between children in one class. The teacher worked with them to develop their oral language and self-regulatory skills so that they could share their feelings verbally without resorting to hitting. In another class involving a "really withdrawn" child, a teacher decided to use her kindergarten's "drama and play center more to build in opportunities for imaginative play" to develop the child's skills in interacting with others.

More is happening in all of these examples than mere self-regulation. Students are acquiring what educators in the Francophone district described as *autonomie*—the ability to learn independently while in the company of others. This capacity for self-regulation, or *autonomie,* is consistent with the argument that well-being can enhance achievement and is also valued in its own right.

Another strategy to complement academic achievement with well-being was the idea of resilience, or what educators called "bounce back," reflecting the Latin origin of resilience in *resilere*—to react back. The resilience framework in the schools in one district stemmed from the research of a consultant who had done workshops with the district. As with growth mindsets, the district wanted its students to know that resilience is something that is developed, rather than a fixed ability. "You build resiliency. You're not born with it," one principal said. One elementary school took the idea of "building" resilience literally. In its principal's own words,

> You know what? We need to do a boost. We dressed up as construction workers. We developed "toolkits" for students. They had their own toolkit of different supports. We built a resiliency wall. Every student had a brick and they could [write] on, "Who supports me when I'm feeling down?"

These resiliency walls and toolkits were erected throughout the school. Students wrote about various sources of support they could draw on from their resiliency toolkits that helped them feel relaxed, calm, or strong enough to move forward. Teachers reported that students sometimes literally searched through these toolkits when they felt they needed help to deal with a frustrating issue.

Another elementary school organized a superhero theme when a student was diagnosed with a serious illness. According to one teacher, this "tied together zones of regulation, mental health, and superheroes all in one. It was fabulous." When the boy passed away later that year, the students "dealt with it very well," according to a superintendent. "Basically, we do better at bouncing back," a teacher at the school added. "When things get tough, we need to find our superhuman powers within ourselves."

One development in student well-being in the districts was students' increasing engagement in this agenda themselves. One district created student-led well-being groups called Sources of Strength. A district-level administrator described how the group consisted of student "leaders from every part of the school. You get kids that aren't the jocks, and they are not the artsy kids. You want it to be representative of everybody." Students volunteered to be part of the group because they felt that by being open about their own struggles with anxiety, depression, or just feeling different because of a speech impairment, for instance, they would be able to help others who were undergoing similar experiences. Their own weaknesses and vulnerabilities became sources of other students' strength.

The students received training from mentors at the school. They organized events such as a Walk for Depression Awareness, so that students and community members wouldn't ignore any student who was struggling. A mental health resources poster displayed at the school encouraged students to "sit in nature," "read a book," or "pet a furry creature" as ways of reversing emotional states that could lead them into tailspins of depression and anxiety.

In these ways, the district was encouraging students to pay attention to each other, to reach out to others with kindness, and to make sure that no one was left alone to suffer in silence. Well-being here was an accomplishment that showed students were learning how to be with one another in a way that didn't lead to individual self-absorption but addressed their aspirations to take care of one another.

Conclusion

The three perspectives on the relationship between achievement and well-being are distinct only analytically. In practice, they overlap. Mindfulness programs were developed alongside programs of self-regulation, for example, in schools that also saw achievement as a way to help children feel successful. But the analytic distinctions do help us understand that psychological strategies to develop well-being, such as emotional regulation, mindfulness, building resiliency, and using growth mindsets, are intrinsically valuable as well as important means to accomplish achievement-related ends.

Decompressing with meditation, moving with yoga, stepping outside for some fresh air, or immersing themselves in a novel or a sketch that might give them a break from academic pressures—these are all ways that young people can develop their well-being. Educators are also endeavoring to improve their students' well-being with climbing walls, calming areas, resiliency programs, meditation, and movement.

Whatever the theory of the relationship between well-being and achievement was, the enthusiasm about well-being initiatives was widespread across all 10 districts. Teachers, leaders, schools, and systems were compassionate about the struggles their students faced and were committed to helping all their students succeed and be well. They responded by initiating programs that helped calm their students' agitated minds; established a range of wraparound supports, including ones that were led by students; and engaged each other and a range of partners to build the capacity for success.

It's easy to take cheap shots against well-being or achievement when they are pursued or presented as singular and opposite goals. On the one hand, we don't want a school system that is obsessed with well-being to the point where young people live in a superficial and self-indulgent world of undemanding happiness. That path will only lead to a nation of over-praised, narcissistic adults who feel that success and earned expertise are unimportant, and that all that matters is the needs and opinions of themselves and of others who happen to agree with them.

Equally, achievement shouldn't be reduced to grades and test scores, with students expected to apply themselves with grim determination even in the face of poor teaching, irrelevant tests, or a curriculum that is so boring they cannot see any value in it. Achievement should be about accomplishing things of purpose, value, and interest for oneself and for others. It should bring a sense of lasting fulfillment, not just relief at test completion or evanescent fun.

Well-being and achievement shouldn't exist in two different worlds, with different specialists populating them—mathematics and literacy people on one side, mental health specialists on the other. At every level, from the school up to the whole system, it's important to establish clear structures that unite those who have portfolios and responsibilities in curriculum and learning with those who have expertise in well-being and mental health. Leaders themselves need to create, articulate, and repeat clear and compelling narratives that bring achievement and well-being together.

Well-being is needed to support achievement, especially when children come from backgrounds that present them with great challenges. Achievement and accomplishment are also sources of well-being. It's hard for young people to maintain their dignity if they feel like they're failing all the time.

Neither well-being nor academic achievement is sufficient in itself for producing well-rounded human beings. We don't want schools to produce nations of happy, smug, and stupid people. But we don't want a world full of clever people who are evil, sick, and twisted either.

Well-being has been a long-overlooked policy priority in education. It is now working its way into schools all over the world. Our work in Ontario points to many different ways in which educators have eagerly seized the opportunities to develop their students' well-being. But when austerity is imminent and budget cuts loom, initiatives in yoga or meditation or support roles in counseling and similar areas can seem like the easiest options for making economies, compared to literacy or mathematics. To sustain its importance and focus, the emphasis on well-being therefore has to find its proper relationship to the learning mission of schools and school systems. Whether we work in times of plenty or in an era of austerity, we shouldn't have to choose between success on the one hand and well-being on the other. We must strive to turn out young adults who are successful *and* fulfilled at the same time. This is what the Prosperity Doctrine should look like in action.

Epilogue: Getting Better

On December 26, 2004, there was a tsunami in Asia. It claimed almost a quarter of a million lives. Its impact on economies and infrastructure was devastating. Former US Presidents Bill Clinton and George H.W. Bush joined forces to coordinate a massive recovery effort. The UN secretary general subsequently appointed Clinton as special envoy for tsunami relief.

It was through this work that the former president introduced the idea of "building back better" after a catastrophe.[420] His same words were employed after other natural and human-induced disasters, as well as in response to the 2008 global economic collapse. By the time of the COVID-19 pandemic, national governments and transnational organizations including the OECD, the UN, and the World Economic Forum were all talking about "building back better."

What did Clinton mean by the phrase? Physically rebuilding schools, roads, hotels, businesses, places of worship, and other infrastructure was the obvious priority. But in his 2006 UN Report, *Key Propositions for Building Back Better,* Clinton went far beyond physical reconstruction. "While a disaster can actually create opportunities to shift development patterns—to *build back better*—recovery can also perpetuate pre-existing patterns of vulnerability and disadvantage," he argued.[421] Disasters often amplified existing inequalities, so it was important that the effort to build back better should not only repair damage but also rectify long-standing problems of unfairness that had preceded it. Clinton's propositions therefore stated that building back better should do the following:

- Enable families and communities to "drive their own recovery."
- "Promote fairness and equity."
- "Enhance preparedness for future disasters."
- "Empower local governments to manage recovery efforts."
- Avoid "rivalry and unhealthy competition."
- "Leave communities safer by reducing risks and building resilience."[422]

"Building back better" is not just a slogan. In June 2020, the OECD reported that building back better meant more than "getting economies and livelihoods quickly back on their feet."[423] Rather, "a central dimension of building back better is the need for a people-centered recovery that focuses on *well-being,* improves *inclusiveness,* and reduces *inequality*" (emphases added).[424] It expresses a need to "reduce the likelihood of future shocks and increase society's resilience to them when they do occur."[425] The OECD called upon governments to work together in addressing environmental objectives and creating "nature-based solutions" to the most difficult challenges, such as climate change.[426]

In response to the pandemic, many governments and transnational organizations adopted the language and spirit of building back better as a way to think about and create a response to recovery. They saw that it would involve more than simply restoring economic growth or repeating and reinforcing existing inequalities and injustices. In *Reimagining Our Future: Building Back Better from COVID-19,* for example, UNICEF urged responses to the pandemic that would "at the same time create a foundation for a greener, more sustainable future for children" and that would also "strengthen . . . systems to better respond to future crises."[427] "Children and young people are watching closely as we deal with this crisis that threatens their future," UNICEF argued.[428] "If we, in turn, keep the focus on them, they can be a touchstone for the unprecedented solidarity we need to overcome COVID-19 and build back better."[429]

Faced with confronting the greatest pandemic in a century, the biggest economic crisis since the 1930s, levels of extreme inequality that had spiraled upward for decades, growing political unrest, disturbing global shifts toward authoritarianism, and an environmental crisis that threatens our very existence, transnational economic organizations didn't merely pivot or pirouette as they had done in response to other crises. They repealed, retracted, and recanted practically everything they had stood for over the previous 40 years.

For example, in July 2020 the World Economic Forum published a paper titled *To Build Back Better, We Must Reinvent Capitalism: Here's How.*[430] It urged "a profoundly positive transformation of the global economy, taking us closer to a world in which everyone can live well, within planetary boundaries."[431] The authors noted the

> need to "build back better," to "reset," if we are to address the deep systemic vulnerabilities the pandemic has exposed. For businesses, building back better is about much more than corporate social responsibility: it is about truly aligning markets with the natural, social and economic systems on which they depend. It is about building real resilience, driving equitable and sustainable growth, and reinventing capitalism itself.[432]

What the Commitment Will Require

The kind of commitment needed to build back better requires intense emotional engagement. In much of the research on well-being and SEL, so-called negative emotions such as anger and fear are supposed to be regulated rather than aroused. Yet figuring out how to deal with human suffering in ways that don't minimize it—or that wrap it up in happy-go-lucky or "keep calm and carry on" mentalities—is essential to restoring long-term health and prosperity. Consider research, including the following, that is never mentioned by mainstream advocates of well-being and SEL:

- *A happy person may be "slower than a fearful person"* to detect a potential threat in the environment. "When a person is confronted with serious threat that requires very fast responses, such a delayed detection" can be catastrophic.[433]
- *"People who lack fear or anger may be at a disadvantage"* when facing a threat "because their bodies are not as well prepared for a fight" compared to those whose increased blood pressure and heart rate make them more alert to environmental challenges.[434]

- *Happiness can "make people more gullible,"* and "people who believe everything they hear can be in serious danger when in a hostile environment."[435]
- *"Individuals in negative moods" are often more creative* than others, because happy people "evaluate the status quo and their own ideas positively," while creativity requires people to "exert high levels of effort and persistence" in the face of adversity or difficulty.[436]
- *"Defensive pessimists" expect the worst and become skilled at anticipating difficulties.* When they are urged to be less pessimistic, their performance declines, because they fail to confront challenges realistically.[437]

The COVID-19 pandemic, racial oppression and injustice, vaccine nationalism, threats to democracy, Brexit, extreme inequality, and being on the brink of catastrophic and irreversible climate change—these things are real and deeply interconnected. *We are in the fight of our lives.* The hyper-competitiveness of GERM-ridden preoccupations with individual achievement and tested basics provides no answer. Nor does the happy-talk and calming-everybody-down of positive psychology and emotional regulation. What's the alternative?

In a VUCA world of inequality and turmoil, we need to embrace, not avoid, our so-called negative emotions. Let's begin with *fear* and *anger.* Celebrity adventurer Bear Grylls explains that people who claim to have no fear are either lying or "not going for anything big enough in their life." Grylls continues, "You have got to move towards the difficult stuff. And the irony is that the things we fear most often dissipate." [438]

We need to become collectively outraged about and challenge leaders who have betrayed public trust and actively perpetuated unfairness, exclusion, and injustice. We mustn't let our fear of push-back from politicians or from some segments of the public make us adopt lily-livered positions that advance only minor tweaks in assessment at the cost of the fundamental movements away from high-stakes testing that are truly needed and completely possible.

We must harness these emotions of anger and fear to ignite change for the better. We must teach our young people to move toward the danger sometimes too.

What about other profane emotions? *Depression,* for example, is something we should neither wallow in nor simply try and snap ourselves out of. Depression is a reasonable emotional response to circumstances that offer no good solutions in situations where we feel we have no control. Acknowledging the existence of depression, though, can lead people to take back some semblance of inner control by developing solutions to shared problems together. Getting children involved in projects about climate change, for example, can lead to a productive career pathway into a booming, new, carbon-neutral economy that can make a difference in saving the world.

Angst and *anxiety* can prompt us to meditate, relax, and breathe deeply. But if this doesn't seem like a sufficient response to significant threats, they can also propel us into surges of frenetic creativity that lead to vaccines being invented in record time or to online learning being delivered from scratch in a matter of days. Recognizing the existence of these emotions can also motivate teenagers to get off their devices and into the outdoors where they can work off their anxieties exuberantly, while engaging in learning that is creative in its own right.

Grief and *bereavement* are not pathologies. They are normal reactions to all kinds of losses. These include losing a family member, witnessing a parental separation, leaving behind a homeland, being dumped by a boyfriend or girlfriend, or experiencing the death of a pet. The best response to grief and loss is not to tell people to buck up, get over it, or even bounce back as soon as they can. Resilience walls and bounce-backs can rush people too quickly through the grieving process, just so everyone can return to work and move on as fast as possible. The pressure to get people back on task is now so great that the American Psychiatric Association classifies grief and depression lasting more than two weeks as a "serious medical illness."[439] We disagree! In dealing with all kinds of losses, including counseling students about alternate career choices, supporting teachers in an online environment, or implementing significant curriculum change, we need to accept the normality of the grieving process. We need to work through it, rather than rush people past it.

Building back better in health or education isn't just about lifting performance, following the evidence, or focusing harder. It also requires attention to the psychic, emotional worlds of those who have suffered or struggled, as well as those who serve, support, and make sacrifices for them. And it calls for us to do this in relation to the whole gamut of people's emotions, not just those that are easier to manage or that yield more immediate benefits for the organization by being regulated.

The mainstream psychological literature on emotional development and emotional intelligence provides important strategies for teachers. Teachers can help students to recognize and manage their emotions. They can introduce meditation to guide students toward greater mindfulness and compassion. They can also create peer support groups for students to channel their energies in more positive directions.

These kinds of supports can contribute to teachers' own emotional development too. Like adult passengers in depressurized flight cabins who are told to put on their own oxygen masks before they help children with theirs, teachers will find it hard to support their students for long if they are in psychological turmoil themselves.

Important as all this psychological guidance is, though, it still misses something. The research we have reported throughout this book goes beyond the findings of positive psychology, the literature on emotional intelligence, Dweck's research on fixed and growth mindsets, Maslow's hierarchy of needs, and the personal benefits of mindfulness and meditation. It addresses students' and educators' emotional lives holistically, including the profane and less easily managed aspects of these lives that schools and other organizations tend to avoid when they bring positive psychology to their aid.

Our earlier take on questioning well-being and our insights into the counterintuitively positive role of negative emotions have enabled us to look into the inner lives of students and their teachers through different lenses. What have these lenses helped us to see, beyond happiness, calmness, grit, resilience, and positive thinking?

- Abraham Maslow's neglected stage of *self-transcendence* can actually inspire us to practice self-sacrifice from time to time.
- Supposedly *negative emotions of grief, frustration, and anger* can prompt us into constructive and corrective action.
- As well as *keeping calm and carrying on* in the face of chaos, in today's world we must also engage with emotional states such as *disgust* (and prejudice) and *ennui* (and entitlement) that cannot be managed by calmness alone.
- Even *growth mindsets* have their limits. Telling children they can be anything they want to be, without any consideration of their particular talents or absence of talents, is a cruel lie. Growth mindsets should definitely encourage greater achievement and ambition, but they should also avoid fostering delusions of limitless success.
- *Mindfulness,* we have shown, can and should be used as a way to focus and strive for greater justice, not only as an inward retreat from the outer world of injustice.

To do all this effectively in order to address the *inner lives* of people, we must also do something about the *outer worlds* in which they work. This message is essential to the Prosperity Doctrine and one that distinguishes our approach from many others.

Consider the monumental challenges faced by all education professionals who struggle to address their students' well-being. How does it feel to deal with students in poverty whose hard-working families can't earn a basic living wage? Knowing there's a teenage suicide waiting to happen while the social work system fails to prioritize counseling support is devastating for any educator. Working in a high-poverty district where countless initiatives drive hundreds of teachers to take online courses in mindfulness so they can recover from the stresses of their jobs is a sure sign there is something amiss with the demands being faced by the system. Why throw vast resources at digital tablets that sit children in front of screens most of the day when there is no parallel impetus or investment to shift more learning and play into healthy, outdoor environments? How far should teachers comply with standardized testing when they know it creates ill-being among their most vulnerable children?

There's nothing wrong with being mindful, calm, and optimistic when we feel everything is getting on top of us. But when the system itself starts making us ill, it's good to start feeling guilty about taking up children's time with test preparation, as this might then stir up organized opposition to the tests. It's right to be angry about inequity and injustice, so we can fight for something better together instead of being left to make all the sacrifices on our own. It's also helpful to capitalize on our frustrations to spark movements for the change and transformation that we need to bring a new age of prosperity into being—which brings us back to the Prosperity Doctrine.

The Prosperity Doctrine—Again

If we truly are in the fight of our lives, we can't go into battle empty-handed. Well-being is best secured when all of us take a proactive role in building back everyone's lives for the better. This is where the Prosperity Doctrine comes in—as an agenda for improving everyone's quality of life and opportunities to flourish and thrive. How can we do this? And what must we also avoid doing?

First, we cannot count on the 26 people who control more than half of the world's wealth to reform themselves. When the Chan Zuckerberg Initiative funded a report on well-being after the pandemic, barely a word was mentioned about the social aspects of well-being, other than teachers' efforts to make sure students were fed, clothed, and sheltered.[440] As this book goes to print, the US Internal Revenue Service is seeking to collect $9 billion in unpaid taxes from Priscilla Chan's husband and Facebook founder, Mark Zuckerberg.[441] Then there are the world's two wealthiest men—Jeff Bezos, founder and former CEO of Amazon, and Elon Musk, founder and CEO of Tesla. They have been spending much of their globally tax-sheltered combined net worth of $363 billion[442] on becoming rocket men who can experience space travel for themselves.[443]

It's time for the world's billionaires to pay their fair tax share and let their fellow citizens exercise democratic control over how the revenues are distributed, rather than asserting their own philanthropic preferences about what's best for everyone else. In an oncoming age of prosperity, well-being for everyone requires ending the privilege of extreme wealth for the few.

Second, we cannot resort to another wave of failed austerity policies to get us back on an even keel after the health pandemic. Recalling the 1948 Marshall Plan in which the United States invested in economic reconstruction in Western Europe, the superintendents of New York City, Los Angeles, and Chicago have called for "a Marshall Plan for the schools." This effort would provide emergency funding, once the peak of the coronavirus passed, for extra in-person instruction and for "mental health support for students to address the significant trauma they are facing."[444] To reinvest in public education is to reinvest in public good and in equal educational opportunity. It is to understand that public-sector jobs and associated increases in economic recovery and social mobility help everyone by assembling the building blocks of a renewed political democracy.

Third, we cannot expect the vested interests of testing companies to reduce the amount of standardized testing in favor of curriculum and assessment reforms that will enrich social studies, expand the arts, and move more learning into the open air—thereby enhancing quality of life, well-being, and prosperity for all young people. A time of prosperity, fulfillment, and thriving in learning and in life must be met with a transformation in educational assessments. With the aid of modern digital technology, these should leave behind large-scale standardized achievement tests (as the state of California announced in 2020 that it would do) and move toward more system-side formative assessments (as the state of Oregon has proposed).[445] As Andy and his fellow advisers have recommended for Scotland, transformed educational assessments can also move away from one-time, win-lose competitive examinations at the end of high school, toward exams that are designed more like driving tests, to be continuously offered and retaken until proficiency is achieved.[446]

Fourth, although we *can* expect technology companies and their partners to inject more digitally based innovation into schools, we *cannot* expect them to police the risks that result from their efforts and enthusiasms. Instead of *hybrid* learning and technology, we should adopt a new terminology and approach of *ethically seamless* learning and technology.

The Prosperity Doctrine embraces digital technology when it enhances all people's quality of life. It also addresses technology's now well-known risks. There are many strategies for doing this.

Schools and school districts can establish technology watchdog committees or working groups that also involve students. Educational institutions and governments can insert clauses into educational contracts with technology and data companies that require them to address harms and risks.

Fifth, the Prosperity Doctrine restores our relationship to nature, including our own human nature. Given the power of technology interests to drive innovation in a post-pandemic school system, educators themselves will need to insist and ensure that outdoor learning in nature is not pushed aside, but protected and expanded. A restorative relationship to nature—and the planet—reconnects us with Indigenous heritages, cultivates environmental respect and responsibility from the first years of life, and combats the ill-being incurred by nature-deficit disorder. It enriches and enhances young people's physical and spiritual health as well as their learning.

Schools can and sometimes already do embrace nature's assets for learning and well-being by scheduling regular outdoor breaks, creating rough rather than manicured play surfaces, reintroducing outdoor activities that have what one Icelandic principal characterized to us as "a little bit of danger," creating gardens outside, caring for plants inside, and organizing regular walks and hikes in the woods and the mountains where these opportunities are available.

Finally, as we report in research elsewhere, the Prosperity Doctrine means paying as much attention to the well-being of the adults as to that of the students.[447] Headteachers (school principals) in Scotland were offered coaches and counselors during the pandemic to support them in their own leadership.[448] This opportunity should be an entitlement for all school and system leaders, always. In Finland, a highly placed country on well-being indicators, teachers get more time out of class to collaborate with other teachers—a key contributing factor to professional well-being—than teachers anywhere else.[449]

In our work in Canada, Norway, and South Korea, teachers' unions collaborate with governments and universities to undertake innovations that support students' learning, as well as their own members' learning and well-being.[450] Surely, when teachers reach the twilight of their careers and some of their tasks may not be as easy as they once were, we also find new roles for them as mentors and coaches. There are many creative ways to reengage them instead of just nudging them aside into early retirement.

Toward Universal Well-Being

Only when we integrate the three uplifting forces of social prosperity, ethical technology use, and restorative nature will we develop schools and societies that allow everyone to flourish. It's not too late to follow the injunction of the 1996 European Commission report we described in Chapter 1 and to learn not only *how to be* as individuals but also *how to live together.* Supporting the development of the whole child means we also have to address the development and transformation of our whole world.

Universal well-being must be an ethical imperative. Academic achievement detached from well-being must become a thing of the past. The single-minded pursuit of economic growth without regard for social welfare or environmental sustainability will soon be joining it. Well-being as the solitary attainment of an individual detached from school and society cannot be our ultimate aspiration.

A tectonic shift is underway. As we have seen, a geological term describing what emerges through such a shift is *uplift.* Our challenge in education today is to make sure this emerging uplift is successful and sustainable. To uplift those we serve, we must also uplift those who serve them.[451] We must promote well-being and learning for all.

More than any other profession, teachers and other educators are in a prime position to influence the young. They can and must become the champions of a world and its educational systems that advance and integrate the hard work of learning and accomplishment with the deep fulfillment of well-being and social prosperity. They must educate the whole child in and for the whole world. This aspiration is the true meaning of what it must take to build back better for the well-being and success of all students everywhere, now and in the future.

Acknowledgments

We are grateful to many people for inviting us to work with them on well-being. Michelle Forge and Michael O'Keefe of the Council of Ontario Directors of Education (CODE) asked us to conduct research on the consortium of 10 Ontario districts that they organized and led. Shaneé Washington-Wangia, Chris Bacon, and Mark D'Angelo served on our Boston College research team and significantly helped develop our thinking in relation to issues of inclusion and identity. Danette Parsley, Mike Siebersma, Matt Eide, and other members of the leadership team on the NW RISE project expanded our horizons about the rewards and challenges of improving education for students in remote rural communities in the Pacific Northwest. We are grateful to our research team on this project who, at different points, comprised Elizabeth Cox, Michael O'Connor, and Minjung Kim.

Dean Elaine Munthe of the University of Stavanger in Norway graciously invited us to be visiting professors from 2014 to 2020, where we worked with her and her colleagues as well as public school educators in the nearby municipalities of Rogaland and Sandnes. We learned a great deal from the quietly deliberate and collaborative ways that Norwegians organize their schools and their society, especially with regard to thriving in nature.

One topic in our discussion of well-being is technology. Andy is the director of CHENINE (Change, Engagement and Innovation in Education: www.chenine.ca) at the University of Ottawa Faculty of Education. CHENINE addresses how digital technology is presenting opportunities for and posing risks to students and teachers in and beyond the COVID-19 pandemic. He would like to thank his colleagues Amal Boultif, Phyllis Dalley, Megan Cotnam-Kappel, Michelle Hagerman, Joel Westheimer, and Jessica Whitley for their many contributions to his thinking about these issues that are expressed within this book.

Dennis would like to thank his colleagues at the Bosch Foundation in Berlin for the award of a Richard von Weizsäcker Fellowship to study the impact of the digitization of learning on educational change and the future of work. The staff, comprising Sandra Breka, Jannik Rust, and Madeleine Schneider, have generously supported his research.

At different times this book references other research articles that we have published together and separately. Parts of our writing here have drawn on these sources. We acknowledge their permission for reuse.[452] Our discussions of well-being during the global pandemic also draw on media editorials we wrote in real time while the coronavirus was unfolding, and we are grateful for permission to include that material too.[453]

Finally, we extend our thanks to our wives, Pauline and Shelley. They have been our companions for many decades now, and we are grateful for their many contributions to the development of our ideas. This is the fourth book that we've written together, and there is no way that we could have kept going without their steadfast support. When John Donne wrote that "no man is an island," he must have been thinking of people like us!

Notes

[1] Barnardo's. (2020, June 30). *Generation lockdown: A third of children and young people experience increased mental health difficulties.* https://www.barnardos.org.uk/news/generation-lock-down-third-children-and-young-people-experience-increased-mental-health

[2] Maslow, A. H. (1954). *Motivation and personality.* Harper.

[3] For example, Gwyneth Paltrow's website, *Goop,* was set up in 2008 and can be found at https://goop.com/whats-goop/.

[4] See, for example, Merisse, T. (2018). *Master your emotions: A practical guide to overcome negativity and better manage your feelings* [Independently published]; Fogg, B. J. (2020). *Tiny habits: The small changes that change everything.* Virgin Books; and Neese, A. (2019). *How to breathe: 25 simple practices for calm, joy, and resilience.* Ten Speed Press.

[5] In a 2008 YouTube video for EmmyTVLegends.org, actor Leonard Nimoy recalls that this phrase was first inserted into the original *Star Trek* series by scriptwriter Theodore Sturgeon, in an episode titled "Amok Time." https://www.youtube.com/watch?v=jmkDOzjfSSY

[6] Ontario Ministry of Education. (2014). *Achieving excellence: A renewed vision for education in Ontario.* Queen's Printer for Ontario.

[7] Hargreaves, A., Shirley, D., Wangia, S., Bacon, C. K., & D'Angelo, M. (2018). *Leading from the middle: Spreading learning, well-being, and identity across Ontario.* Council of Ontario Directors of Education.

[8] Ontario Ministry of Education. (2014). *Achieving excellence: A renewed vision for education in Ontario.* Queen's Printer for Ontario.

[9] Ontario Ministry of Education. (2019). Education facts 2019–2020. http://www.edu.gov.on.ca/eng/educationFacts.html

[10] OECD. (2020). *PISA 2018 results (Volume I): What students know and can do.* https://www.oecd-ilibrary.org/sites/5f07c754-en/index.html?itemId=/content/publication/5f07c754-en

[11] Campbell, C. (2020). Educational equity in Canada: The case of Ontario's strategies and actions to advance excellence and equity for students. *School Leadership & Management*; Hargreaves, A., & Shirley, D. L. (2020). Leading from the middle: Its nature, origins, and importance. *Journal of Professional Capital and Community, 5*(1), 92–114.

[12] OECD. (2020). *PISA 2018 results (Volume I): What students know and can do.* https://www.oecd-ilibrary.org/sites/5f07c754-en/index.html?itemId=/content/publication/5f07c754-en

[13] See Van Pelt, D., & Macleod, A. (2017, June 27). More parents turning away from public school system. *Toronto Sun.* https://torontosun.com/2017/06/27/more-parents-turning-away-from-public-school-system; Fullan, M., & Rincón-Gallardo, S. (2016). Developing high-quality public education in Canada: The case of Ontario, in F. Adamson, B. Astrand, & L. Darling-Hammond (Eds.). *Global education reform: How privatization and public investment influence education outcomes.* Routledge.

[14] Hargreaves, A. (2020). Large-scale assessments and their effects: The case of mid-stakes tests in Ontario. *Journal of Educational Change, 21,* 393–420.

[15] Campbell, C. (2020). Educational equity in Canada: The case of Ontario's strategies and actions to advance excellence and equity for students. *School Leadership & Management.*

[16] Ontario Ministry of Education. (2014). *Achieving excellence: A renewed vision for education in Ontario.* Queen's Printer for Ontario, note 7, p. 1.

[17] For the technical report of our research, see Hargreaves, A., Shirley, D., Wangia, S., Bacon, C. K., & D'Angelo, M. (2018). *Leading from the middle: Spreading learning, well-being, and identity across Ontario.* Council of Ontario Directors of Education.

[18] Sigalos, M. (2020, November 10). Biden's economic recovery plan, called *Build Back Better,* would spend more than $7.3 trillion and invest in green infrastructure, health care, and more. CNBC. https://www .cnbc.com/2020/11/10/president-elect-joe-bidens-plan-for-the-economy-jobs-and-covid-19-.html

[19] Green, E. L. (2020, July 13). DeVos abandons a lifetime of local advocacy to demand schools reopen. *New York Times.* https://www.nytimes.com/2020/07/13/us/politics/betsy-devos-schools-coronavirus .html; Coughlan, S. (2020, June 29). Penalty fines for missing school next term. BBC. https://www .bbc.com/news/education-53221741

[20] Christakis, N. A. (2020). *Apollo's arrow: The profound and enduring impact of coronavirus on the way we live.* Little, Brown, Spark.

[21] World Health Organization Constitution. https://www.who.int/about/governance/constitution

[22] America's Promise Alliance. (2020). The state of young people during COVID-19: Findings from a nationally representative survey of high school youth. https://www.americaspromise.org/sites /default/files/d8/YouthDuringCOVID_FINAL%20%281%29.pdf

[23] Biesta, G. J. J. (2010). *Good education in an age of measurement: Ethics, politics, democracy.* Routledge.

[24] Delors, J., et al. (1996). *Learning: The treasure within.* Report to UNESCO of the International Commission on Education for the Twenty-First Century. UNESCO.

[25] Faure, E., et al., International Commission on the Development of Education. (1972). *Learning to be: The world of education today and tomorrow.* UNESCO.

[26] Delors, J., et al., (1996). *Learning: The treasure within.* Report to UNESCO of the International Commission on Education for the Twenty-First Century. UNESCO, p. 13.

[27] Ibid., p. 11.

[28] Ibid., pp. 86–98.

[29] Ibid., p. 21.

[30] Ibid., p. 21.

[31] Ibid., p. 20.

[32] Ibid., p. 21.

[33] Fallace, T. D. (2006). The origins of Holocaust education in American public schools. *Holocaust and Genocide Studies, 20*(1), 80–102. The website for Facing History and Ourselves is accessible at https://www.facinghistory.org/about-us.

[34] Strom, M. S. (2003). A work in progress. In S. Totten (Ed.), *Working to make a difference: The personal and pedagogical stories of Holocaust educators across the globe.* Lexington Books, p. 76.

[35] Strom, M. S. (1994). *Facing history and ourselves: Holocaust and human behavior.* Facing History and Ourselves National Foundation, p. xiv.

[36] Green, G. (Writer), & Chomsky, M. J. (Director). (1978). *Holocaust* [TV miniseries]. NBC.

[37] Strom, M. (1994). *Facing history and ourselves: Holocaust and human behavior.* Facing History and Ourselves National Foundation, p. xiv.

[38] Facing History and Ourselves. (2019). *How do we know it works? Researching the impact of Facing History and Ourselves since 1976.*

[39] Ibid.

[40] See https://www.facinghistory.org/about-us

[41] See https://www.facinghistory.org/resource-library/support-teachers-coronavirus-covid-19-outbreak

[42] See www.rootsofempathy.org

[43] See https://rootsofempathy.org/roots-of-empathy/

[44] HundrED organization lists the world's top 100 innovations in education. These include Roots of Empathy. See https://hundred.org/en/innovations/roots-of-empathy

[45] See https://rootsofempathy.org/roots-of-empathy/

[46] Santos, R. G., Chartier, M. J., Whalen, J. C., Chateau, D., & Boyd, L. (2011). Effectiveness of school-based violence prevention for children and youth. *Healthcare Quarterly, 14*(2), 80–91; Schonert-Reichl, K. A., Smith, V., Zaidman-Zait, A., & Hertzman, C. (2012). Promoting children's prosocial behaviours in school: Impact of the "Roots of Empathy" program on the social and emotional competence of school-aged children. *School Mental Health, 4*(1), 1–21; Cain, G., & Carnellor, Y. (2008). Roots of Empathy: A research study on its impact on teachers in Western Australia. *Journal of Student Well-Being, 2*(1), 52–73.

[47] Quoted in an interview with DeCanniere, A. (2014), for *UR Chicago Magazine Online,* January 20. http://www.urchicago.com/interviews/2014/1/20/mary-gordon-from-roots-of-empathy.html

[48] Ibid.

[49] Smith, A. (1809). *The theory of moral sentiments* (12th ed., first published in 1759). Glasgow: R. Chapman.

[50] UNICEF. (2020). *Worlds of influence: Understanding what shapes child well-being in rich countries.* Innocenti Report Card 16.

[51] OECD. (2017). *PISA 2015 results (Volume III): Students' well-being.* https://www.oecd.org/education/pisa-2015-results-volume-iii-9789264273856-en.htm

[52] Hargreaves, A. (2020). Large-scale assessments and their effects: The case of mid-stakes tests in Ontario. *Journal of Educational Change, 21,* 393–420.

[53] Youth Development Committee, Ontario Ministry of Children and Youth Services. (2012). *Stepping stones: A resource on youth development.* Ontario Ministry of Children and Youth Services, pp. 12–13.

[54] Ibid.

[55] Ontario Ministry of Education. (2014). *Achieving excellence: A renewed vision for education in Ontario.* Queen's Printer for Ontario, p. 15.

[56] Boak, A., et al. (2016). *The mental health and well-being of Ontario students, 1991–2015: Detailed OSDUHS findings.* Centre for Addiction and Mental Health.

[57] Ontario Human Rights Commission. (n.d.). *Gender identity and gender expression* [Brochure]. http://www.ohrc.on.ca/en/gender-identity-and-gender-expression-brochure

[58] Ontario Ministry of Education. (2014). *Achieving excellence: A renewed vision for education in Ontario.* Queen's Printer for Ontario, p. 16.

[59] Ibid., p. 12.

[60] Ontario Ministry of Education. (2016). *Well-being in our schools, strength in our society: Deepening our understanding of well-being in Ontario schools and how to support it, in kindergarten to grade 12.* Queen's Printer for Ontario, p. 6.

[61] Ibid., p. 7.

[62] Ibid., p. 7.

[63] Ontario's well-being framework and affiliated documents and reports have been removed from the ensuing Conservative government's Ministry of Education website.

[64] Edmonds, R. (1979). Effective schools for the urban poor. *Educational Leadership, 37*(1): 15–18, 20–24; Rutter, M., Maughan, B., Mortimore, P., & Ouston, J. (1979). *Fifteen thousand hours: Secondary schools and their effects on children.* Open Books.

[65] Centers for Disease Control and Prevention. (n.d.). Health-related quality of life: Well-being concepts. https://www.cdc.gov/hrqol/wellbeing.htm

[66] ASCD. (2018). *The Learning Compact renewed: Whole child for the whole world,* p. 28.

[67] Lewin, K. (1943). Psychology and the process of group living. *Journal of Social Psychology, 17*(1), 113–131.

[68] Maslow, A. H. (1943). A theory of human motivation. *Psychological Review, 50*(4), 370–396.

[69] Maslow, A. H. (1970). *Religions, values, and peak experiences.* Penguin.

[70] Maslow, A. H. (1982). In R. J. Lowery (Ed.) & J. Freedman (Abridger), *The journals of A. H. Maslow.* Lewis, p. 204.

[71] Maslow, A. H. (1969). The farther reaches of human nature. *Journal of Transpersonal Psychology, 1*(1), p. 4.

[72] Maslow, A. H. (1979). In R. J. Lowery (Ed.). *The journals of A. H. Maslow, Volumes 1–2.* Brooks/Cole, p. 799.

[73] Blackstock, C. (2011). The emergence of the breath of life theory. *Journal of Social Work Values and Ethics, 8*(1), 1–16; see also Blackstock, C. (2019, June). Revisiting the breath of life theory, *British Journal of Social Work, 49*(4), 854–859.

[74] Seligman, M. E. P. (1975). Learned helplessness. *Annual Review of Medicine, 23*(1), 407–412.

[75] Seligman M. E. P. (2002). *Authentic happiness: Using the new positive psychology to realize your potential for lasting fulfillment.* Free Press.

[76] Maslow, A. H. (1968). *Toward a psychology of being.* D. Van Nostrand.

[77] Seligman, M. E. P. (2002). *Authentic happiness: Using the new positive psychology to realize your potential for lasting fulfillment.* Free Press, p. 128.

[78] Seligman, M. E. P. (2011). *Flourish: A visionary new understanding of happiness and well-being.* Atria, p. 89.

[79] The interaction between Martin Seligman and Prime Minister Cameron, its context and consequences, is reported in C. Cederström & A. Spicer, (2015), *The wellness syndrome,* Polity Press, pp. 75–80.

[80] Csikszentmihalyi, M. (1975). *Beyond boredom and anxiety: Experiencing flow in work and play.* Jossey Bass; Csikszentmihalyi, M. (1990). *Flow: The psychology of optimal experience.* Harper & Row.

[81] Seligman, M. E. P. (2011). *Flourish: A visionary new understanding of happiness and well-being.* Atria, pp. 237–241.

[82] Adler, A. (2016). Teaching well-being increases academic performance: Evidence from Bhutan, Mexico, and Peru. University of Pennsylvania ScholarlyCommons. https://repository.upenn.edu/edissertations/1572/

[83] The website for CASEL can be retrieved at https://casel.org.

[84] See Goleman, D. (1995). *Emotional intelligence: Why it can matter more than IQ.* Bantam Books; Goleman, D. (1998). *Working with emotional intelligence.* Bantam Books; Goleman, D., Boyatzis, R., & McKee, A. (1995). *Primal leadership: Learning to lead with emotional intelligence.* Harvard Business Review Press.

[85] The core competencies are described on the CASEL website. https://casel.org/what-is-sel/

[86] See https://casel.org/what-is-sel/

[87] See https://casel.org/impact/

[88] See https://casel.org/collaborative-state-initiative/

[89] Rivera, J. (Producer), & Docter, P. H. (Director). (2015). *Inside out* [Film]. Pixar Animation Studios.

[90] Keltner, D. (2009). *Born to be good: The science of a meaningful life.* Norton.

[91] Darwin, C. (1872). *The expression of the emotions in man and animals.* John Murray.

[92] Kuypers, L. (2011). *The zones of regulation: A curriculum designed to foster self-regulation and emotional control.* Think Social Publishing.

[93] Dweck, C. S. (2006). *Mindset: The new psychology of success.* Ballantine; Dweck, C. S. (2014). *The power of believing you can improve* [TED Talk]. https://www.ted.com/talks/carol_dweck_the_power_of_believing_that_you_can_improve

[94] See https://yidanprize.org/the-prize/overview/.

[95] Dweck, C. S. (2006). *Mindset: The new psychology of success.* Ballantine, p. 7.

[96] Ibid., p. 7.

[97] Ibid., p. 75.

[98] Ibid., p. 73.

[99] Dion, C. (Performer), & Leff, A., Pollack, M., Perloff-Giles, N., & Koehike, D. (Writers). (2019). *Imperfections* [Song]. Columbia Records.

[100] Dweck, C. S. (2006). *Mindset: The new psychology of success.* Ballantine, p. 74.

[101] Ibid., p. ix.

[102] Ibid., p. 195.

[103] Ibid., p. 17.

[104] French, R. P. (2016). The fuzziness of mindsets: Divergent conceptualizations and characterizations of mindset theory and praxis. *International Journal of Organizational Analysis, 24*(4), 673–691.

[105] Quoted in Dickens, J. (2015, June 18). Carol Dweck says mindset is not "a tool to make children feel good." *Schools Week.* https://schoolsweek.co.uk/why-mindset-is-not-a-tool-to-make-children-feel-good

[106] Dweck, C. (2015, September 22). Carol Dweck revisits the "growth mindset." *Education Week.* https://www.edweek.org/leadership/opinion-carol-dweck-revisits-the-growth-mindset/2015/09

[107] Farrarons, E. (2016). *Moments of mindfulness: Anti-stress coloring and activities for busy people.* The Experiment.

[108] Retrievable from https://books.google.com/ngrams/graph?content=mindfulness&year_start=1950&year_end=2005&corpus=15&smoothing=3

[109] See ramdass.org/about-ram-dass

[110] Ram Dass. (1978). *Be here now.* Harmony.

[111] Nhat Hanh, T. (1998). *Interbeing: Fourteen guidelines for engaged Buddhism.* Parallax Press.

[112] Nhat Hanh, T. (1975). *The miracle of mindfulness.* Beacon Press, p. 41.

[113] Nhat Hanh, T. (1998). *Interbeing: Fourteen guidelines for engaged Buddhism.* Parallax Press, p. 17.

[114] Maslow, A. H. (1971) *The farther reaches of human nature.* Viking.

[115] Kabat-Zinn, J. (2005). *Full catastrophe living: Using the wisdom of your body and mind to face stress, pain, and illness.* Delta.

[116] Kabat-Zinn, J., et al. (1998). Influence of a mindfulness meditation-based stress reduction intervention on rate of skin clearing in patients with moderate to severe psoriasis undergoing phototherapy (UVB) and photochemotherapy (PUVA). *Psychosomatic Medicine, 60*(5), 625–632.

[117] Davidson, R. J., & Lutz, A. (2008). Buddha's brain: Neuroplasticity and meditation. *IEEE Signal Processing Magazine, 25*(1). https://www.ncbi.nlm.nih.gov/pmc/articles/PMC2944261/

[118] Shirley, D., & MacDonald, E. (2016). *The mindful teacher* (2nd ed.). Teachers College Press.

[119] Hassed, C., & Chambers, R. (2015). *Mindful learning: Reduce stress and improve brain performance for effective learning*. Shambhala; Jennings, P. A. (2015). *Mindfulness for teachers: Simple skills for peace and productivity in the classroom*. Norton; Rechtschaffen, D. (2014). *The way of mindful education: Cultivating well-being in teachers and students*. Norton.

[120] Quote retrieved from www.mindfulschools.org.

[121] Flook, L., Goldberg, S. B., Pinger, L., & Davidson, R. J. (2015). Promoting prosocial behavior and self-regulatory skills in preschool children through a mindfulness-based kindness curriculum. *Developmental Psychology, 51*(1), 44–51, p. 44.

[122] Flook, L., et al. (2010) Effects of mindful awareness practices on executive functions in elementary school children. *Journal of Applied School Psychology, 26*(1), 70–95, p. 70.

[123] Quach, D., Jastrowski Mano, K., & Alexander, K. (2015). A randomized control trial examining the effect of mindfulness meditation on working memory capacity of adolescents. *Journal of Adolescent Health, 58*(5), 489–496, pp. 493–494.

[124] Department for Education. (2019, February 4). One of the largest mental health trials launches in schools. https://www.gov.uk/government/news/one-of-the-largest-mental-health-trials-launches-in-schools

[125] Shirley, D., & MacDonald, E. (2016). *The mindful teacher* (2nd ed.). Teachers College Press.

[126] Morcum, L. A. (2017). Indigenous holistic education in philosophy and practice. *Foro de educacion, 15*(23), 121–138.

[127] Dewey, J. (1916/2013). *Democracy and education: An introduction to the philosophy of education*. CreateSpace, p. 46.

[128] Gupta, U. D. (Ed.). (2009). *The Oxford India Tagore: Selected writings on education and nationalism*. Oxford University Press.

[129] Montessori, M. (1912/1964). *The Montessori method*. Schocken Books.

[130] Lilley, I. M. (Ed.). (1967). *Friedrich Froebel: A selection from his writings*. Cambridge University Press.

[131] For more on the World Education Fellowship, go to http://wef-international.org/about.

[132] Brehony, K. J. (2004). A new education for a new era: The contribution of the conferences of the New Education Fellowship to the disciplinary field of education 1921–1938. *Paedagogica Historica, 40*(5–6), 733–755.

[133] Berman, P., & McLaughlin, M. W. (1978). *Federal programs supporting educational change: Implementing and sustaining innovations (Vol. III)*. RAND.

[134] Honig, M. I. (2004). Where's the "up" in bottom-up reform? *Educational Policy, 18*(4), 527–561.

[135] Mary Hindle, who is now deceased, submitted these quotations to the school in longhand for its centennial in 1999. They are included in a document presented by the school governors to Andy on May 6, 2004, titled *Odd Notes from Childhood*.

[136] In 2004, Andy was invited to lay the foundation stone for the new building at his old school, Spring Hill Community Primary School, which he suggested should be done with his former teacher, Mary Hindle. As a gift, the governors of the school made a collection for him of old records of the school such as class lists, logbook entries, and excerpts from this inspection report.

[137] Central Advisory Council for Education. (1967). *Children and their primary schools (the Plowden Report)* (Vol. 1). HMSO, p. 185.

[138] Ibid.

[139] McInerney, L. (2014, December 2). Feature: Tim Brighouse. *Schoolsweek*. https://schoolsweek.co.uk/tim-brighouse/

[140] Quote retrieved from https://www.wholeeducation.org/ on March 20, 2021.

[141] Quote retrieved from https://www.wholeeducation.org/lawet/ on March 20, 2021.

[142] Ibid.

[143] Quotes retrieved from https://www.wholeeducation.org/braunstone-frith-local-community/ on March 20, 2021.

[144] See Abrams, S. E. (2016). *Education and the commercial mindset*. Harvard University Press; Levinson, M. (2012). *No citizen left behind*. Harvard University Press.

[145] Quote retrieved from ASCD (n.d.), *The whole child approach to education* at http://www.ascd.org/ASCD/pdf/siteASCD/publications/wholechild/WC-One-Pager.pdf on March 20, 2021.

[146] ASCD. (2018). *The Learning Compact renewed: Whole child for the whole world*, p. 6.

[147] Ibid., p. 12.

[148] Ibid., pp. 11–12.

[149] Ibid., pp. 27–41.

[150] ASCD. (2018, March 24). Washington's Hamilton Elementary School named winner of 2018 Vision in Action: The Whole Child Award.

[151] Ibid.

[152] ASCD. (2017, March 25). Arkansas's Butterfield Middle School named 2017 Vision in Action winner: The Whole Child Award.

[153] See Brighouse, T. (2008). Sir Alec Clegg. *Education 3–13, 36*(2), 103–108.

[154] Clarkson, K. (Performer), & busbe & Geringas, A. (Writers). (2012). *Dark side* [Song]. RCA.

[155] Mayo, E. (1933). *The human problems of an industrial civilization.* Macmillan.

[156] Taylor, F. W. (1911). *The principles of scientific management.* Harper & Brothers.

[157] Roethlisberger, F. J., & Dickson, W. J. (1961). *Management and the worker: An account of a research program conducted by the Western Electric Company, Hawthorne Works, Chicago.* Harvard University Press.

[158] Rosenzweig, P. (2007). *The halo effect . . . and the eight other business delusions that deceive managers.* Free Press.

[159] Davies, W. (2016). *The happiness industry: How the government and big business sold us well-being.* Verso.

[160] The following paragraphs draw on Davies, W. (2016). *The happiness industry: How the government and big business sold us well-being.* Verso; and Cederström, C., & Spicer, A. (2015). *The wellness syndrome.* Polity Press.

[161] Cederström, C., & Spicer, A. (2015). *The wellness syndrome.* Polity Press, pp. 75–80.

[162] Davies, W. (2016). *The happiness industry: How the government and big business sold us well-being.* Verso, p. 11.

[163] Cederström, C., & Spicer, A. (2015). *The wellness syndrome.* Polity Press, p. 133.

[164] Berliner, D. (2013, September). Effects of inequality and poverty vs. teachers and schooling on America's youth. *Teachers College Record, 115*(12), 1–26; Cook, W. (2013). *How intake and other external factors affect school performance.* Research and Information on State Education (The RISE Trust). http://www.risetrust.org.uk/pdfs/EReview-4.pdf

[165] See Fineman, S. (1993). Organizations as emotional arenas. In S. Fineman (Ed.), *Emotions in organizations.* Sage. Also, Matthews, G., Zeidner, M., & Roberts, R. D. (Eds.). (2004). *Emotional intelligence: Science and myth.* MIT Press.

[166] Abolitionist Teaching Network. (2020). *Guide for racial justice and abolitionist social and emotional learning.* https://abolitionistteachingnetwork.org/guide

[167] Ibid.

[168] See https://karanga.org/

[169] See Kohn, A. (2015). The "mindset" mindset: What we miss by focusing on kids' attitudes. https://www.alfiekohn.org/article/mindset/

[170] Dweck, quoted in Gross-Loh, C. (2016, December 16). How praise became a consolation prize: Helping children confront challenges requires a more nuanced understanding of the "growth mindset." *The Atlantic.* https://www.theatlantic.com/education/archive/2016/12/how-praise-became-a-consolation-prize/510845/

[171] Ris, E. (2016, May 10). The problem with teaching "grit" to poor kids? They already have it. Here's what they really need. *Washington Post.* https://www.washingtonpost.com/news/answer-sheet/wp/2016/05/10/the-problem-with-teaching-grit-to-poor-kids-they-already-have-it-heres-what-they-really-need/

[172] Sanyaolu, A., Okori, C., Qi, X., Locke, J., & Rehman, S. (2019). Childhood and adolescent obesity in the United States: A public health concern. *Global Pediatric Health, 6.* https://www.ncbi.nlm.nih.gov/pmc/articles/PMC6887808/

[173] Fuhrman, J. (2018). The hidden dangers of fast and processed food. *American Journal of Lifestyle Medicine, 12*(5), 375–381.

[174] For evidence from the World Bank and UNESCO, see Psacharopoulos, G., Rojas, C., & Velez, E. (1992). *Achievement evaluation of Colombia's Escuela Nueva: Is multigrade the answer?* Policy Research Working Papers. http://documents.worldbank.org/curated/en/887031468770448877/pdf/multi-page.pdf; and Cassasus, J. et al. (2000). *First international comparative study of language, mathematics, and associated factors for students in the third and fourth grade of primary school, 2nd report.* Latin American Laboratory for Assessment of Quality in Education. http://unesdoc.unesco.org/images/0012/001231/123143eo.pdf. Vicky Colbert is the recipient of the $1 million 2013 WISE Prize for Education Laureate and the $4 million 2017 Yidan Prize for Education Development. https://yidanprize.org/global-community/laureates/ms-vicky-colbert/

[175] Baumeister, R. F., Campbell, J. D., Krueger, J. I., & Vohs, K. D. (2003). Does high self-esteem cause better performance, interpersonal success, happiness, or healthier lifestyles? *Psychological Science in the Public Interest, 4*(1), 1–44.

[176] Ibid. Also Baumeister, R. F., & Vohs, K. D. (2018). Revisiting our reappraisal of the (surprisingly few) benefits of high self-esteem. *Perspectives on Psychological Science, 13*(2), 137–140.

[177] Cederström, C., & Spicer, A. (2015). *The wellness syndrome.* Polity Press, p. 133.

[178] Freud, S. (2008) On narcissism: An introduction. In J. Sandler, E. S. Person, & P. Fonagy (Eds.). *Freud's "On narcissism: An introduction."* Routledge, pp. 1–32.

[179] American Psychiatric Association. (2013). *Diagnostic and statistical manual of mental disorders* (4th ed.), p. 714.

[180] Lasch, C. (1979). *The culture of narcissism: American life in an age of diminishing expectations.* Norton.

[181] Kluger, J. (2014). *The narcissist next door: Understanding the monster in your family, in your office, in your bed—in your world.* Riverhead Books, p. 13.

[182] Storr, W. (2018). *Selfie: How we became so self-obsessed and what it's doing to us.* Abrams Press.

[183] This section draws on Storr, W. (2018). *Selfie: How we became so self-obsessed and what it's doing to us.* Abrams Press.

[184] Branden, N. (1969). *The psychology of self-esteem.* Bantam.

[185] Baumeister, R. F., et al. (2003). Does high self-esteem cause better performance, interpersonal success, happiness, or healthier lifestyles? *Psychological Science in the Public Interest, 4*(1), 1–44.

[186] Baumeister, R. F., & Vohs, K. D. (2001). Narcissism as addiction to esteem. *Psychological Inquiry, 12*(4), 206–210.

[187] Twenge, J. M., & Campbell, W. K. (2009). *The narcissism epidemic: Living in the age of entitlement.* Simon & Schuster.

[188] Ibid., p. 14.

[189] Ibid., p. 30.

[190] Papageorgiou, K. A., Denovan, A., & Dagnall, N. (2018). The positive effect of narcissism on depressive symptoms through mental toughness: Narcissism may be a dark trait but it does help with seeing the world less grey. *European Psychiatry, 55*, 74–79.

[191] St. John of the Cross. (2003). *Dark night of the soul.* Dover Press. (The Spanish language original was published in 1618.)

[192] Sameer, C. (2021, March 16). Are we raising the "strawberry generation"—entitled and rude brats? *The Asian Parent.* https://www.asiaone.com/lifestyle/are-we-raising-strawberry-generation-entitled-and-rude-brats

[193] See Shirley, D., & Hargreaves, A. (2021). *Five paths of student engagement: Blazing the trail to learning and success.* Solution Tree.

[194] Campbell, D. T. (1975). Assessing the impact of planned social change. In G. M. Lyons (Ed.), *Social research and public policies: The Dartmouth/OECD conference.* Public Affairs Center, Dartmouth College, p. 35.

[195] The concept of mid-stakes testing was first introduced in relation to assessment policies in South Korea, by Lee, J., & Kang, C. (2019). A litmus test of school accountability policy effects in Korea: Cross-validating high-stakes test results for academic excellence and equity. *Asia Pacific Journal of Education, 39*(4), 517–531.

[196] Wilson, R., Piccoli, A., Hargreaves, A., Ng, P. T., & Sahlberg, P. (2021). *Putting students first: Moving on from NAPLAN to a new educational assessment system (The Gonski Institute Policy Paper #2-2021).* Sydney: UNSW Gonski Institute.

[197] For extended accounts of Ontario's large-scale assessments, see Hargreaves, A. (2020). Large-scale assessments and their effects: The case of mid-stakes tests in Ontario. *Journal of Educational Change, 21,* 393–420; and Shirley, D., & Hargreaves, A. (2021). *Five paths of student engagement: Blazing the trail to learning and success.* Solution Tree.

[198] Fullan, M. (2012, February). *Lead the change series: Q&A with Michael Fullan.* AERA Educational Change Special Interest Group, Issue 16. https://michaelfullan.ca/wp-content/uploads/2016/06/13514675730.pdf

[199] Hargreaves, A. (2020). Large-scale assessments and their effects: The case of mid-stakes tests in Ontario. *Journal of Educational Change, 21,* 393–420; Shirley, D., & Hargreaves, A. (2021). *Five paths of student engagement: Blazing the trail to learning and success.* Solution Tree.

[200] Campbell, C., et al. (2018). *Ontario: A learning province.* Queen's Printer.

[201] Strauss, V. (2020, June 21). It looks like the beginning of the end of America's obsession with student standardized tests. *Washington Post.* https://www.washingtonpost.com/education/2020/06/21/it-looks-like-beginning-end-americas-obsession-with-student-standardized-tests/

[202] Ibid.

[203] Kelley, J. P. (2020, May 30). Ohio House passes bill to further limit state school testing. *Dayton Daily News*. https://www.daytondailynews.com/news/local-education/ohio-house-passes-bill-further-limit -state-school-testing/HJTZxlgVcIMBEPPht8gYJL/

[204] Hubler, S. (2020, May 21). University of California will end use of SAT and ACT in admissions. *New York Times*. https://www.nytimes.com/2020/05/21/us/university-california-sat-act.html

[205] Ravitch, D. (2020). *Slaying Goliath: The passionate resistance to privatization and the fight to save America's public schools*. Knopf, pp. 89–114.

[206] Tucker, M. (2020, June 26). COVID-19 and our schools: The real challenge. National Center on Education and the Economy. https://ncee.org/2020/06/covid-19-and-our-schools-the-real-challenge/

[207] Finn, C. (2020, November 25). How badly has the pandemic hurt K–12 learning? Let state testing in the spring tell us. *Washington Post*. https://www.washingtonpost.com/opinions/2020/11/25/how-badly -has-pandemic-hurt-k-12-learning-let-state-testing-spring-tell-us/

[208] Editorial Board. (2021, January 8). Why we shouldn't abandon student testing this spring. *Washington Post*. https://www.washingtonpost.com/opinions/why-we-shouldnt-abandon-student-testing-this -spring/2021/01/08/839eb860-4ed4-11eb-83e3-322644d82356_story.html

[209] Jimenez, L. (2020, September 10). Student assessment during COVID-19. *Center for American Progress*. https://www.americanprogress.org/issues/education-k-12/reports/2020/09/10/490209/student -assessment-covid-19/

[210] Strauss, V. (2021, March 24). Education Secretary Cardona stands firm on standardized testing mandate amid criticism. *Washington Post*. https://www.washingtonpost.com/education/2021/03/24/cardona -stands-firm-on-standardized-testing-mandate-amid-criticism/

[211] McGaw, B., Louden, W., & Wyatt-Smith, C. (2020). *NAPLAN review: Final report*. New South Wales Department of Education.

[212] Carey, A. (2020, August 28). Push for NAPLAN to be expanded into new test for all students. *Sydney Morning Herald*. https://www.smh.com.au/education/push-for-naplan-to-be-expanded-into-new-test -for-all-students-20200828-p55q9v.html

[213] Sahlberg, P. (2021, January 5). The epidemic Australia is failing to control. *Sydney Morning Herald*. https://www.smh.com.au/education/the-epidemic-australia-is-failing-to-control-20201229-p56qq3.html

[214] See Ravitch, D. (2020). *Slaying Goliath: The passionate resistance to privatization and the fight to save America's public schools*. Knopf; and Sahlberg, P. (2021). *Finnish lessons 3.0: What can the world learn from educational change in Finland?* Teachers College Press.

[215] Burkeman, O. (2012). *The antidote: Happiness for people who can't stand positive thinking*. Faber & Faber.

[216] Davies, W. (2016). *The happiness industry: How the government and big business sold us well-being*. Verso.

[217] Burkeman, O. (2012). *The antidote: Happiness for people who can't stand positive thinking*. Faber & Faber, p. 8.

[218] Coward, H. (2008). *The perfectibility of human nature in eastern and western thought*. SUNY Press; Koltko-Rivera, M. E. (2006). Rediscovering the later version of Maslow's hierarchy of needs: Self-transcendence and opportunities for theory, research, and unification. *Review of General Psychology, 10*(4), 302–317; Blackstock, C. (2011). The emergence of the breath of life theory. *Journal of Social Work Values and Ethics, 8*(1), 1–16.

[219] See Li, J. (2012). *Cultural foundations of learning: East and west*. Cambridge University Press.

[220] Dickens, C. (1854/2016). *Hard times*. MacMillan, p. 11.

[221] Raworth, K. (2017). *Doughnut economics: Seven ways to think like a 21st century economist*. Chelsea Green.

[222] Saez, E., & Zucman, G. (2014). *Wealth inequality in the United States since 1913: Evidence from capitalized income tax data*. Working Paper 20625. National Bureau of Economic Research.

[223] Mazzucato, M. (2018). *The value of everything: Making and taking in the global economy*. Public Affairs.

[224] Eaton, G. (2020, May 4). Top economists warn the UK not to repeat austerity after the COVID-19 crisis. *The New Statesman*. https://www.newstatesman.com/politics/economy/2020/05/top -economists-warn-uk-not-repeat-austerity-after-covid-19-crisis

[225] Wilkinson, R., & Pickett, K. (2009). *The spirit level: Why greater equality makes societies stronger*. Bloomsbury Publishing.

[226] Booth, R., & Butler, P. (2018, November 16). UK austerity has inflicted "great misery" on citizens, UN says. *The Guardian*. www.theguardian.com/society/2018/nov/16/uk-austerity-has-inflicted-great -misery-on-citizens-un-says

[227] See Cederström, C., & Spicer, A. (2015). *The wellness syndrome*. Polity Press, pp. 75–80.

[228] Stein, J. (2018, June 6). An explosive U.N. report shows America's safety net was failing before Trump's election. *Washington Post*. https://www.washingtonpost.com/news/wonk/wp/2018/06/06/an -explosive-un-report-shows-americas-safety-net-was-failing-before-trumps-election/

[229] See Sahlberg, P. (2021). *Finnish lessons 3.0: What can the world learn from educational change in Finland?* Teachers College Press.

[230] For accounts of how GERM-like strategies spread in the United States, see Hargreaves, A., & Shirley, D. (2009) *The fourth way: The inspiring future for educational change*. Corwin; and Hargreaves, A., & Shirley, D. (2012). *The global fourth way: The quest for educational excellence*. Corwin.

[231] Hargreaves, A., & Shirley, D. (2012). *The global fourth way: The quest for educational excellence*. Corwin.

[232] See Klees, S. J., et al. (2020). The World Bank's SABER: A critical analysis. *Comparative Education Review, 64*(1). https://www.journals.uchicago.edu/doi/full/10.1086/706757

[233] OECD. (2000). *Measuring student knowledge and skills: The PISA assessment of reading, mathematical and scientific literacy.*

[234] Robinson, K., & Aronica, L. (2018). *You, your child and school: Navigate your way to the best education*. Penguin Books.

[235] OECD. (2017). *PISA 2015 results: Student well-being.*

[236] Han, B.-C. (2015). *The burnout society*. Stanford University Press.

[237] Bennis, W., & Nanus, B. (1985). *Leaders: The strategies for taking charge*. HarperCollins; US Army Heritage & Education Center. (2019, May 7). Who first originated the term VUCA (Volatility, Uncertainty, Complexity and Ambiguity)? https://usawc.libanswers.com/faq/84869; Bennett, N., & Lemoine, G. J. (2014, January–February). What VUCA really means for you. *Harvard Business Review*. https://hbr.org/2014/01/what-vuca-really-means-for-you

[238] Bon Jovi, J. (Writer & Performer). (2020). *Limitless* [Song]. Island Records.

[239] Lavis, P., & Robson, C. (2015). *Promoting children and young people's emotional health and wellbeing: A whole school and college approach*. Public Health England, p. 6.

[240] Sirin, S. R., & Rogers-Sirin, L. (2015). *The educational and mental health needs of Syrian refugee children*. Migration Policy Institute.

[241] Bunn, C., Cottman, M. H., Gaines, P., Charles, N., & Harriston, K. (2021). *Say their names: How Black Lives Matter came to America*. Grand Central Publishing; Maqbool, A. (2020, July 10). Black Lives Matter: From social media post to global movement. BBC News. https://www.bbc.com/news/world -us-canada-53273381

[242] Santora, M. (2020, July 7). London police stop star athletes, setting off racial profiling debate. *New York Times*. https://www.nytimes.com/2020/07/07/world/europe/uk-police-bianca-williams-racial-profiling .html; Dodd, V. (2020, August 18). Black Met inspector stopped by police while driving home from work. *The Guardian*. https://www.theguardian.com/uk-news/2020/aug/18/black-met-police-inspector -stopped-by-officers-while-driving-home-from-work

[243] Case, A., & Deaton, A. (2020). *Deaths of despair and the future of capitalism*. Princeton University Press; Case, A., & Deaton, A. (2017, March 17). *Mortality and morbidity in the 21st century*. Brookings Papers on Economic Activity. Brookings Institution. https://www.brookings.edu/ wp-content/uploads/2017/08/casetextsp17bpea.pdf

[244] Mattinson, D. (2020). *Beyond the red wall: Why Labour lost, how the Conservatives won and what will happen next*. Biteback; and Wuthnow, R. (2018). *The left behind: Decline and rage in rural America*. Princeton University Press.

[245] PA Media. (2020, August 27). A third of girls say they won't post selfies without enhancement. *The Guardian*. https://www.theguardian.com/society/2020/aug/27/a-third-of-girls-say-they-wont-post -selfies-without-enhancement

[246] Twenge, J. M. (2017). *iGen: Why today's super-connected kids are growing up less rebellious, more tolerant, less happy—and completely unprepared for adulthood*. Simon & Schuster.

[247] Geddes, L., & Marsh, S. (2021, January 22). Concerns grow for children's health as screen times soar during COVID crisis. *The Guardian*. https://www.theguardian.com/world/2021/jan/22/children -health-screen-times-covid-crisis-sleep-eyesight-problems-digital-devices; McGinn, D. (2020, July 20). Parents struggle to wean children off "perfect storm" of screen time during pandemic. *Globe and Mail*. https://www.theglobeandmail.com/canada/article-parents-struggle-to-wean-children-off-perfect

-storm-of-screen-time/; Ponti, M. (2019, June 6). Digital media: Promoting healthy screen use in school-aged children and adolescents. *Paediatric Child Health, 24*(6), 402–408. https://www.cps.ca /en/documents/position/digital-media

[248] Wolf, M. (2020, August 24). Screen-based online learning will change kids' brains. Are we ready for that? *The Guardian.* https://www.theguardian.com/commentisfree/2020/aug/24/deep-literacy -technology-child-development-reading-skills

[249] Nature Canada. (2018, November 23). *Screen time vs green time: The health impacts of too much screen time.* https://naturecanada.ca/enjoy-nature/for-children/screen-time-vs-green-time/

[250] Schwarzfischer, P., et al. (2020). Effects of screen time and playing outside on anthropometric measures in preschool aged children. *PLoS ONE, 15*(3); Moore, S. A., et al. (2020, July 6). Impact of the COVID-19 virus outbreak on movement and play behaviours of Canadian children and youth: A national survey. *International Journal of Behavioral Nutrition and Physical Activity, 17*(85); Hinkley, T., Brown, H., Carson, V., & Teychenne, M. (2018). Cross sectional associations of screen time and outdoor play with social skills in preschool children. *PlOS one, 13*(4), e0193700.

[251] Hobbs, T. (2019). Three decades of school shootings: An analysis. *Wall Street Journal.* https://www .wsj.com/graphics/school-shooters-similarities/

[252] Booth, R. (2019, February 5). Anxiety on rise among the young in social media age. *The Guardian.* https://www.theguardian.com/society/2019/feb/05/youth-unhappiness-uk-doubles-in-past-10-years

[253] Whang, O. (2020, October 28). Greta Thunberg reflects on living through multiple crises in a "post-truth society." *National Geographic.* https://www.nationalgeographic.com/environment/article /greta-thunberg-reflects-on-living-through-multiple-crises-post-truth-society

[254] UNESCO. (2020). *COVID-19 impact on education.* https://en.unesco.org/covid19/educationresponse

[255] World Bank. (2021, January 22). *Urgent, effective action required to quell the impact of COVID-19 on education worldwide.* https://www.worldbank.org/en/news/immersive-story/2021/01/22/urgent -effective-action-required-to-quell-the-impact-of-covid-19-on-education-worldwide; OECD. (2020, June 29). *Education and COVID-19: Focusing on the long-term impact of school closures.* https://www .oecd.org/coronavirus/policy-responses/education-and-covid-19-focusing-on-the-long-term-impact -of-school-closures-2cea926e/

[256] Dorn, E., Hancock, B., Sarakatsannis, J., & Viruleg, E. (2020, June 1). COVID-19 and student learning in the United States: The hurt could last a lifetime. McKinsey & Co. https://www.mckinsey.com /industries/public-and-social-sector/our-insights/covid-19-and-student-learning-in-the-united-states -the-hurt-could-last-a-lifetime; UNESCO Office Santiago and Regional Bureau for Education in Latin America and the Caribbean & Inter-American Development Bank. (2021, January 20). *Reopening schools in Latin America and the Caribbean: Key points, challenges, and dilemmas to plan a safe return to in-person classes.* UNESCO.

[257] Balingit, M. (2021, February 25). Unprecedented numbers of students have disappeared during the pandemic. Schools are working harder than ever to find them. *Washington Post.* https://www .washingtonpost.com/education/pandemic-schools-students-missing/2021/02/25/f0b27262-5ce8 -11eb-a976-bad6431e03e2_story.html

[258] Whitley, J., et al. (2020, November 5). Diversity via distance: Lessons learned from families supporting students with special education needs during remote learning. *EdCan Network Magazine.* https:// www.edcan.ca/articles/diversity-via-distance/

[259] Whitley, J. (2020, June 1). Coronavirus: Distance learning poses challenges for some families of children with disabilities. *The Conversation.* https://theconversation.com/coronavirus-distance -learning-poses-challenges-for-some-families-of-children-with-disabilities-136696

[260] UN Women. (2020). *The shadow pandemic: Violence against women during COVID-19.* https://www .unwomen.org/en/news/in-focus/in-focus-gender-equality-in-covid-19-response/violence-against -women-during-covid-19; Owen, B. (2020, October 15). Calls to Canadian domestic violence helplines jump during pandemic. CTV News. https://www.ctvnews.ca/canada/calls-to-canadian -domestic-violence-helplines-jump-during-pandemic-1.5145983; Twohey, M. (2020, April 7). New battle for those on coronavirus front lines: Child custody. *New York Times.* https://www.nytimes .com/2020/04/07/us/coronavirus-child-custody.html

[261] Batty, D. (2020, August 5). Lockdown having "pernicious impact" on LGBT community's mental health. *The Guardian.* https://www.theguardian.com/society/2020/aug/05/lockdown-having-pernicious -impact-on-lgbt-communitys-mental-health

[262] Bloom, B. S. (1956). *Taxonomy of educational objectives: The classification of educational goals.* Longman.

[263] Bintliff, A. V. (2020, September 8). How COVID-19 has influenced teachers' well-being: A new study shows decreases in teacher well-being during the pandemic. *Psychology Today.* https://www.psychologytoday.com/ca/blog/multidimensional-aspects-adolescent-well-being/202009/how-covid-19-has-influenced-teachers-well

[264] Kamenetz, A. (2020, June 29). US pediatricians call for in-person school this fall. NPR. https://www.npr.org/sections/coronavirus-live-updates/2020/06/29/884638999/u-s-pediatricians-call-for-in-person-school-this-fall; Sick Kids. (2020, July 29). COVID-19: Guidance for school re-opening. https://www.sickkids.ca/siteassets/news/news-archive/2020/covid19-recommendations-for-school-reopening-sickkids.pdf

[265] Buck, N. (2020, November 12). Children face a deluge of excess screen time—inside the classroom. *Globe and Mail.* https://www.theglobeandmail.com/opinion/article-children-face-a-deluge-of-excess-screen-time-inside-the-classroom/

[266] Loades, M. E., et al. (2020). Rapid systematic review: The impact of social isolation and loneliness on the mental health of children and adolescents in the context of COVID-19. *Journal of the American Academy of Child and Adolescent Psychiatry, 59*(11), 1218–1239.e3.

[267] Bethune, S. (2014, April). Teen stress rivals that of adults: APA's Stress in America™ survey finds unhealthy behavior in teens, especially during the school year. *American Psychological Association, 45*(4). https://www.apa.org/monitor/2014/04/teen-stress

[268] Press Association. (2017, October 5). Growing social media backlash among young people, survey shows. *The Guardian.* https://www.theguardian.com/media/2017/oct/05/growing-social-media-backlash-among-young-people-survey-shows

[269] Roxby, P. (2020, June 13). Coronavirus social-contact curbs "put adolescents at risk." https://www.bbc.com/news/health-53022369

[270] BBC News. (2020, August 24). Coronavirus: Teens' anxiety levels dropped during pandemic, study finds. https://www.bbc.com/news/uk-53884401

[271] BBC News. (2020, April 20). Coronavirus: Denmark lets young children return to school. https://www.bbc.com/news/world-europe-52291326

[272] Leaders. (2020, July 18). The risks of keeping schools closed far outweigh the benefits. *The Economist.* https://www.economist.com/leaders/2020/07/18/the-risks-of-keeping-schools-closed-far-outweigh-the-benefits

[273] See Green, E. L. (2020, July 13). DeVos abandons a lifetime of local advocacy to demand schools reopen. *New York Times.* https://www.nytimes.com/2020/07/13/us/politics/betsy-devos-schools-coronavirus.html

[274] See Coughlan, S. (2020, June 29). Penalty fines for missing school next term. BBC News. https://www.bbc.com/news/education-53221741

[275] Mahoney, J. (2020, November 1). Students miss out and teachers feel overwhelmed as school boards blend in-person and virtual classes. *Globe and Mail.* https://www.theglobeandmail.com/canada/article-students-miss-out-and-teachers-feel-overwhelmed-as-school-boards-blend/

[276] Baskin, K. (2020, December 30). Your school district's reopening survey. *McSweeney's Internet Tendency.* https://www.mcsweeneys.net/articles/your-school-districts-reopening-survey

[277] Durkheim, É. (1897). *Suicide: A study in sociology* (1951 Ed., J. A. Spaulding & G. Simpson, Trans.). London: Routledge.

[278] Kumar, M. B., & Tjepkema, M. (2019, August 28). Suicide among First Nations people, Métis and Inuit (2011–2016): Findings from the 2011 Canadian Census Health and Environment Cohort (CanCHEC). Statistics Canada. Ottawa, Canada. https://www150.statcan.gc.ca/n1/pub/99-011-x/99-011-x2019001-eng.htm; The Trevor Project. (2020). *National Survey on LGBTQ Youth Mental Health 2020.* https://www.thetrevorproject.org/survey-2020/?section=Introduction; Greenhalgh, S. (2016, December 9). The hidden costs of Asia's high test scores. *The Diplomat.* https://thediplomat.com/2016/12/the-hidden-costs-of-asias-high-test-scores/

[279] Helliwell, J. F., Layard, R., Sachs, J., & De Neve, J.-E. (Eds.). (2020). *World happiness report 2020.* Sustainable Development Solutions Network.

[280] Transparency International. (2020). *Corruption perceptions index 2020.* https://www.transparency.org/en/cpi/2020/index/nzl

[281] The Economist Intelligence Unit. (2021). *Democracy index 2020: In sickness and in health?* London. https://www.eiu.com/n/campaigns/democracy-index-2020/

[282] UNICEF. (2020). *Worlds of influence: Understanding what shapes child well-being in rich countries.* Innocenti Report Card 16.

[283] Wilkinson, R., & Pickett, K. (2009). *The spirit level: Why greater equality makes societies stronger.* Bloomsbury.

[284] Ibid., p. 25.

[285] Godoy, M., & Wood, D. (2020, May 30). What do coronavirus racial disparities look like state by state? NPR. https://www.npr.org/sections/health-shots/2020/05/30/865413079/what-do-coronavirus-racial -disparities-look-like-state-by-state

[286] Campbell, D., & Siddique, K. (2020, June 2). COVID-19 death rate in England higher among BAME people. *The Guardian.* https://www.theguardian.com/world/2020/jun/02/covid-19-death-rate-in -england-higher-among-bame-people

[287] Public Health England. (2020). Beyond the data: Understanding the impact of COVID-19 on BAME groups. https://assets.publishing.service.gov.uk/government/uploads/system/uploads/attachment _data/file/892376/COVID_stakeholder_engagement_synthesis_beyond_the_data.pdf

[288] Case, A., & Deaton, A. (2020). *Deaths of despair and the future of capitalism.* Princeton University Press; Case, A., & Deaton, A. (2017, March 17). *Mortality and morbidity in the 21st century.* Brookings Papers on Economic Activity. Brookings. https://www.brookings.edu/wp-content /uploads/2017/08/casetextsp17bpea.pdf

[289] Wilson, W. J. (1997). *When work disappears: The world of the new urban poor.* Vintage.

[290] Case, A., & Deaton, A. (2020). *Deaths of despair and the future of capitalism.* Princeton University Press, p. 5.

[291] Johns, G. (2012). Presenteeism: A short history and a cautionary tale. In J. Houdmont, S. Leka, & R. R. Sinclair (Eds.). *Contemporary occupational health psychology: Global perspectives on research and practice, Vol. 2* (pp. 204–220). Wiley Blackwell.

[292] Case, A., & Deaton, A. (2020). *Deaths of despair and the future of capitalism.* Princeton University Press, p. 8.

[293] Wilkinson, R., & Pickett, K. (2018). *The inner level: How more equal societies reduce stress, restore sanity, and improve everyone's well-being.* Penguin.

[294] Jones, O. (2011). *Chavs: The demonization of the working class.* London: Verso; Sandel, M. J. (2020). *The tyranny of merit: What's become of the common good?* Farrar, Straus & Giroux.

[295] Edsall, T. B. (2020, December 9). The resentment that never sleeps. *New York Times.* https://www .nytimes.com/2020/12/09/opinion/trump-social-status-resentment.html

[296] Hargreaves, A. (2020). *Moving: A memoir of education and social mobility.* Solution Tree.

[297] Mattinson, D. (2020). *Beyond the red wall: Why Labour lost, how the Conservatives won, and what will happen next.* Biteback.

[298] Martin, L. (Producer), & Edwards, P. (Cinematographer & Editor). (2020, December 1). *Burnley: "Children ripping bags open for food" during pandemic* [Video]. BBC News. https://www.bbc.com /news/av/uk-55133081

[299] Hochschild, A. R. (2016). *Strangers in their own land: Anger and mourning on the American right.* New Press.

[300] Metzl, J. M. (2019). *Dying of whiteness: How the politics of racial resentment is killing America's heartland.* Basic Books.

[301] DuBois, W. E. B. (1975). *Black reconstruction: An essay toward a history of the part Black folk played in the attempt to reconstruct democracy in America: 1860–1880.* Athenaeum, p. 21.

[302] Lammy, D. (2019). Foreword to Williamson, S. (2019). *Fighting for deep social justice.* SSAT (The Schools Network), p. 1.

[303] Ibid., p. 2.

[304] Baker, B. D. (2018). *Educational inequality and school finance: Why money matters for America's schools.* Harvard University Press.

[305] Lee, N. T. (2020, March 2). Bridging digital divides between schools and communities. Brookings. https://www.brookings.edu/research/bridging-digital-divides-between-schools-and-communities/

[306] Wilkinson, R., & Pickett, K. (2009). *The spirit level: Why greater equality makes societies stronger.* Bloomsbury, p. 193.

[307] Davies, R. (2019, March 8). Norway's $1tn wealth fund to divest from oil and gas exploration. *The Guardian.* https://www.theguardian.com/world/2019/mar/08/norways-1tn-wealth-fund-to-divest -from-oil-and-gas-exploration

[308] See, for example, Sahlberg, P. (2021). *Finnish lessons 3.0: What can the world learn from educational change in Finland?* Teachers College Press.

[309] See Hargreaves, A. (2016, March 2). Teachers and professional collaboration: How Sweden has become the ABBA of educational change. Albert Shanker Institute. http://www.shankerinstitute.org/blog /teachers-and-professional-collaboration-how-sweden-has-become-abba-educational-change; and Hjelm, S. (2020, December 31). Vouchers and market-driven schools in Sweden. *Larry Cuban on School Reform and Classroom Practice.* https://larrycuban.wordpress.com/2020/12/31/vouchers -and-market-driven-schools-in-sweden-sara-hjelm/

[310] UNICEF. (2020). *Worlds of influence: Understanding what shapes child well-being in rich countries.* Innocenti Report Card 16, p. 11.

[311] Mandela, N. (1995, May 8). Speech by President Nelson Mandela at the launch of the Nelson Mandela children's fund, Mahlamba'ndlopfu, Pretoria, South Africa.

[312] O'Hara, M. (2014, March 8). Robert Reich: Austerity is a terrible mistake. *The Guardian.* https://www .theguardian.com/society/2014/mar/18/robert-reich-attacks-economic-austerity

[313] Andrew, S. (2020, June 30). The US has 4% of the world's population but 25% of its coronavirus cases. CNN. https://www.cnn.com/2020/06/30/health/us-coronavirus-toll-in-numbers-june-trnd/index.html

[314] Eaton, G. (2020, May 4). Top economists warn the UK not to repeat austerity after the COVID-19 crisis. *The New Statesman.* https://www.newstatesman.com/politics/economy/2020/05/top -economists-warn-uk-not-repeat-austerity-after-covid-19-crisis

[315] Raworth, K. (2017). *Doughnut economics: Seven ways to think like a 21st century economist.* Chelsea Green.

[316] Reich, R. (2020). *The system: Who rigged it, how we fix it.* Knopf.

[317] Ibid., p. 69.

[318] Freeland, C. (2012). *Plutocrats: The rise of the new global super-rich and the fall of everyone else.* Doubleday Canada.

[319] Giridharadas, A. (2019). *Winners take all: The elite charade of changing the world.* Alfred Knopf, pp. 122–123.

[320] See https://www.dictionary.com/browse/prosperity.

[321] Scottish Government. (2020, January 22). *Health and well-being as fundamental as GDP.* https://www .gov.scot/news/health-and-well-being-as-fundamental-as-gdp/

[322] Andy develops this argument in Hargreaves, A. (2020). *Moving: A memoir of education and social mobility.* Solution Tree.

[323] Lynch, K., & Deegan, P. (2020, April 1). Five lasting implications of COVID-19 for Canada and the world. *Globe and Mail.* https://www.theglobeandmail.com/business/commentary/article-five-lasting -implications-of-covid-19-for-canada-and-the-world/

[324] Boushey, H. (2020, October 19). Economic inequality made the US more vulnerable to the pandemic: If core inequalities aren't addressed by American policy-makers, the recovery will be further slowed down. *Policy Options.* https://policyoptions.irpp.org/magazines/october-2020/economic-inequality -made-the-u-s-more-vulnerable-to-the-pandemic/

[325] Boushey, H. (2019). *Unbound: How inequality constricts our economy and what we can do about it.* Harvard University Press, p. 30.

[326] OECD. (2019). *TALIS 2018 results. Volume 1.* Table 1.2.4. "Change in teaching practices from 2013–2018."

[327] Whitley, J. (2020, June 1). Coronavirus: Distance learning poses challenges for some families of children with disabilities. *The Conversation.* https://theconversation.com/coronavirus-distance -learning-poses-challenges-for-some-families-of-children-with-disabilities-136696

[328] Black, S. (2020, September 5). Learning in lockdown: "The largest social experiment we've ever done." *The Guardian.* https://www.theguardian.com/australia-news/2020/sep/06/learning-in-lockdown-the -largest-social-experiment-weve-ever-done

[329] Gouëdard, P., Pont, B., & Viennet, R. (2020). *Education responses to COVID-19: Implementing a way forward.* Working Paper No. 224. Paris: OECD, p. 31. http://www.oecd.org/officialdocuments /publicdisplaydocumentpdf/?cote=EDU/WKP(2020)12&docLanguage=En

[330] Hagerman, M. S., & Kellam, H. (2020). *Learning to teach online: An open educational resource for pre-service teachers.* http://onlineteaching.ca

[331] The original description of this teacher's work is reported in Heintz, A., Hagerman, M. S., Boltz, L. O., & Wolf, L. G. (2017). Teacher awareness and blended instruction practices: Interview research with K–12 teachers. In A. Marcus-Quinn & T. Hourigan (Eds.), *Handbook on digital learning for K–12 schools* (pp. 465–482). Springer.

[332] Alberta Teachers Association. (2020, June). Alberta teachers responding to Coronavirus (COVID-19): Pandemic research study initial report, p. 15. https://www.teachers.ab.ca/COVID-19/2020-School -Re-entry/Pages/Covid-19-Survey.aspx

[333] Miller, S. (2020, October 3). A message from Stuart Miller, director of the Halton School Board. https://hdsb.ca/our-board/Pages/Administration%20and%20Superintendents/Messages-From-Director.aspx. Details passed on by Susan Thrasher and Stuart Miller of the Halton School Board.

[334] Pajalic, A. (2020, July 7). I hated remote teaching during the COVID-19 lockdown. It should never replace the classroom. *The Guardian.* https://www.theguardian.com/commentisfree/2020/jun/08/i-hated-remote-teaching-during-the-covid-19-lockdown-it-should-never-replace-the-classroom

[335] Herold, B., & Kurtz, H. Y. (2020, May 11). Teachers work two hours less per day during COVID-19: 8 key *EdWeek* survey findings. *Education Week.* www.edweek.org/ew/articles/2020/05/11/teachers-work-an-hour-less-per-day.html

[336] Ziebell, N., Acquaro, D., Pearn, C., & Seah, W. T. (2020). *Australian education survey: Examining the impact of COVID-19.* Melbourne, Vic: Melbourne Graduate School of Education. https://education.unimelb.edu.au/__data/assets/pdf_file/0008/3413996/Australian-Education-Survey.pdf

[337] Natanson, H., & Meckler, L. (2020, November 26). Remote school is leaving children sad and angry. *Washington Post.* https://www.washingtonpost.com/education/2020/11/27/remote-learning-emotional-toll/?arc404=true

[338] Biel is quoted in Natanson, H., & Meckler, L. (2020, November 26). Remote school is leaving children sad and angry. *Washington Post.* https://www.washingtonpost.com/education/2020/11/27/remote-learning-emotional-toll/?arc404=true

[339] Barkan, R. (2020, December 30). This year proved once and for all: Screens are no substitute for real life. *The Guardian.* https://www.theguardian.com/commentisfree/2020/dec/30/coronavirus-screens-no-substitute-schools

[340] Willingham, D., & Riley, B. (2020, July 9). Why calls to "reinvent schooling" in response to the pandemic are wrong. *Washington Post.* https://www.washingtonpost.com/education/2020/07/09/why-calls-reinvent-schooling-response-pandemic-are-wrong/

[341] Christakis, E. (2020, December 15). School wasn't so great before COVID, either. *The Atlantic.* https://www.theatlantic.com/magazine/archive/2020/12/school-wasnt-so-great-before-covid-either/616923/

[342] Eisen, L. (Producer, Director, & Writer). (2020). *Kids vs screens: How screens affect our children's development, learning abilities and mental health* [Documentary]. The Nature of Things series. CBC TV.

[343] McGinn, D. (2020, October 29). All that excess screen time parents were told not to worry about at the start of COVID-19? It's time to worry. *Globe and Mail.* https://www.theglobeandmail.com/canada/article-parents-rethink-more-screen-time-for-kids-in-covid-19-pandemic-as/

[344] Rhodes, L. (Producer), & Orlowski, J. (Director). (2020). *The social dilemma* [Documentary]. Netflix.

[345] Fowler, G. A., & Kelly, H. (2020, April 9). "Screen time" has gone from sin to survival tool. *Washington Post.* https://www.washingtonpost.com/technology/2020/04/09/screen-time-rethink-coronavirus/

[346] World Health Organization. (2018). Managing epidemics: Key facts about major deadly diseases, p. 11. https://www.who.int/emergencies/diseases/managing-epidemics-interactive.pdf

[347] Camus, A. (1991). *The plague.* First Vintage International Edition, p. 37. (First published 1948, Alfred Knopf.)

[348] Gouëdard, P., Pont, B., & Viennet, R. (2020). Education responses to COVID-19: Implementing a way forward. *OECD Education Working Papers,* No. 224. OECD.

[349] ARC Education Project. (2020). *System highlights: Uruguay.* http://atrico.org/wp-content/uploads/2020/04/COVID-19-in-Uruguay-Educational-Disruption-and-Response.pptx.pdf

[350] Republic of Korea Ministry of Education. (2020, June). *Responding to COVID 19: Online classes in Korea: A challenge toward the future of education.*

[351] See Ng, P. T. (2021). Timely change and timeless constants: COVID-19 and educational change in Singapore. *Educational Research for Policy and Practice, 20,* 19–27, p. 24.

[352] See https://www.etymonline.com/word/hybrid

[353] Spencer, C. (Producer), & Moore, R., & Johnson, P. (Directors). (2018). *Ralph breaks the internet* [Film]. Walt Disney Pictures.

[354] Parmar, B. (2020, October 12). Screen time is as addictive as junk food—how do we wean children off? *The Guardian.* www.theguardian.com/commentisfree/2020/oct/12/screen-time-addictive-social-media-addiction

[355] See data on Denmark as the leader in teachers' use of technology for projects in OECD (2019) *TALIS 2018 Results. Volume 1.* Table 1.2.4., "Change in teaching practices from 2013–2018"; and for Denmark's use of outdoor strategies during the pandemic, see Noack, R. (2020, September 16). In Denmark, the forest is the new classroom. *Washington Post.* https://www.washingtonpost.com/world/2020/09/16/outdoor-school-coronavirus-denmark-europe-forest/

356 See Hargreaves, A., & O'Connor, M. T. (2018). *Collaborative professionalism: When teaching together means learning for all.* Corwin.

357 These examples come from our research with the NW RISE network in the Pacific Northwest, which we discuss in Shirley, D., & Hargreaves, A. (2021). *Five paths of student engagement: Blazing the trail to learning and success.* Solution Tree.

358 CBC Television: *The National* (2016). The KPDSB Hockey Solution. https://www.youtube.com/watch?v=T721qBLlA8A

359 St-Denis, N., & Walsh, C. (2016). Reclaiming my Indigenous identity and the emerging warrior: An autoethnography. *Journal of Indigenous Social Development, 5*(1), 8.

360 First Nations Education Steering Committee. (2014). *First People's principles of learning.* http://www.fnesc.ca/first-peoples-principles-of-learning

361 Watts, J. (2021, January 21). Jane Goodall: "Change is happening: There are many ways to start moving in the right way." *The Guardian.* https://www.theguardian.com/environment/2021/jan/03/jane-goodall-change-is-happening-there-are-many-ways-to-start-moving-in-the-right-way

362 Ardoin, N. M., Bowers, A. W., Roth, N. W., & Holthuis, N. (2017). Environmental education and K–12 student outcomes: A review and analysis of research. *Journal of Environmental Education, 49*(1), 1–17.

363 International Council of Education Advisers. (2020). *International Council of Education Advisers Report 2018–2020.* Scottish Government.

364 Details of the Ottawa Forest School can be retrieved from https://childnature.ca.

365 See https://novascotia.ca/news/release/?id=20210413001.

366 UNESCO. (2020). *Education for sustainable development: A roadmap.*

367 Louv, R. (2005). *Last child in the woods: Saving our children from nature-deficit disorder.* Algonquin Books.

368 Renner, E., Nisti, M., & Lobo, L. (Producers), & Terra, R. (Director). (2020). *The beginning of life 2: Outside* [Documentary]. Netflix.

369 Barry, E. (2018, March 10). In Britain's playgrounds, "bringing in risk" to build resilience. *New York Times.* https://www.nytimes.com/2018/03/10/world/europe/britain-playgrounds-risk.html

370 McGonigal, K. (2019). *The joy of movement: How exercise helps us find happiness, hope, connection, and courage.* Avery.

371 Chatwin, B. (1988). *The songlines* (Reprint ed.). Penguin.

372 Kierkegaard, S. (2014). *Kierkegaard's writings. Vol. 25.* Princeton University Press, p. 214.

373 Robinson, K. (2006). *Do schools kill creativity?* [TED Talk]. https://www.ted.com/talks/sir_ken_robinson_do_schools_kill_creativity

374 Education Scotland. (2021). *What Scotland learned: Building back better,* p. 38. https://education.gov.scot/media/nwibvl2q/what-scotland-learned-building-back-better.pdf

375 McNamara, L. (2021). Redesigning the recess experience: Lessons from COVID-19. In C. Vaillancourt (Ed.), *Children and schools during COVID-19 and beyond: Engagement and connection through opportunity.* Royal Society COVID-19 Working Group on Children and Schools, Royal Society of Canada.

376 Kraemer, D. (2021, July 23). Greta Thunberg: Who is the climate campaigner and what are her aims? BBC News. https://www.bbc.com/news/world-europe-49918719

377 The Roots and Shoots website can be retrieved from http://www.rootsandshoots.org.

378 See https://www.nps.gov/articles/quick-nps-history.htm.

379 Clarke, T. (2020) Children's well-being and their academic achievement: The dangerous discourse of "trade-offs" in education. *Theory and Research in Education, 18*(3), pp. 1–32. Quote from p. 1.

380 Ibid., p. 23.

381 OECD. (2017). *PISA 2015 results: Students' well-being,* p. 232.

382 Wilkinson, R., & Pickett, K. (2009). *The spirit level: Why greater equality makes societies stronger.* Bloomsbury.

383 Lai, C. (2018, March 15). City of sadness? Hong Kong drops five spots to 76th in UN World Happiness Report, *Hong Kong Free Press.* https://hongkongfp.com/2018/03/15/city-sadness-hong-kong-drops-five-spots-76th-un-world-happiness-report/; Wong, M. (2018, September 27). Why the wealth gap? Hong Kong's disparity between rich and poor is greatest in 45 years, so what can be done? *South China Morning Post.* https://www.scmp.com/news/hong-kong/society/article/2165872/why-wealth-gap-hong-kongs-disparity-between-rich-and-poor

384 Tucker, M. (2019). *Leading high-performance school systems: Learning from the world's best.* ASCD and NCEE; OECD. (2011). *Strong performers and successful reformers in education: Lessons from PISA for the United States.*

[385] Bray, M. (2006). Private supplementary tutoring: Comparative perspectives on patterns and implications. *Compare, 36*(4), 515–530.

[386] Sato, M. (2011). Imagining neo-liberalism and the hidden realities of the politics of reform: Teachers and students in a globalized Japan. In D. B. Willis & J. Rappleye (Eds.), *Reimagining Japanese education: Borders, transfers, circulations, and the comparative* (pp. 225–246). Symposium Books, p. 226; Lee, D. D. & Park, C.-K. (2020, December 13). Young South Korean women are turning to suicide in ever greater numbers. COVID-19 is just the start of their problems. *South China Morning Post*. https://www.scmp.com/week-asia/people/article/3113655/young-south-korean-women-are-turning-suicide-ever-greater-numbers; Ting, V. (2018, May 31). Hong Kong children overwhelmed by academic pressure, with suicide accounting for a third of young unnatural deaths, government review of Coroner's Court cases reveals. *South China Morning Post*. https://www.scmp.com/news/hong-kong/society/article/3012666/hong-kong-children-overwhelmed-academic-pressure-suicide

[387] Lee, M., & Larson, R. (2000). The Korean "examination hell": Long hours of studying, distress, and depression. *Journal of Youth and Adolescence, 29,* 249–271; Goh, D.-S. (2019, October 23). Why Korean students are obsessed with university admission. *Asia Times.* https://asiatimes.com/2019/10/why-korean-students-are-obsessed-with-the-university-admission/

[388] Chu, L. (2017). *Little soldiers: An American boy, a Chinese school, and the global race to achieve.* HarperCollins.

[389] Sahlberg, P., & Doyle, W. (2019). *Let the children play: How more play will save our schools and help children thrive.* Oxford University Press.

[390] Ng, P. T. (2017). *Learning from Singapore: The power of paradoxes.* Routledge.

[391] Tucker, M. S. (Ed.). (2011). *Surpassing Shanghai: An agenda for American education built on the world's leading systems.* Harvard Education Press.

[392] Chu, L. (2017). *Little soldiers: An American boy, a Chinese school, and the global race to achieve.* HarperCollins.

[393] Zhao, Y. (2017, September 27). Torture is not good education: A response to WSJ's Why American Students Need Chinese Schools. National Education Policy Center. https://nepc.colorado.edu/blog/torture-not-good

[394] Rushowy, K. (2015, December 8). More Ontario parents opting for private tutoring, survey finds. *Toronto Star.* https://www.thestar.com/yourtoronto/education/2015/12/08/more-ontario-parents-opting-for-private-tutoring-survey-finds.html

[395] Major, L. E., & Machin, S. (2018). *Social mobility and its enemies.* Pelican.

[396] Honoré, C. (2009). *Under pressure: Rescuing our children from the culture of hyper-parenting.* Harper One, p. 258, p. 116.

[397] Heller Sahlgren, G. (2018) *The achievement-well-being trade-off in education.* Centre for Education Economics, p. 13.

[398] Ibid., p. 13.

[399] Ibid., p. 18.

[400] Ibid., p. 5.

[401] Tranter, D., Carson, L., & Bolland, T. (2018). *The third path: A relationship-based approach to student well-being and achievement.* Nelson.

[402] Gyeonggi-do Office of Education. (2019). *Gyeonggi Hyukshin Education,* Suwon-si, South Korea: Author. Gloudemans, P. (2019) High achievement, with dignity. *Boston College News.* https://www.bc.edu/bc-web/bcnews/nation-world-society/education/education-in-korea.html

[403] Meeting with Illugi Gunnarsson, Minister of Education, Science, and Culture, Reykjavik, Iceland, June 8, 2016.

[404] Ronay, B. (2016, June 8). Football, fire and ice: The inside story of Iceland's remarkable rise. *The Guardian.* https://www.theguardian.com/football/2016/jun/08/iceland-stunning-rise-euro-2016-gylfi-sigurdsson-lars-lagerback

[405] Milkman, H. (2017, December 6). Iceland succeeds at reversing teenage substance abuse the US should follow suit. *Huffington Post.* https://www.huffpost.com/entry/iceland-succeeds-at-rever_b_9892758

[406] Meeting of Pasi Sahlberg, University of New South Wales, and Andy with the mayor of Reykjavik, Dagur Eggertsson, and his team to develop an educational vision for the city, February 5, 2018.

[407] Meeting with Lilja Dögg Alfreðsdóttir, Minister of Education, Science, and Culture, Reykjavik, Iceland, October 12, 2019. The official publication of Iceland's PISA results can be located at OECD (2019) Education GPS: Iceland. https://gpseducation.oecd.org/CountryProfile?primaryCountry=ISL&treshold=10&topic=PI

[408] At the time this book went to press, this policy document was available in Icelandic only. It is retrievable at https://www.stjornarradid.is/efst-a-baugi/frettir/stok-frett/2021/03/26/Menntastefna -samthykkt-a-Althingi/.

[409] Mustachi, J. (2016). *The time to act is now: Ontario children can't wait: 2016 report card on child and family poverty in Ontario*. Ontario Campaign 2000: End Child & Family Poverty. https://campaign 2000.ca/wp-content/uploads/2016/11/ReportCardOntarioNov182016.pdf

[410] Fathers, F. (2015). *Overcoming the odds: Creating possibilities for youth in Windsor-Essex*. United Way/ Centraide Windsor-Essex County.

[411] Dweck, C. S. (2006). *Mindset: The new psychology of success*. Ballantine, p. 7.

[412] Ibid., p. 13.

[413] Ibid., p. 12.

[414] OECD. (2015). *Improving schools in Scotland: An OECD perspective*. https://www.oecd.org/education /school/Improving-Schools-in-Scotland-An-OECD-Perspective.pdf

[415] UN General Assembly. (1948, December 10), Universal Declaration of Human Rights. United Nations, p. 217 A (III).

[416] See https://www.lexico.com/definition/dignity

[417] Sennett, R., & Cobb, J. (1973). *The hidden injuries of class*. Knopf, p. 121.

[418] Ibid., p. 147.

[419] Shanker, S. (2013). *Calm, alert, and learning: Classroom strategies for self-regulation*. Pearson.

[420] Clinton, W. J. (2006). *Key propositions for building back better: Lessons learned from tsunami recovery*. United Nations.

[421] Ibid., p. 1.

[422] Ibid., p. 1.

[423] OECD. (2020). *Building back better: A sustainable, resilient economy after COVID-19*, p. 2.

[424] Ibid., p. 5.

[425] Ibid., p. 1.

[426] Ibid., p. 1.

[427] UNICEF. (2020). *Reimagining our future: Building back better from COVID-19*, p. 1.

[428] Ibid., p. 10.

[429] Ibid.

[430] Bakker, P., & Elkington, J. (2020, July 13). To build back better, we must reinvent capitalism: Here's how. World Economic Forum. https://www.weforum.org/agenda/2020/07/to-build-back-better-we -must-reinvent-capitalism-heres-how/

[431] Ibid.

[432] Ibid.

[433] Gruber, J., Mauss, I., & Tamir, M. (2011). A dark side to happiness? How, when, and why happiness is not always good. *Perspectives on Psychological Science, 6*(3), 222–233. Quote from p. 225.

[434] Ibid.

[435] Ibid.

[436] George, J. M., & Zhou, J. (2002). Understanding when bad moods foster creativity and good ones don't: The role of context and clarity of feelings. *Journal of Applied Psychology, 87*(4), 687–697. Quote from p. 687.

[437] Gasper, K., Lozinski, R. H., & LeBeau, L. S. (2009). If you plan, then you can: How reflection helps defensive pessimists pursue their goals. *Motivation and Emotion, 33,* 203–216. Quote from p. 203.

[438] Jeffries, S. (2021, February 16). Bear Grylls: There's no point getting to the summit if you're an arsehole. *The Guardian*. https://www.theguardian.com/tv-and-radio/2021/feb/16/bear-grylls-tv -adventurer-interview-you-vs-wild-movie-netflix

[439] American Psychiatric Association. (2020). What is depression? https://www.psychiatry.org/patients -families/depression/what-is-depression

[440] EdSurge Research. (2020). *Research eclipsed: How educators are reinventing research-informed practice during the pandemic*. https://d3btwko586hcvj.cloudfront.net/uploads/pdf/file/212 /Research_Eclipsed_FINAL-1600884157.pdf

[441] Rubin, R. (2021, February 8). Facebook and IRS prepare for $9 billion US tax court fight. *Wall Street Journal*. https://www.wsj.com/articles/facebook-and-irs-prepare-for-9-billion-u-s-tax-court-fight -11581177600

[442] Levin, T. (2021, March 16). Elon Musk is once again the world's richest person, as Tesla's upward tear continues. *Business Insider*. https://www.businessinsider.com/elon-musk-jeff-bezos-net-worth-worlds -richest-tesla-amazon-stock-2021-1

[443] Hyde, M. (2021, June 11). In space, nobody can hear Jeff Bezos. So can Richard Branson go too? *The Guardian*. https://www.theguardian.com/commentisfree/2021/jun/11/space-jeff-bezos-richard-branson-amazon-virgin

[444] Carranza, R., Beutner, A., & Jackson, J. (2020, December 13). We need a Marshall Plan for the schools. And we need it now. *Washington Post*. https://www.washingtonpost.com/opinions/2020/12/13/we-need-marshall-plan-our-schools-we-need-it-now/

[445] See Hubler, S. (2020, May 21). University of California will end use of SAT and ACT in admissions. *New York Times*. https://www.nytimes.com/2020/05/21/us/university-california-sat-act.html; and Oregon Department of Education. (2021, January 22). *Oregon's statewide assessment and accountability 2020–21 strategic waiver request*. https://www.oregon.gov/ode/educator-resources/assessment/Documents/Oregon_AssessAccountWaiverRequest_2020_21.pdf

[446] International Council of Education Advisers. (2020). *International Council of Education Advisers Report 2018–2020*. Scottish Government.

[447] Shirley, D., Hargreaves, A., & Washington-Wangia, S. (2020). The sustainability and unsustainability of teachers' and leaders' well-being. *Teaching and Teacher Education 92*, pp. 1–12. https://dennisshirley.com/wp-content/uploads/2020/12/TATE-Sustainability-of-Well-being-.pdf

[448] Education Scotland. (2021, February 4). *Education Scotland launches new online 1:1 coaching and mentoring*. https://education.gov.scot/education-scotland/news-and-events/education-scotland-launches-new-online-1-1-coaching-and-mentoring/

[449] See Sahlberg, P. (2021). *Finnish lessons 3.0: What can the world learn from educational change in Finland?* Teachers College Press.

[450] Shirley, D. (2019). *The untapped power of international partnership for educational change: The Norway Canada project (NORCAN)*. Utdanningsforbundet. https://www.utdanningsforbundet.no/globalassets/varpolitikk/publikasjoner/rapporterutredninger/international_norcan_report_2019.pdf; Sung, Y.-K., & Lee, Y. (2018). Politics and the practice of school change: The Hyukshin school movement in South Korea. *Curriculum Inquiry, 48*(2), 238–252.

[451] Hargreaves, A., Boyle, A., & Harris, A. (2014). *Uplifting leadership: How organizations, teams, and communities raise performance*. Jossey-Bass.

[452] Articles, reports, and book chapters we draw on comprise the following: Hargreaves, A. (2020). Austerity and inequality; or prosperity for all? Educational policy directions beyond the pandemic. *Educational Research for Policy and Practice, 20*, 3–10; Hargreaves, A. (2020). Large-scale assessments and their effects: The case of mid-stakes tests in Ontario. *Journal of Educational Change, 21*, 393–420; Hargreaves, A., & Shirley, D. (2018, November 29). Well-being and success: Opposites that need to attract. *Education Canada*. https://www.edcan.ca/articles/well-being-and-success/; Hargreaves, A., & Shirley, D. (2018). What's wrong with well-being? *Educational Leadership, 76*(2), 58–63; Hargreaves, A., Shirley, D., Wangia, S., Bacon, C. K., & D'Angelo, M. (2018). *Leading from the middle: Spreading learning, well-being, and identity across Ontario*. Council of Ontario Directors of Education.

[453] These opinion pieces comprise Hargreaves, A. (2020, August 6). The education technology students will need—and won't—after coronavirus. *Washington Post*. www.washingtonpost.com/education/2020/08/06/education-technology-students-will-need-wont-after-covid-19/; Hargreaves, A. (2020, December 11). Is this how to make schools pandemic-proof? *TES*. https://www.tes.com/news/Covid-19-coronavirus-how-pandemic-proof-schools

Index

The letter *f* following a page locator denotes a figure.

About the Authors

 **Andy Hargreaves** is director of CHENINE (Change, Engagement and Innovation in Education) at the University of Ottawa, research professor at the Lynch School of Education and Human Development at Boston College, and honorary professor at Swansea University in the UK. He is cofounder and president of the ARC Education Project, a group of nations committed to broadly defined excellence, equity, well-being, inclusion, democracy, and human rights in education. He was president of the International Congress for School Effectiveness and Improvement 2017–2019, served as education advisor to the premier of Ontario 2015–2018, and is currently an advisor to the first minister of Scotland. He holds honorary doctorates in the Education University of Hong Kong and the University of Uppsala in Sweden. He is a fellow of the Royal Society of Arts.

Andy has consulted with the OECD, the World Bank, governments, universities, and teacher unions worldwide. His more than 30 books have attracted multiple writing awards—including the prestigious 2015 Grawemeyer Award in Education for *Professional Capital* (with Michael Fullan). He has been honored in the United States, the UK, and Canada for services to public education and educational research. Andy is ranked by *Education Week* among the top scholars with most influence on US education policy debate. In 2015, Boston College gave him its Excellence in Teaching with Technology Award.

Dennis Shirley is Duganne Faculty Fellow and professor of education at the Lynch School of Education and Human Development at Boston College. Dennis dedicates his life to the improvement of teaching and learning for students so that they may flourish, wherever they may be.

Dennis has led and advised many educational change initiatives. He was the principal investigator of the Massachusetts Coalition for Teacher Quality and Student Achievement, a federally funded improvement network that united 18 urban schools, 7 higher education institutions, and 16 community-based organizations. He has conducted in-depth studies about school innovations in England, Germany, Canada, and South Korea. Dennis has been a visiting professor at Harvard University in the United States, Venice International University in Italy, the National Institute of Education in Singapore, the University of Barcelona in Spain, and the University of Stavanger in Norway. Some of his recent initiatives include multiple innovations in the digital environment, an online master's degree program on Global Perspectives: Teaching, Curriculum and Learning Environments, and research the human-technology frontier in education and work, supported by a Richard von Weizsäcker Fellowship from the Bosch Foundation in Berlin, Germany. He is a fellow of the Royal Society of Arts.

Dennis's previous book is *The New Imperatives of Educational Change: Achievement with Integrity.* He holds a doctorate from Harvard University.

❋ ❋ ❋

Well-Being in Schools: Three Forces That Will Uplift Your Students in a Volatile World is the fourth book that Andy and Dennis have written together. Their last coauthored book is *Five Paths of Student Engagement: Blazing New Paths for Learning and Success.*